T0053659

The
EVERYTHING
EASY LARGE-PRINT
CROSSWORDS
BOOK

Dear Reader,

There are about 50 million crossword solvers in the United States. But there are also 250 million who have not yet decided to become crossword solvers; everyday folk who just aren't that familiar with crossword puzzles. People like my parents and in-laws. There's nothing wrong with having never been a crossword solver. In fact, maybe you are one of those 50 million solvers, and just prefer your puzzles on the friendly and easy side. This book will work for you, too. Or maybe you're in another country, and there are too many pop culture references in most crosswords to make them worth your time. No matter who you are, dig in and enjoy!

Douglas Fink

The EVERYTHING Series

Editorial

Publisher	Gary M. Krebs
Director of Product Development	Paula Munier
Managing Editor	Laura M. Daly
Associate Copy Chief	Sheila Zwiebel
Acquisitions Editor	Lisa Laing
Production Editor	Casey Ebert

Production

Director of Manufacturing	Susan Beale
Production Project Manager	Michelle Roy Kelly
Prepress	Erick DaCosta Matt LeBlanc
Interior Layout	Heather Barrett Brewster Brownville Colleen Cunningham Jennifer Oliveira
Cover Design	Erin Alexander Stephanie Chrusz Frank Rivera

THE EVERYTHING® EASY LARGE-PRINT CROSSWORDS BOOK

Bigger and easier than ever!

Douglas R. Fink

Adams Media
New York London Toronto Sydney New Delhi

Adamsmedia

Adams Media
An Imprint of Simon & Schuster, Inc.
100 Technology Center Drive
Stoughton, MA 02072

An Everything® Series Book.
Everything® and everything.com® are registered trademarks of Simon & Schuster, Inc.

ADAMS MEDIA and colophon are trademarks of Simon and Schuster.

For information about special discounts for bulk purchases, please contact Simon & Schuster Special Sales at 1-866-506-1949 or business@simonandschuster.com.

The Simon & Schuster Speakers Bureau can bring authors to your live event. For more information or to book an event contact the Simon & Schuster Speakers Bureau at 1-866-248-3049 or visit our website at www.simonspeakers.com.

Manufactured in the United States of America

23 2024

Library of Congress Cataloging-in-Publication Data has been applied for.

ISBN 978-1-59869-237-2

Contents

Acknowledgments

I would like to acknowledge the following people for their hard work on this book, as welll as give due credit to those whose names I do not know specificially. Lisa Laing at Adams Media was the editorial wrangler, in charge of keeping me on schedule. Past copyeditors (a freelance position that does not get Production/Editorial page credit) have included Valeria Shea, Ellen Ripstein (of "Wordplay" fame), and David Dickerson. *Ghost Magazine* and *Justine Magazine* have regularly featured my puzzles. And lastly, I'd like to thank you, the reader, for pursuing the worthy diversion of crosswords.

Introduction

This book is intended to be an introduction to crossword puzzles. It is one thing to write a book without the hard and obscure stuff. It is another to weed out answers and trivia in a crossword puzzle book to make it more approachable to more people. What do I mean by this? Words, terms, or trivia that leave out certain age groups, or those who haven't necessarily gotten into this whole crossword thing. The author's own parents and in-laws are not crossword people, and younger kids may lack the trivia and vocabulary common in many of today's crosswords. This is a book that a grandparent and grandkid can do together, without either having a distinct disadvantage.

So, here I present you with an introductory book to crosswords, designed to be fair toward all ages and backgrounds. Grab your favorite writing utensil, kick back, and enjoy!

1. Off to a Good Start

ACROSS

1 Skirt edges
5 Architect's drawing
9 Close a jacket
12 It steams away wrinkles
13 Fair feature
14 Cold cubes
15 The biggest bear, in "Goldilocks and the Three Bears"
16 Copycat
18 Schoolroom spinner
20 Color for a baby girl
21 Mouth edge
24 Awaken
26 Turns a book into a movie, say
28 Mountain top
32 Biblical interjection
33 VCR button
34 Samples a flavor
36 "Don't break it!"
37 Mini earthquake
39 The __ Commandments
40 Border
43 Personal box, at daycare
45 It usually goes "ding-dong!"
47 Dentist's request
51 Lodging house
52 Goofing off
53 Olympic sled
54 Golf peg
55 Bird home
56 "How was I to __?"

DOWN

1 Leg joint
2 Significant time
3 Swab the deck
4 Plan problem
5 Previous convictions, casually
6 Under-the-stick dance
7 French farewells
8 Butterfly catcher
9 Tubular pasta
10 Symbolic picture
11 Prepare coffee
17 The Missing Link
19 Shaving foam
21 Final
22 Cartoon "light bulb"
23 Buddies
25 Excellent
27 The sound of little feet
29 Mixed-breed dog
30 Gilligan's home
31 High-school student
35 Leave, as the Union
36 Drinking glass
38 Ponders, with "over"
40 Change one's words
41 Test-takers' "ta-da!"
42 "Going, going, __"
44 Egg center
46 Vegetable holder
48 Play on words
49 Inflated __
50 "Turn over a __ leaf"

Skirt edges

solution on page 300

ACROSS

1 Body covering
5 Snug
9 Dancing-shoe attachment
12 Reverse, on a PC
13 Hang __ (keep)
14 Yearly count
15 Lowly drudge
16 Next-door resident
18 Choose
20 "Now I __ me down to sleep . . ."
21 Kind of hygiene
23 Story line
27 Farm vehicle
31 Keep out of sight
32 Superman or Spiderman
33 Knee's locale
35 Not odd
36 Computer person
37 Recency
39 Night sky light
40 Rational
41 Fireplace dust
43 Fixed a manuscript
48 Type of phone
52 Waiter's need
53 Bread that's often seeded
54 Where to get 53 Across
55 Successfully treat
56 "Is it soup __?"
57 Blueprint detail
58 Hugged

DOWN

1 Has dinner
2 Leg joint
3 Thing that's worshiped
4 Poor dog's portion
5 Be in charge
6 Half of two
7 Not moving
8 Cross-legged exercises
9 Bill at the bar
10 "A long, long time __ . . ."
11 Miles __ hour
17 Word connector
19 Camp bed
22 Field of battle
24 Not on tape
25 Ballads
26 Double-digit bills
27 In this fashion
28 Musical break
29 __ code (phone number prefix)
30 The OK, for one
34 Having no brand name
38 Join in marriage
40 Lug, slangily
42 Foam
44 Poison-ivy result
45 Not false
46 Countess' husband
47 Redid a color
48 Go "wah!"
49 Hole in a needle
50 Allow
51 Ginger __

Body covering

solution on page 300

ACROSS

1 Close loudly
5 Use an oar
8 Shipwreck site
12 Part of a scale
13 Big monkey
14 Prod
15 Suffered
17 Wise man
18 "__ Goes the Weasel"
19 People might stick them out
21 Poetic lines
22 Alien spaceship
25 Items on a tribal pole
28 Holy
30 Fairy-tale meanie
31 __ my warning
32 Frightens
35 Bends
37 Dawn drops
38 Beat at the pie contest
40 Tried to influence politicians
42 Popular title starter
45 "Hansel and Gretel" prop
47 Cotton or denim
49 Barbed __
50 Anger
51 Eye feature
52 "More or __" (somewhat)
53 La Brea __ Pits
54 "A __ formality"

DOWN

1 Ginger __
2 Company symbol
3 On
4 Fellows
5 Father's Day gifts
6 Unseals
7 Pie slices
8 Bit of trickery
9 Crossword solvers' smudges
10 Easter-__ hunt
11 Expense
16 Thing
20 Our country
21 Swerve
23 12-inch units
24 __ and ends
25 Warty critter
26 Eye slyly
27 Net-dragging ships
29 __-chat
33 Rowdy bunch
34 Turn in
35 __-totter
36 Go in ankle-deep
39 Princess crown
41 Single bills
42 Car wheel
43 Beard material
44 "So what __ is new?"
45 Bird that hunts at night
46 Compete
48 Basketball-hoop part

Close loudly

solution on page 300

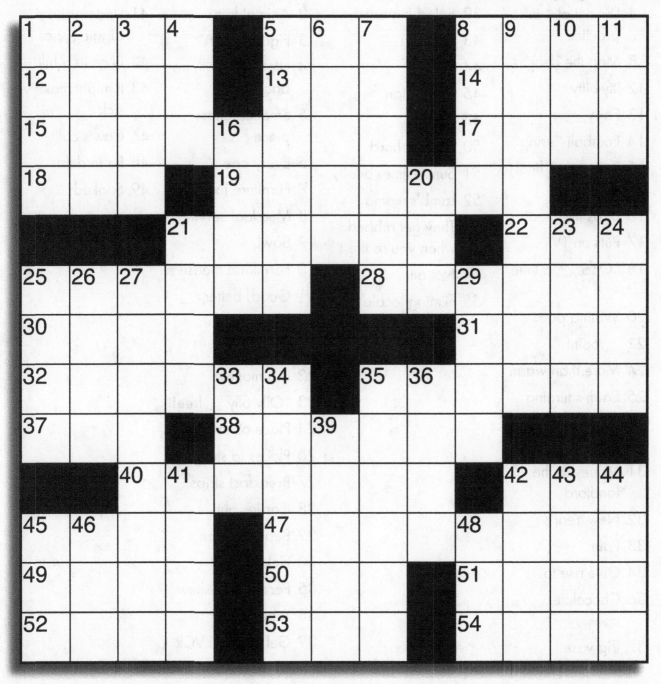

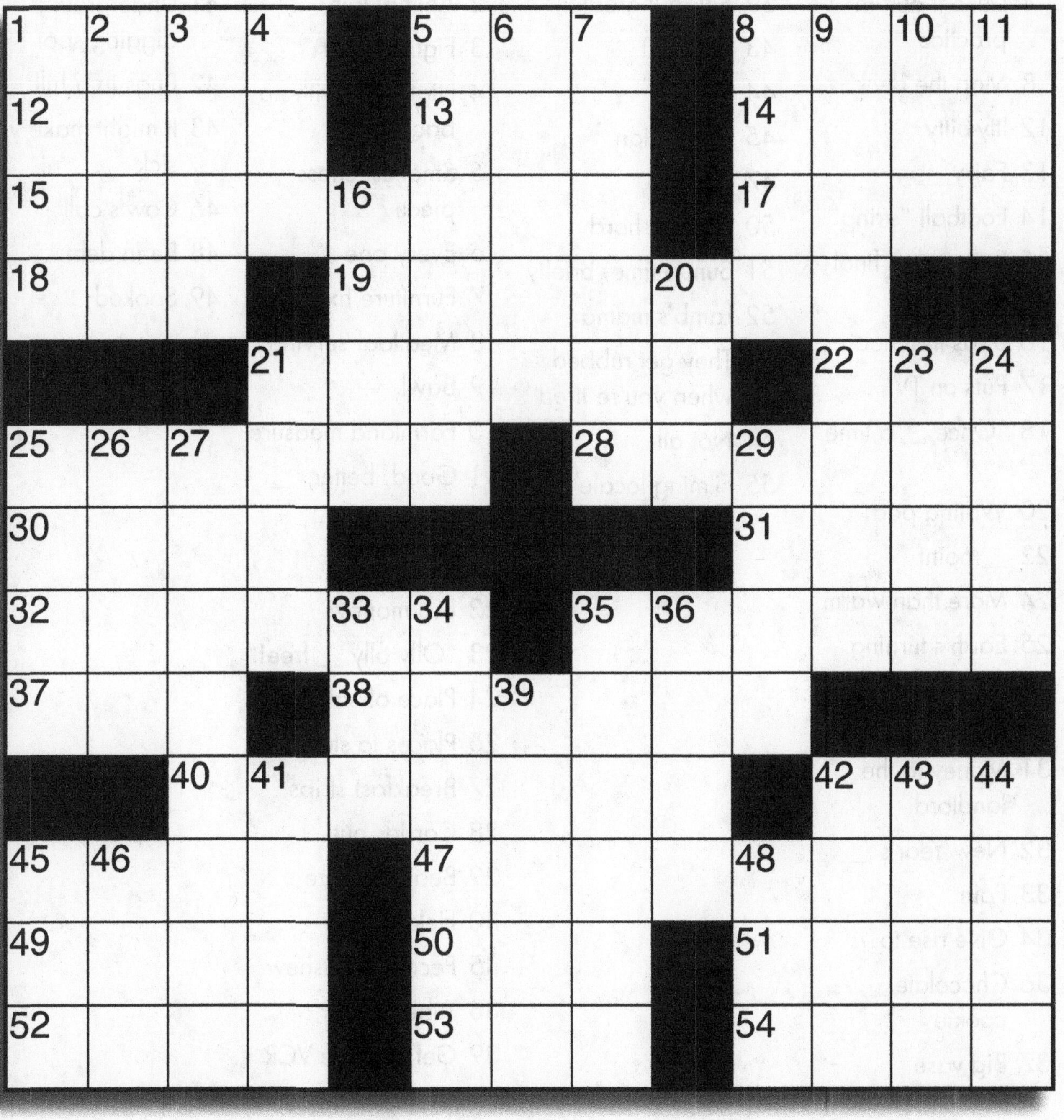

ACROSS

1 Combine, in math
4 Duke it out, in practice
8 Mop the deck
12 Itty-bitty
13 Fairy __
14 Football "string"
15 Fairy tale's final word
16 Birds that hoot
17 Puts on TV
18 "Once __ a time . . ."
20 Writing pad
22 __ point
24 More than warm
25 Earth's turning point
26 Without a saddle
31 Money to the landlord
32 New Year's __
33 Pain
34 Give rise to
36 Chocolate __ cookie
37 Big vase
38 Pencil tip
39 Salad ingredient
43 DNA bit
44 Alike
45 Seer's sign
47 Promise
50 Breathe hard
51 Sunup time, briefly
52 Lamb's mama
53 They get rubbed when you're tired
54 Not all
55 Filming locale

DOWN

1 Amaze
2 Animal lair
3 Figuring out
4 High seat with no back
5 Smallest chess piece
6 Every one
7 Furniture fixer
8 Meatloaf serving
9 Bawl
10 Farmland measure
11 Good, better, __
19 Thick glue
21 Gobbled up
22 Bus money
23 "Olly olly __ free!"
24 Place of safety
26 Places to sleep
27 Breakfast strips
28 Carries out
29 Beard's place
30 Held onto
35 Pecan or cashew
38 Tube pasta
39 Get with the VCR
40 "Sure, why not?"
41 Underground digging spot
42 Bugs in a hill
43 It might make you sick
46 Cow's call
48 Be in debt
49 Soaked

Combine, in math

solution on page 300

ACROSS

1 Prison cell walls
5 Hammer or saw
9 Place with a sauna
12 All over again
13 DC office shape
14 "Neither here __ there"
15 Syringe, informally
16 Summer bloom
18 Lion's noise
20 Stray dogs
21 Gave a PG to, say
24 Young boy
25 Cry of triumph
26 Nothing more than
29 "Be good to __ other"
33 "Welcome" item
34 Archeologist's finds
36 "Skip to my __, my darling"
37 "Hey, you!"
39 Words in print
40 Cratchit's son
41 Commercials
43 Golf-bag items
45 William Tell's target
48 Two minus two
50 Cooking vessel
52 Chooses
56 Shade tree
57 Darn socks
58 Expensive fur
59 Hi-fi item
60 Simon __
61 Abominable Snowman

DOWN

1 Scrooge's word
2 ". . . have you __ wool?"
3 Iron-pumper's unit
4 Cursed
5 Roman garment
6 "Your turn," in radio talk
7 Rowboat paddle
8 Andes pack animal
9 Bad mood
10 Look sad
11 Tentacles
17 Naked
19 Stench
21 Prance
22 Shouts of triumph
23 Little kids
24 Small wildcat
27 Brownie ingredient
28 "I cannot tell a __" (cherry–tree-tale word)
30 Glee-club member
31 Penny or dime
32 Sings without words
35 Mix the batter
38 Baby-powder ingredient
42 Considers
44 Having lots of space
45 Sailing
46 Part of a hand that's read
47 Tire inflator
48 Goofy
49 "Trying to make __ meet"
51 Ball in a pod
53 "As easy as __"
54 Blaster's need
55 Go down the bunny slope

Prison cell walls

solution on page 300

ACROSS

1 Groundhog __
4 Cries
8 " . . . and threw up the __"
12 Gold and iron come from it
13 Angel topper
14 Canyon comeback
15 Came forth
17 Gore or Cheney
18 Waffle topper
19 Working for minimum __
21 Bumped into
23 Small bay
27 Thick lump
30 Horse foot
33 "__ we there yet?"
34 Dr. Frankenstein's lair
35 Pottery or woodworking
36 Moving truck
37 Get some good out of
38 Big Bad Wolf verb
39 Speedy
40 Kitchen herb
42 Knight's title
44 Was in debt
47 Join together
51 "Hold up!"
54 Making it fizzy
56 Car bar that holds the wheels
57 Dirty air
58 Mouth cover
59 Farmer's place, in a song
60 Phone-athon giveaway bag
61 Home for a hog

DOWN

1 "Easy __ it!"
2 Salvation __
3 Time between birthdays
4 Circle or square
5 Cheerio grain
6 Tried to make a bubble
7 Fizzy drink
8 Days in a week
9 Pro flier
10 "Thar __ blows!"
11 Jump like a bunny
16 Feeling no pain
20 Birthday present
22 By way of, for short
24 Volcanic flow
25 Historic ages
26 Camp shelter
27 Oversupply
28 Eye hair
29 Follow orders
31 Clumsy one
32 Ons and __
35 Munch
39 Worry
41 Lodging place
43 Picture
45 From California to Virginia
46 Floor model
48 18-wheelers
49 Annoying insect
50 Like an omelet
51 A __ of used chewing gum
52 Chopping tool
53 Sick
55 Decompose

Groundhog

solution on page 300

ACROSS

1 Ball
4 Fishing poles
8 Bushy hairdo
12 "__ attention!"
13 On vacation
14 Hawaiian party
15 Woofer's kin
17 Leave off the list
18 Black-ink item
19 Mother chickens
20 Yodeler's range
23 "__ of Good Feelings"
25 Actors' jobs
27 Funny
31 Water-temperature tester
32 Bit of glass that can make a rainbow
34 Twosome
35 Place for a ball game
37 "Beer Barrel __"
39 "__ a Wonderful Life"
40 Open a banana
41 Garden creeper
44 Baseball-card deal
48 Confused actor's request
49 Coat with plastic
53 Cheerios, basically
54 ". . . lived happily __ after"
55 ". . . from __ to shining . . ."
56 Horse's gait
57 Fender damage
58 "__ the Bunny" (children's book)

DOWN

1 Choose
2 Uncooked
3 "See ya!"
4 "Phooey!"
5 Uses credit
6 Schoolyard challenge
7 "All __ go!"
8 Island greetings
9 Sulk angrily
10 Picnic spoiler
11 An inning has six
16 "Ill at __" (uncomfortable)
20 Industrial __
21 Burglar's take
22 "Guilty" or "not guilty"
24 __ roast
26 Dentist's request after rinsing
27 "Ready, __, fire!"
28 Not in motion
29 Microwave, in slang
30 Objective
33 Stole cattle
36 Reader's __
38 "__ sesame!"
41 Coin hole
42 Teller of fibs
43 "Do __ others . . ."
45 Rant and __
46 Closing word in church
47 What a vacuum vacuums
50 Deadly Egyptian snake
51 British drink
52 All-you-can-__ buffet

Ball

solution on page 301

ACROSS

1 Family group
5 Does simple arithmetic
9 Janitor's tool
12 Greasy
13 Attendance cry
14 Brewpub order
15 Flower with thorns
16 Wingspread
17 __ York City
18 Shoelace bindings
20 Lent a hand
22 Like testimony
24 ". . . by the __'s early light . . ."
27 "Let 'er __!"
30 Aardvark's prey
31 Be of one mind
32 Not at sea
34 Not ours
35 Glimmer
36 Cube with spots
37 Fisherman's tool
38 Bench or stool
39 Sub spotter
41 Free throws, say
43 "Me too!"
47 "So, it's YOU!"
49 Exam without pencils
51 You're filling it in now
52 Took first place
53 This clue is on one
54 __-and-go-seek
55 __ off steam
56 Raced
57 Santa's sackful

DOWN

1 Bulletin-board material
2 "The __ King"
3 "Not to mention . . ."
4 Russian no's
5 Checkup sounds
6 Leave
7 Bathtub hole
8 E-mail order
9 __ orange
10 Bullring cry
11 Church bench
19 Bunch of bees
21 Rim
23 "It's just __ of those things"
25 Used to be
26 Bird's home
27 "From __ to riches"
28 Dot in the ocean
29 Game bird served "under glass"
31 In the future
33 Swearing-in words
34 Material for a toy soldier
36 Medicine portion
39 Seatbelt part
40 Correct
42 "How clumsy of me!"
44 Threesome
45 Neat and orderly
46 Flowery verses
47 Hole-making tool
48 Garden digging tool
50 Was in charge

Family group

solution on page 301

ACROSS

1 Not young
4 Good's opposite
8 Auction offers
12 Pirate's yes
13 The __ Star State
14 Neighborhood
15 Powder __ (explosive container)
16 Perform with a chorus
17 Block of bread
18 Rod and __
20 Mystery or sci-fi
21 Door sound
23 Needing a massage
26 High or low time at the beach
27 __ sale (sale of castoff items)
32 50/50
33 Payment for service
34 Ocean color
35 Interfered
37 Tap a golf ball
38 Golden Calf, for one
40 "I couldn't care __"
41 Cluster
45 __ book store
47 "Superman" reporter Lois __
48 Social skill
50 "Blech!"
53 Helps out
54 Fairy-tale baddie
55 Pigeon's cry
56 Paid athletes
57 Chick's sound
58 Do a tugboat chore

DOWN

1 Acorn tree
2 Soap-making ingredient
3 Dishonored
4 "If all __ fails . . ."
5 "Presto!"
6 No room at the __
7 "Break a __" (good luck)
8 Hay bundle
9 Shirt presser
10 Beloved
11 Ump's call
19 Fix text
20 Workout room
21 Flower stalk
22 "As I __ and breathe!"
24 Belief
25 Color
28 Pancake syrup
29 Water channel of ancient Rome
30 Courage
31 Has food
33 Gave food to
36 It might get chapped
39 "Filthy" money
41 Applaud
42 Bear's den
43 Word processor's "back as it was"
44 It needs cleaning up
46 "Mother May I" unit
48 "Let's take it from the __"
49 Birthday number
51 Sticky stuff
52 "__ do you do?"

Not young

solution on page 301

1	2	3	■	4	5	6	7	■	8	9	10	11
12			■	13				■	14			
15			■	16				■	17			
■	■	18	19			■		20			■	■
21	22			■	23	24	25		■	■	■	■
26				■		27			■	28	29	30	31
32				■	33			■	34			
35				36			■	■	37			
■	■	■	38			■	39	■	40			
41	42	43	44		■	■	45	46			■	■
47				■	48	49			■	50	51	52
53				■	54				■	55		
56				■	57				■	58		

ACROSS

1 "Thanks a __!"
4 Catch some rays
8 Comfy
12 Bedazzle
13 Like some fruit
14 Pinocchio's stand-out
15 Toothpaste type
16 Warning of things to come
17 Cooking chamber
18 Correct a pencil error
20 Informed
21 Was nuts about
23 "What's up, __?"
25 Related
26 The H in H2O
31 King's home
33 Criticize meanly
34 Unpleasant sights
36 Dart about
37 "Like father, like __"
38 Attacks with snowballs
39 Breeze
43 "Neither here nor __"
45 Tug-of-war need
46 Accurate
47 __-a-tat
50 Comic-strip light bulb
51 "SOS!"
52 Decorate a cake
53 Annoying one
54 Electric swimmers
55 Didn't go hungry

DOWN

1 Be a straggler
2 Run up a tab
3 Broadcast for cable, say
4 Wide
5 Tries to get a bulls-eye
6 Quick
7 Barbie's boyfriend
8 "__ White and the Seven Dwarves"
9 __ Scotia
10 One who logs in
11 Actor Wilder who played Willy Wonka
19 Monopoly payments
20 Farm unit
21 Bridal-gown trim
22 Give the go-ahead to
24 __ or evens
26 One who says, "I'll save you!"
27 Make a bid
28 Indoor mall region
29 Radiate
30 Tennis-court dividers
32 In need of a map
35 Main course
38 Chirps
39 Faucet problem
40 Came by horse
41 Chimps and baboons
42 Accomplishment
44 Ship's bottom
46 Fifth word of The Pledge of Allegiance
48 Behave
49 Golf ball holder

Thanks a __!

solution on page 301

ACROSS

1 Baby cow
5 Freshly
9 Craft or skill
12 Racetrack shape
13 "The Hunchback of Notre __"
14 Not high
15 Details for calculations
16 Idiot
18 Sales __
19 Long, slippery fish
20 Up to the task
21 It's what you breathe
22 Without clothes
23 Supermarket need
24 Piano student's exercises
26 Mother's flower
28 Parrot's word
29 Fuzzy fruit
33 "Your point being . . . ?"
35 School study unit
36 __ and proper
39 Picture on a PC screen
41 Basketball hoop
42 Heavenly glow
43 Took a chair
44 A deer, a female deer
45 Type of saw
47 Big jars
49 Color gotten at the beach
50 Response to "Marco!"
51 Pal, in England
52 Clever
53 Poses a question
54 Attention-getter

DOWN

1 Cape __, MA
2 A Deadly Sin
3 Sideways
4 __ your wings
5 Suzette's so-longs
6 Titled
7 Symbol
8 Tiny
9 Court excuse
10 Dinner breads
11 Canary sound
17 Made less frantic
21 Cinder
22 Sign light
25 Mountain pack animals
27 "Once __ a time . . ."
30 Night lights
31 Customers
32 Skirt edge
34 '70s dance halls
35 Watchwords
36 Agreements
37 Urban's opposite
38 Literary twist
40 Make the cracks watertight
44 Landfill
46 Health club
48 "Ready, __, go!"

Baby cow

solution on page 301

ACROSS

1 Change to another house
5 __ milk
9 Quick swim
12 A wad of Washingtons
13 __ and cheese party
14 "Winner takes __"
15 Immediately, in the ER
16 Ingredient
17 Go by plane
18 Serious
20 Santa's landing area
22 Number of sides on stop signs
24 Commuter's destination
27 Santa's entry
30 Song from long ago
31 That guy
32 Build
34 Bitter cold
35 Lancelot's suit
37 Stinging plants
39 ". . . partridge in a __ tree"
40 Brief film role
41 Drop shed while crying
43 Got rid of a pencil mark
47 Winter ailment
49 __ on the cob
51 Cola
52 Rowboat need
53 Owl's call
54 Barbershop order
55 Female sheep
56 Make __ meet (get by)
57 Movie backdrops

DOWN

1 Tree-trunk growth
2 Latch __
3 __ Parmesan
4 Self-__
5 Lively person, slangily
6 First-aid __
7 Not active
8 Brief note
9 Yellow flower
10 Unhealthy
11 Two-__ tissue
19 Person who digs underground
21 Friend of Pooh
23 "Laughing" animal
25 __-a-Roni
26 Door openers
27 English fellow
28 Give a job to
29 Young
30 Frisky swimmer
33 Bonds together
36 Refinery item
38 Browns the bread
40 Sing sweetly
42 Hurt
44 "Don't be a __ loser"
45 Fix text
46 Beavers' barriers
47 "Who goes there, friend or __?"
48 Judge's concern
50 Lightning __

Change to another house

solution on page 301

ACROSS

1 Poison __
4 Barbershop sound
8 Cut reminder
12 Comment before "I told you so"
13 "Don't take that __ with me, young man!"
14 __ down the runway
15 ABC and NBC
17 Used a credit card
18 Court case
19 Toy on a string
21 Do needlework
23 Combined, as numbers
27 Boring
30 Done
33 Card with the fewest symbols
34 Start of the Lord's Prayer
35 Sandwich need
36 "__ sells seashells . . ."
37 Patriotic Uncle
38 Allows
39 "__ 'til you drop"
40 Japanese menu item
42 Shaggy ox
44 Makes a choice
47 Squeeze
51 Grizzly __
54 Spicy pepper
56 Eye feature
57 Happily __ after
58 "Charlotte's __"
59 Baseball event
60 "Try to make ends __"
61 1 + 1

DOWN

1 "Small world, __ it?"
2 Turn sharply
3 Hairy Himalayan
4 Robbed
5 "Neither rain __ sleet . . ."
6 Stained with writing fluid
7 Mexican currency
8 Arose
9 Cornfield cry
10 Paul Bunyan's tool
11 Get __ of (dispose of)
16 Do laundry
20 Scotland __
22 Was dressed in
24 100-yard __
25 Sound response
26 ____ Impact
27 Office manager
28 Oahu feast
29 Octopus's eight
31 Pet doc
32 Simple
35 Radar spot
39 Get under one's __
41 Basketball game for two
43 Fall __ (disintegrate)
45 "Let __ eat cake"
46 Put in the bank
48 Witches' brew ingredient
49 Boat personnel
50 Tramp
51 Jumbo
52 Baseball stat
53 Get in one's crosshairs
55 Hive insect

Poison

solution on page 302

ACROSS

1 Eye impolitely
5 Engrave
9 "So near and yet so __"
12 Need to retake the class
13 Carbonated drink
14 Tell a fib
15 Flew the coop
16 Thief's gain
17 Put two and two together
18 Not out of one's mind
19 Purpose
21 Maple-syrup source
23 Some cooking liquids
26 Stuck-up sort
30 Bacon unit
31 "What do __ want?"
32 Within __ (close by)
34 "You are my __ and only."
35 Any answer word in this puzzle
37 Groomed oneself
39 Highway rig
40 Peculiar
41 Musical dramas
45 Calamine-lotion target
49 Blow the __ off (reveal)
51 Teeth surrounders
52 Scrabble piece
53 "__ you kidding me?"
54 __ club (chorus)
55 Type of history
56 Nighty-night place
57 Yearnings
58 Rip apart

DOWN

1 Switch positions
2 Black-tie event
3 Bank claim
4 Most mature
5 Blotting out of the sun or moon
6 Mickey Mouse or Bugs Bunny
7 Stop flowing
8 Strong dislike
9 Pressing device
10 First-__ kit
11 "Rudolph the __-Nosed Reindeer"
20 "Believe it or __!"
22 Well ventilated
24 "Sign on the dotted __"
25 Went fast
26 A sight for sore __
27 Auction's last word
28 Old-fashioned and inappropriate
29 Phone cut-in
30 Home for a mower
33 Church symbols
36 Mr. Van Winkle
38 Newspaper worker
42 Like French toast
43 The Golden __ (Do unto others . . .)
44 Grace ender
46 Spare __
47 Tribal unit
48 Embraced
49 Chemist's lair
50 Ill will

Eye impolitely

solution on page 302

ACROSS

1 James __ Jones
5 Woodcutting tool
8 Big smile
12 Elmer's __
13 Bullfight cry
14 "All __!" (court phrase)
15 Lady's man
16 What Jack Sprat couldn't eat
17 Just hanging around
18 Russian rulers, once
20 Give food to
21 Bunch
24 Mixed-breed dog
26 Pound part
27 __ Galahad
28 Lawn piece
31 Dozing
33 Art on one's skin
35 Honor __ parents
36 Baby lion or bear
38 Bandage material
39 By way of, shortly
40 __ tube
41 Curly hairstyle
44 Oil __
46 __ machine (gambling device)
47 Santa's helper
48 Deep female voice
52 "At __!" (army command)
53 Fight official
54 Train-track part
55 Like some wines or cheeses
56 Pig pen
57 Changed colors

DOWN

1 Have __ on one's face
2 British brew
3 Try to get elected
4 Salad leaves
5 Couch
6 Frightens
7 Diver's outfit
8 Cheat by conning
9 Be a passenger
10 Bit of land in the ocean
11 Require
19 Words from the podium
21 Farm animal associated with tin cans
22 Be hasty
23 "If and __ if…"
25 Sad
28 Astonish
29 Seep
30 Busy person
32 Ship's treasurers
34 Pub mug
37 Ammo item
39 Lugged
41 On a cruise
42 It hangs from a pole
43 Woke up
45 Doubtful
49 __ down the law
50 Equal finish
51 "__ Yeller"

James __ Jones

solution on page 302

2. Start-up

ACROSS

1 Gain in return for labor
5 Awful actors
9 Plead
12 Zone
13 Don't include
14 "A long, long time __ . . . "
15 Appear
16 Kelly of "Singin' in the Rain"
17 Also
18 __ in a tie (required overtime)
20 Horse sound
22 Caught at the rodeo
24 Desert wanderer
27 Flower holder
29 Hibernation locale
30 Graduate school papers
34 Adeptly
36 __-door neighbor
37 Caesar's robe
39 Groups of three
41 Church officials
46 Hindu mystic
48 Green eye color
49 Make a choice
51 Baby's first "word"
53 Deal with it
54 "__, fie, fo, fum . . . "
55 Likened
56 Leg joint
57 Temporary craze
58 Faxed
59 Shrill bark

DOWN

1 Artist's stand
2 Bullring
3 Hollow marsh stalks
4 Phone book listings
5 Road __ (two-lane user)
6 Alters a law
7 Greedy cry
8 Beer mug
9 It makes the shower safer
10 Head sweller
11 Moo __ gai pan
19 Love bird
21 "Fore!" game
23 Toward sunrise
25 Suffer
26 Not wet
28 On __ (nervous)
30 Miner's need
31 ". . . eating __ curds and whey"
32 Were
33 Pack
35 Apiece
38 Root cause
40 Long stories
42 Full of kitsch
43 __ layer (UV ray blocker)
44 Behave like Teflon
45 Catch some Zs
47 Create
49 "Wipe that smile __ your face"
50 "The Princess and the __"
52 Six-legged sidewalk critter

Gain in return for labor

solution on page 303

ACROSS

1 Watermelon shape
5 Good places for a hot bath
9 Had one's fill
12 Jet-set need
13 __ of Fame
14 Came in first
15 Lodge members
16 Took to a higher court
18 Crow's-__ (place to cry "Land ho!" from)
19 Hoarse
20 Once around the track
22 Come to __ with (deal with)
26 Newspaper editorial hub
31 Circus animal with a ball
32 Hairy jungle beast
33 Bad guy's expression
35 Get older
36 In one __ swoop
38 Like castaways
40 Go in
42 "I __ you a debt of gratitude"
43 Ma's or Pa's sisters
46 "__, wanna buy a watch, cheap?"
50 Local mythology
53 Saint's light
54 "I caught you in the act!"
55 Break-__ point
56 Send forth
57 Signal yes with your head
58 Autumn tool
59 Ties the knot

DOWN

1 Microwave __
2 Nasty
3 Interrogates
4 Finally
5 Puts a point on
6 Baby's father
7 Swiss mountains
8 "George Washington __ here"
9 Piercing tool
10 Tic-tac-__
11 "I am at my wit's __!"
17 Sinbad's si's
21 Words from your sponsors
23 "__ 'em and weep"
24 Sorcerer
25 Snowy-weather toy
26 Outdoor eatery
27 Hit the __ road
28 Hit with snowballs
29 "At your mark, get __ . . ."
30 Lamp fuel
34 __ deal
37 Plumber's problem
39 Sister's son
41 Measuring stick
44 Star's kablooey
45 "Star __" (classic sci-fi show)
47 Identical
48 Slipped
49 Sippy-cup users
50 Admirer
51 "NOW I see!"
52 Lass's guy

Watermelon shape

solution on page 303

ACROSS

1 Lasso
5 "__, crackle, pop!"
9 "__ aboard!"
12 Times to remember
13 Mystical emanation
14 Dove's cry
15 Soldiers of yore
16 Colors in a printer cartridge
17 __-been
18 Do a trucker's job
20 Robbery
22 Does one's bidding
24 "And __ we go!"
26 Ping-pong divider
27 "Or __!" (threat)
29 "The __ Panther"
33 Pin the __ on the donkey
35 __ and vinegar dressing
36 Bird of ill __
37 Singly
38 Puts together
40 Calf cry
41 Page or clerk
43 Nuclear power __
45 Golf club handle
48 Fisherman's supply
49 Candle substance
50 Pottery substance
53 Use a straw
56 Sick
57 Oprah or Regis
58 Based on a __ story
59 "__ whiz!"
60 Oxen harness
61 You ain't __ nothing yet!

DOWN

61 "You ain't __ nothin' yet!"
1 __ the engine
2 Metal-bearing rock
3 Pitiful
4 School report
5 __ the seven seas
6 Convent sister
7 The __ of the Covenant
8 Spaghetti or macaroni
9 Be sore
10 Meat __ (box-shaped entree that's sliced)
11 "Little Bo-Peep has __ her sheep . . ."
19 __ to your own advantage
21 Vaccine holder, for short
22 __ the matter at hand
23 Mexican jumping __
24 "All kidding __ . . ."
25 Join metal
28 Laundromat collection
30 Childish
31 Gas used in lights
32 Tie one's shoelaces
34 Turn over a new __
39 Health resort
42 An __ trigger finger
44 Grocery store needs
45 Quick drink
46 He played the Skipper
47 Rod between wheels
48 Computer unit
51 British toilet
52 "__ not what your country . . ."
54 Actor's hint
55 Boyfriend of Barbie

Lasso

solution on page 303

ACROSS

1 Hammered item
5 Place for pastrami
9 Lighthouse locale
12 Moreover
13 What a magnet responds to
14 A taste of one's __ medicine
15 Pots and __
16 Circle parts
17 Was in first place
18 High regard
20 "Be __ to your web-footed friends . . ."
22 Steal
24 Tries to lose some pounds
27 Lasagna seasoning
31 Addams Family adjective
32 "Been there, __ that"
33 Speck
35 Penny
36 __ out (gives out portions)
38 Withdraws
40 Box-office hit
41 Asphalt
42 Harvest
44 Solar __
49 Cost an arm and a __
51 __ as a pancake
53 It spews from a volcano
54 Sailor's yes
55 Work hard
56 Tums target
57 Say "I do"
58 Nimble
59 Burrowing animal

DOWN

1 __ of the neck
2 Word of sorrow
3 "__ it a pity"
4 Misplace
5 Baseball field shape
6 "To __ is human"
7 Under __ and key
8 Not outdoors
9 Welded
10 Flock female
11 "__ then what happened?"
19 Geologic division
21 Dorothy, to Auntie Em
23 Brag
25 Fork feature
26 Readies the table for a meal
27 __-on favorite
28 Hotel offering
29 Made bigger
30 Honking birds
34 Cruel
37 Elevator passages
39 Shed tears
43 "Kerplunk"
45 __ dunk (basketball shot)
46 __ Bell
47 Demonic
48 Created
49 Mother-in-__
50 A real __-opener
52 Telecast

Hammered item

solution on page 303

ACROSS

1 __ Wednesday
4 Harry Potter has one
8 Rural plot
12 Pursue romantically
13 The Stooges, e.g.
14 Train sound
15 Popular street name
16 Hot __ (racecars)
17 __ in there (stay tough)
18 Spectacular
20 Get up and go
22 Haul
24 At the center of
25 Juicy fruit
26 Map out
27 "__ had so many children . . ."
30 Coffeepot with a spigot
31 Task
32 Frying __
33 "And not one __ cent more!"
34 Wacky
35 Three feet
36 "The Old Grey __" (kid's song)
37 "Ten __ a-leaping . . ."
38 State to be true
41 Guided trip
42 An ear of __
43 "Ship __!"
45 Bizarre
48 Barking up the wrong __
49 Fizzy drink
50 "__ is me!"
51 One who can tell the future
52 Shout
53 Mend

DOWN

1 Wondrous fear
2 Do, re, mi, fa, __, la, ti, do
3 Country of origin
4 __ the bed (remove the linens)
5 Captain Hook's fear
6 Assist
7 ". . . parsley, sage, __ and thyme"
8 Had a pain
9 Scorch
10 Step on a ladder
11 Like nog
19 Rate word
21 "__, ten, a big fat hen"
22 On the __ of the moment
23 Dog caller's word
24 "Leave well enough __"
26 Drugstore
27 Small songbirds
28 Not easy
29 Odds and __
31 Russian ruler of long ago
35 "__ betcha!"
36 Clementine's dad, e.g.
37 True-blue
38 Feats
39 Golfer's cry
40 At no cost
41 __ bridge (place with a fee)
44 Work on the garden
46 Bambi's mom, for one
47 Morning moisture

___ Wednesday

solution on page 303

ACROSS

1 Yawn-inducer
5 Try to win
8 Sideways walker
12 Break not just a little bit
13 Sherman Antitrust __
14 Pork fried __
15 Very happy
17 Getting on in years
18 "__ of Fortune"
19 Professional cook
21 Virginia __ (square dance)
23 Coral ring surrounding a lagoon
27 Strong impulse
30 Air outlet
32 The Dynamic __
33 Band assistant
35 Accompany
37 "Oh no, __ again!"
38 Gunfight command
40 What Noah's neighbors needed
41 Baseball maneuver
43 Night sky twinkler
45 Car horn sound
47 Olympic award
51 Low-singing female
54 Scatter
56 Sudden attack
57 Frenzy
58 Coral __
59 "He's not my __" (date reject line)
60 Casual shirt
61 Wallop a fly

DOWN

1 Witch's __
2 "That hurt!"
3 "__ and shine!"
4 Went in
5 Big barrel
6 Winter hanger
7 Cut into, artistically
8 Artistic skill
9 Jury-__ (improvise)
10 An __ up one's sleeve
11 It may be next to an alarm clock
16 Pub pint
20 Grabs a snack
22 "If you're __ in a jam, here I am"
24 Skunk's weapon
25 Skulk
26 Tons
27 Large vases
28 __ beer (type of soda)
29 Fence door
31 Certain salamander
34 __ chatter
36 Jobs
39 Dream of self-improvement
42 "Welcome to my humble __"
44 Concert cube
46 Cut and paste
48 Sketched
49 Going through the water
50 Skedaddled
51 Dali design
52 __ it on the line
53 Just the __ of the iceberg
55 "We're off to __ the wizard . . ."

Yawn-inducer

solution on page 303

ACROSS

1 Line-__ veto
5 Sloped walkway
9 Member of a civic group
12 Not yep
13 Length × width
14 Squirt __
15 Make a sweater
16 E-mailed
17 Cheer for the bullfighter
18 Windowpane holder
20 Magazine edition
22 Fairy-tale bridge master
24 "Coming __ to a theater near you"
26 ". . . __ a farm, E-I-E-I-O"
27 Sign of boredom
29 Breakfast grains
33 Eye part
35 Lex Luthor, to Superman
36 Down to the __ (at the last minute)
37 __ of the woods
38 Valentine's Day flower
40 Checkerboard sequence
41 Revered image
43 Sleeveless suit parts
45 Purple Popsicle flavor
48 "May I __ you?"
49 Sprinted
50 Pretentious
53 Large tubs
56 __ cream cone
57 Alphabet __
58 Copy, sound-wise
59 Church seating
60 On the cutting __
61 Sunflower snack

DOWN

1 Pen and __
2 2,000 pounds
3 Like soap operas
4 __ detector
5 Poison ivy response
6 "Where the Boys __"
7 ". . . three __ in a tub"
8 __ furniture
9 Self-images
10 Humdinger
11 Place for a jeans patch
19 Crafty
21 Winter weather
22 Slender
23 Infrequent
24 Faint away
25 "Weren't we the lucky __!"
28 Hairstyle likely to need a pick
30 No-fly zone, say
31 Horse gait
32 Does needlework
34 Annoyance on a record or CD
39 Night before
42 Halt
44 Santa's helpers
45 Clench
46 Run like mad
47 From the top
48 Exaggerate ad-wise
51 Baseballer Carew
52 __ of war (rope event)
54 None of __ above
55 Instant lawn

Line-__ veto

solution on page 304

ACROSS

1 Bite __ more than you can chew
4 "The Tortoise and the __"
8 Animal's stomach
12 Speak falsely
13 Yoked pair
14 Homeless wanderer
15 Salad's "sauce"
17 Place to be stranded
18 Basil sauce
19 Windows of the soul
20 Go __ over (adore)
23 Sports judge
25 Tellers of fibs
27 To a ripe old __
28 "Gosh!"
31 The long __ of the law
32 Place for a clip-on mike
34 "Say what?"
35 Recolor
36 "Look __ below!"
37 Baby mushroom
39 "__ Beginning to Look a Lot Like Christmas"
40 Not difficult
41 Ugly Duckling's adulthood
44 Multiplication __
48 Diplomat's skill
49 Matched
53 Turn __ a new leaf
54 A grand slam scores four of these
55 Boat paddle
56 Cancun cash
57 The opposite of west
58 "__ not to be late"

DOWN

1 "In the Good __ Summertime"
2 Evergreen tree
3 Finder's __
4 Garden sprayer
5 The __ of Evil
6 Tenant's payment
7 Eat until full, or more
8 Tribal leader
9 Cheerful
10 Skilled
11 Troubles
16 Go a few rounds
20 Happy
21 Light as a feather
22 Boggle or Scrabble
24 Squiggly swimmers
26 Vending machine opening
27 Fitting
28 Stop, stallion
29 It's for you and me
30 ". . . eating her curds and __"
33 Tight, budgetwise
38 Banana skin
39 Lead-in
41 Red 8-sided sign
42 Signal hello or goodbye
43 Ones in a card deck
45 Blue-green
46 Hot cross __
47 Have the __ laugh
50 "It's beginning to look a __ like Christmas"
51 An __ of corn
52 Towel off

Bite __ more than you can chew

solution on page 304

ACROSS

1 Give the __-over
5 A law __ itself
9 Baseball hat
12 Ring, as a bell
13 Lowly laborer
14 "And now, a word from __ sponsor"
15 Clothing labels
16 Little Dutch boy's place to plug
17 Breakfasted
18 Cheap liner accommodations
20 Feed the hogs
21 __ food (cultural cuisine)
23 What Weebles do
27 Pounds one's feet
31 Cognizant
32 Frog sound
33 4-door cars
35 The __ of relativity
36 Cheap cigar
38 Elegant
41 Bleeped
46 Monkey's uncle
47 __-Pong
48 Impatient chess request
49 As thick as __ soup
50 "The Duke of __"
51 Get __ with (avenge)
52 Leaf cutter
53 Rhymed word in "Rudolph the Red-Nosed Reindeer"
54 Eagle's home

DOWN

1 Picks
2 Tidy
3 Zoo enclosure
4 "Or __ what?"
5 "This just in" item
6 Stallion's sound
7 Video arcade "coins"
8 __ and the same
9 Frosty's eyes
10 Ford or Chevy
11 __ school (private precollege place)
19 Show some humanity
20 "Four __ and seven years ago . . ."
22 You'll want to scratch them
23 "It __ a dark and stormy night . . ."
24 "What do I __ you?"
25 Not good
26 Cheeky
28 Dairy sound
29 Golf score to shoot for
30 "The __ is falling!"
34 Church supper
35 Prickling sensation
37 Style
38 Dad
39 "Try to keep an __ mind"
40 "May I show you to a __?"
42 Sign of things to come
43 Roam
44 Nights before
45 Fender bender
47 A square __ in a round hole

Give the ___-over

solution on page 304

ACROSS

1 Mosquito bite symptom
5 Detective's cry
8 What gears do
12 Drive-__ window
13 Rhyme __ reason
14 Division word
15 Swing and Big Band
16 Mark Twain's "__ Sawyer"
17 Skedaddle
18 Wool-eating insect
19 Place where you get cucumbers on your eyes
20 Raid the fridge
21 Use a broom
23 Coo
26 Place to keep one's socks
29 Expert
30 Kid's chase game
33 The __ on the cake
34 "Quiet on the __!"
35 Lubricate
36 "What's the __ with you?"
38 Wore away
40 "Same here!"
44 Piece of soap
45 Conceit
48 Get bigger
49 Go out with socially
50 Do a lawn chore
51 Bugle or trumpet
52 Operates
53 Green around the gills
54 Schlep
55 Places for the weary
56 Promos
57 Zoomed

DOWN

1 12 __ or less (fast-moving checkout line)
2 __ for a loop (confuse)
3 Wooden box
4 Asked to be quiet
5 "The __ come marching one by one, hurrah, hurrah"
6 Hula __
7 Weapon
8 Greedy one
9 Puts down stakes for the night
10 Prestige
11 "Pease porridge __"
22 Like a number that can't be divided
24 Encouraged
25 Decompose
27 School-related stuff
28 Clever comedian
30 From head to __
31 Military pilot's post
32 Boasted
37 Civil __
39 Gown
41 Boy Scout unit
42 Linzer __
43 Privately __
46 Top Olympic-medal material
47 Night birds
49 Redo the words, like in a movie

Mosquito bite symptom

solution on page 304

ACROSS

1 "You have a certain __ about you"
5 Decide
8 Family __ (ancestry)
12 Surprise problem
13 Like uncooked steak
14 "__ goes nothing!"
15 "Go fly a __!"
16 Scientific
18 Awful smell
20 Sound pitch
21 Grownup tadpole
23 Ability
26 Kept out of view
29 Garbage
31 By means of
32 Tram load
33 A __ in the pool
34 Stately tree
35 "Snap, crackle, __"
36 Credit
38 Ham on __
39 Military mistake
41 New __'s Eve
43 __ and rave
45 Hung like a curtain
49 Opinion
52 Went headfirst into the water
53 Palm reader, say
54 Pricker
55 All in the family
56 Mats
57 Sounds with tongue depressors
58 Depend

DOWN

1 Solicits
2 Textbook division
3 Speed
4 Secret __ (spy)
5 Fruit farms
6 Sidekick
7 English idiot
8 "Try to __ for yourself"
9 Footballer who catches a pass
10 Jurassic, for one
11 Squiggly swimmer
17 Have a snack
19 Portable bed
22 Donald Duck's girlfriend
24 Easter flower
25 Like a weak excuse
26 Moves like a bunny
27 Strong metal
28 Left
30 Radar road targets
36 Polly, to Tom Sawyer
37 Road-paving material
40 Carnivals
42 Screen with blips
44 Big brass horn
46 __ fun at
47 Vileness
48 ". . . nobody can __"
49 African cobra
50 The Boston __ Party
51 "Obviously!"

You have a certain __ about you

solution on page 304

ACROSS

1 Diner's food catalog
5 Enjoys dinner
9 "__ he's a jolly good fellow . . ."
12 Cake baker
13 Bigger-than-life
14 Sheep sound
15 __ between the lines
16 "From Here to __"
18 Made a mistake
20 Sailing
21 __ of lamb
23 Goes limp
27 Collie comment
30 Song for two
32 Conceal
33 Basement
35 "What's on the __ for today?"
37 "Hey, what's the big __?"
38 Big book
40 It's on a lawn at dawn
41 People of action
43 "And not a __ out of you!"
45 Stare
47 Shish-__
51 News-flash intro
55 "Let's not forget"
56 "To thine __ self be true"
57 Simmer
58 Make unusable
59 Apprehend
60 Attendant
61 Tire hiss

DOWN

1 "The __ the merrier"
2 "Be it __ so humble . . ."
3 __-sighted
4 "Check __ the hood"
5 __ no evil . . .
6 Comprehension
7 Facial weapons for clowns
8 Fastener that's turned to go in or out
9 G-man's org.
10 Breakfast grain
11 A __ of sunshine
17 Inexperienced
19 Crib cry
22 Blunt
24 __ a hand (assist)
25 Coastal water rise and fall
26 Cole __
27 Citric __
28 Update the decor
29 Run away
31 Subdued
34 Big
36 Nerd
39 Began on Broadway
42 Chips and __
44 Oyster's jewel
46 Tunnel-like noodle
48 Sky color
49 The sun never sets on it
50 Hit one's head, like five bed-bouncing monkeys
51 Man's best friend
52 Stand in __ of
53 It makes a blast
54 Baa maid

Diner's food catalog

solution on page 304

ACROSS

1 Laser __
5 Teacher, for short
9 Doggy __
12 Hankering
13 Villain's opponent
14 Once and for __
15 Soccer cry
16 Squished circle
17 London lavatory
18 Watch the kids
19 Giraffe feature
20 Weep loudly
21 __ Man ("Wizard of Oz" role)
22 Wishing __ (place to throw a coin)
23 Quaint diner
24 Threw a party
26 "Here's mud in your __!"
28 Gain admission
29 Arm bender
33 Use a needle
35 Deli meat in an Italian sub
36 A __ on one's record
39 Gobbles up
41 "I __ your pardon"
42 "Where are __?"
43 Light, like a ghost
44 Note after fa
45 Cabin material
46 Patron
47 Broke a garden bed
49 Volcano dust
50 Simple
51 "I think you're __ something"
52 Waterlogged
53 Low voice
54 "Get over here!"

DOWN

1 Insect
2 Rivers slowly cause it
3 For or __
4 Thaw
5 Hit *69, say
6 Make merry
7 Prophecy seer
8 People
9 Model wood
10 Unsociable
11 World model, in 3-D
21 "Save __ best for last"
22 "If I __ King of the Forest"
23 __ phone
25 __ one's mettle
27 __ and nays
30 Monkeys
31 Egg creations
32 Hair for up there
34 "Pop Goes the __"
35 Two-speaker system
36 Rule
37 Not tight
38 "That __ to be a law!"
40 Red __ (crisis warning)
43 Cougar
44 "Little __ of Horrors"
48 Decimal point

Laser ___

solution on page 305

ACROSS

1 Money
5 Calamine-lotion target
9 Olympic chant
12 What sore muscles do
13 Lot-size measure
14 Complain constantly
15 Fisherman's need
16 Be responsible for
17 Yahtzee cube
18 Writing end of a pencil
20 Make a hospital corner
21 ". . . to get __ poor dog a bone"
24 Rough textured
26 Takes in a foundling
28 Banana color
32 Beauty pageant winner crown
33 Cheek reddener
34 Try to do better
36 Not married
37 Lower in rank
39 "__, a mouse!"
40 Sherry or Chablis
43 Woman's handbag
45 Break the __ (socialize)
46 "I got it!"
47 From the get-go
51 Deer's mother
52 Softball paths
53 PTA bake __
54 Until the __ of time
55 Golf bag items
56 Lad

DOWN

1 Bumper __
2 Champion
3 ". . . __ loves me not"
4 "Not if I can __ it!"
5 Proportions
6 Boxing match site
7 Military guard
8 "Mary __ a little lamb"
9 Reverse
10 Go by boat
11 Like some wine
19 Musical scale
20 Criminal
21 Bonnets and sombreros
22 Revise
23 The __ of the ocean
25 Things in a row
27 Lion group
29 Downhill racer
30 Make goo-goo eyes at
31 7-day period
35 "The __ Strikes Back"
36 ". . . and I can't __ this enough"
38 "An __ of prevention is . . ."
40 __ awake
41 Religious image
42 Have to have
44 Right, on most maps
46 Wrestling pad
48 Negative vote
49 Moose relatives
50 Little

Money

solution on page 305

ACROSS

1 Enjoyed the buffet
4 An open and __ case
8 Nose-in-the-air type
12 Solidify
13 Melody
14 Expect great things
15 Make weaker
17 __ the score (establish a balance)
18 Go skyward
19 Manufacturing __
20 Snub
23 Dirt
25 Dancer's clicker
26 Tidal waves
30 "Have you had __?" (ready to cry uncle?)
33 What some hairlines do
34 Refers to
36 Flamenco shout
37 __ or false
38 Trimmed the grass
40 Written slander
43 Cornfield pest
45 Smell
46 Allowances
50 Skedaddled
51 __ into it]
52 "Let the cat __ of the bag"
53 __ dog (Arctic transport)
54 Big boats
55 Hula hoop or jack-in-the-box

DOWN

1 Birthday cake candle count
2 "__ Little Indians"
3 Keebler employee
4 Pub mug
5 Well-connected airports
6 "__ I miss my guess . . ."
7 Golf gadget
8 Varnish
9 Big boom in the night sky
10 __ for business
11 All __ out of shape
16 Make a mistake
19 Tree with cones
20 Cherry leftover
21 Window section
22 "Once __ a Mattress"
24 Not theirs
26 Commandment start word
27 Kitten sound
28 Motionless
29 Gardener's purchase
31 Said
32 What a pink birth announcement means
35 Hummingbird's food
38 Broods
39 Be in debt
40 Oodles
41 Divine image
42 Tiresome talker
44 "But is it worth the __?"
46 "The Old Man and the __"
47 __ a snowball's chance
48 Pair
49 Porky's pad

Enjoyed the buffet

solution on page 305

3. Head Start

ACROSS

1 Joke
4 "Right away!"
8 Troublesome insect
12 "I see it all now!"
13 Game on horseback
14 Pained
15 Where to go when you've got to go
17 Pirate __
18 Courtroom ritual
19 Advice to a sinner
20 Bedtime reading
23 Drafty
25 Hairpieces
26 "__ It Romantic?"
27 Nay negater
30 "You're under __" (follow-up to "Book 'em")
32 Gong relative
34 Spelling __
35 Fly-swatter material
37 Civic group
38 Smoke
39 A gaggle of __
40 "I dunno" expression
43 "See __ run"
45 Little piggies
46 Sunshade umbrellas
50 Takes advantage of
51 Vent outward
52 Be under the weather
53 Go against
54 Tees
55 Under lock and __

DOWN

1 Lump
2 "Gotcha!"
3 "You've __ Mail"
4 Spritz
5 Honk
6 Hawaiian hellos
7 Circus midget __ Thumb
8 Rather pale
9 "Hello" to "Hello," say
10 Under-the-table kicking spot
11 Use a keyboard
16 "Neigh!" sayer
19 Over the top
20 Cotton __
21 Become fatigued
22 Mythical meanie
24 Move at a snail's pace
26 Part
27 Talented
28 Babbles
29 End of a veiled threat
31 Holier than thou
33 Tournaments
36 "__ Street" (PBS show)
38 Finicky
39 Bearded animals
40 Rhinestone, say
41 Hydrant hookup
42 The Great Barrier __
44 Goody two shoes
46 __ rally
47 Symbol of strength
48 Phony story
49 "You __ dog, you!"

Joke

solution on page 306

ACROSS

1 Fill to the __
5 Generation __
8 Casino coin
12 Steak order
13 Mine find
14 Motorcar
15 Nature's building block
16 Stereo component
17 Place where you may hear peeps
18 Singing cowboy Autry
19 Wigwam
21 Required
23 Circle segment
26 Snitch on
29 Ceremony
31 Sneeze sound
32 Small drum
33 Like potato chips or saltines
35 Coming to a point, shape-wise
36 __-L Ration (dog food brand)
37 Less difficult
39 Give entry to
40 Hankering
44 Got bigger
47 Came together
48 "If the __ fits . . ."
49 A seer may sense it
50 Holiday lead-in
51 "Root, root, root for the home __"
52 Remain
53 Cherry's color
54 Goes down, like the sun

DOWN

1 Boast
2 __ of return
3 Item used to attach a shirt decal
4 Souvenirs
5 Small beard
6 ". . . should be considered __ and dangerous"
7 Salt and __
8 Candy __
9 Shade
10 "__ been real!"
11 Crib user
20 Fit for food
22 Ran off to get married
23 Cousin's mom
24 Go berserk
25 Numbskull
26 Bulletin-board pin
27 43,560 square feet
28 Slim
30 Sightseers
34 Chat a lot
35 Like a suit after tailoring
38 Colander
39 Frittered __
41 "Get __ to a nunnery"
42 Paint layer
43 Clothing seams
44 It's pumped at the pump
45 "My life is stuck in a __"
46 "The end of an __"

Fill to the ___

solution on page 306

ACROSS

1 Groaner
4 Bottle tops
8 Chooses
12 Outrage
13 Harbinger
14 "Shop till you __"
15 Powerful explosive
16 The Golden Arches, for McDonald's
17 Knight's wife
18 Gradually deprive
20 Followed orders
22 Garbage __
24 Stares
26 Like an apple with a hole through it
28 Winter warming devices
32 "You have but to __" (anything you want)
33 Perch
35 Swimmer's unit
36 Sherlock Holmes story type
38 Tex-Mex sauce
40 What a belt goes around
42 Shreds
43 "Take it all in __" (deal with it calmly)
46 Way on or off a turnpike
48 Part of the eye
49 Orderly
51 Watched the kids
54 Salon color job
55 "Yo quiero __ Bell"
56 __ trip
57 Like meringue
58 "__, together, kick!"
59 Luke, to Darth Vader

DOWN

1 Hole used for trapping
2 Vase
3 Various computer systems
4 Fizzy grape or orange drink
5 "You are __ friends"
6 Wooden nail
7 Naps
8 Least normal
9 Use rosary beads
10 Heavy piece of literature
11 Hurried
19 She who might be sheared
21 Pounds, like a drum
22 Ripoff
23 Comfy
25 Sailor's hellos
27 Terror
29 Ovals
30 Scratchy voice
31 Places for a mud bath
34 Becomes accustomed to
37 Like an S
39 Slot-machine feature
41 "Gone without a __"
43 Web __
44 High-school math class about angles
45 Diamond engagement __
47 Upon
50 "You are what you __"
52 Gone by
53 Heavy load

Groaner

solution on page 306

ACROSS

1 James __ Carter
5 Make flour more fine
9 Where to fly a kite
12 Atlas continent usually on two pages
13 " . . . with a banjo on my __"
14 __ the knot (marry)
15 Monopoly collection
16 Castaway's home
17 Tiny army member
18 Without clothes
20 "That's __ nonsense!"
22 Rock and __ music
24 Rapid
27 Health resort
30 Prom partner
32 "Scram!"
33 Habit
35 "Mrs. Robinson, you're __ to seduce me"
37 St. Louis landmark
38 At a snail's __
40 Soup veggie
41 Parts of a forest
43 Took off, like a snake's old skin
45 Russian refusals
47 Devilish one
51 __ up to (amount to)
53 Muck
55 Lagoon
56 Drain cleaner
57 "__ flies when you're having fun"
58 "Somewhere __ the Rainbow"
59 Headed up
60 Gush
61 Tear to pieces

DOWN

1 Make a salary
2 Adrift
3 Skating __
4 "See ya __ alligator"
5 Glide down the slope
6 Verbal slap in the face
7 "How long have you __ this way?"
8 "All I Want for Christmas Is My Two Front __"
9 UFO
10 Next of __ (relatives)
11 "So near and __ so far"
19 Numbskull
21 Word in this book's title
23 Genie's home
25 "Leave your message at the __"
26 Eastern exercise discipline
27 "Scram!"
28 Happy cat sound
29 Climbed up
31 __-a-Sketch
34 "__ went thataway!"
36 Marsh grass
39 Presuppose
42 Religious groups
44 Ornamentation
46 Fall over one's feet
48 Change to a new house
49 __ mitt
50 Geek
51 "For __ the marbles"
52 Hide grey hairs, say
54 Morning lawn sight

James __ Carter

solution on page 306

ACROSS

1 "__ the deck!"
4 A __ on the wrist
8 Thick slice of bacon
12 An __ in the hole
13 Bee's place
14 Slinky, essentially
15 Japanese money
16 Pulpit word
17 Was a passenger
18 Raptor's claw
20 Took part in an election
21 Intelligent
23 Preowned
25 "If you can't say something __ . . ."
26 Fellow
27 Item used to swab the deck
30 Not coastal
32 It's swabbed before taking blood
34 " . . . blackbirds baked in a __"
35 The Far __ (the Orient)
37 Afresh
38 Bread spread, for short
39 Braid
40 "Made for each __"
43 "Hurray for our team" cry
45 Intention
46 Pond __ (algae)
47 Puncturing tool
50 Bowling alley
51 __ with the dishes
52 Lion in the Zodiac
53 Advantage
54 Notable periods
55 Stitch together

DOWN

1 Baled farm item
2 Skating-rink surface
3 Arm with sucker
4 "Thou __ not kill"
5 Car for the stars
6 Street
7 "The __ is mightier than the sword"
8 New England food fish
9 Winnings
10 Lieutenant
11 Ran in the wash
19 Square footage
20 Nix by a President
21 Haircut sound
22 Itty-bitty
24 Grumpy mood
26 Australian greeting
27 Vitamins and __
28 Last column in addition
29 Sunday sermon seating
31 "__ and dear"
33 Go against the odds
36 Game where your hands can't touch the ball
38 Battle
39 Fill-in workers
40 Flirty look
41 Warty animal
42 "__ onto your seats!"
44 __ hoop
46 "Ain't __ Sweet?"
48 Tiny
49 Close to the ground

___ the deck!

solution on page 306

ACROSS

1 Tarot suit
5 Be very talkative
8 Tacks on
12 Bushy hairdo
13 Be wrong
14 Trickle through
15 Screwdriver or wrench
16 12th word of "My Bonnie Lies Over the Ocean"
17 Long truck with lots of storage
18 English assignment
20 Chance __ (meet by accident)
21 Oohs and __
24 100 centimes
26 Stops
28 Reader's __
32 American bald __
33 Musical medley
34 Noble stallions
36 Hi-tech weapons
37 Blinker with lashes
39 Volleyball obstacle
40 Spill liquid
43 Yielded to pressure
45 Crosby costar
46 Bread that might have seeds
47 Golden Rule word
51 Exploiter
52 "Slippery as an __"
53 Chilly
54 Change for a twenty
55 Attempt
56 Crushed underfoot

DOWN

1 "The __ in the Hat"
2 ET craft
3 Paid athlete
4 Lone
5 They're not no's
6 Zones
7 Sought Divine help
8 Calms
9 __-dish pizza
10 Display model
11 Twirl
19 Rapid
21 Air heroes
22 Put on the stove
23 Respected elder
25 Wild talk
27 Fall film surprises
29 Equal in quantity
30 Just to be __
31 IQ __
35 "I can't tell you—it's a __"
36 Active
38 Seven-__ cake
40 "You __ your mouth!"
41 __ one's temper
42 "Chestnuts roasting on an __ fire . . ."
44 __ tape
48 "Neither here __ there"
49 None __ pretty
50 "A chip off the __ block"

Tarot suit

solution on page 306

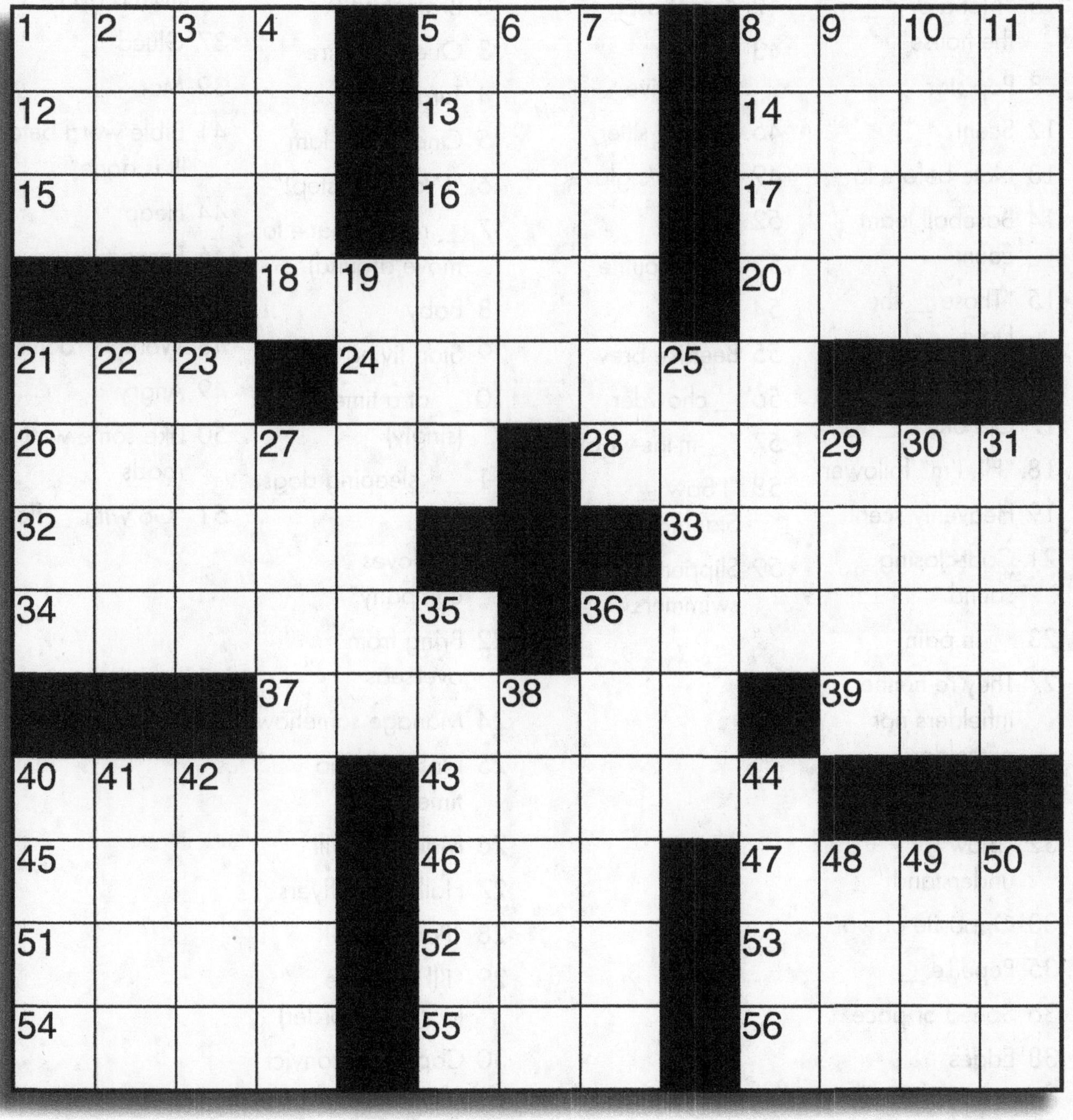

ACROSS

1 Spat
5 "Not a dry __ in the house"
8 Pop star
12 Scent
13 Note before la
14 Baseball team count
15 "Those __ the Days"
16 Baby bear
17 Get one's __ wet
18 "Hi, I'm" follower
19 Heavenly scent
21 Coat-closing sound
23 __ in pain
27 They're neither infielders nor outfielders
31 Wood-burning __
32 "Now I understand!"
33 Opposite of war
35 Pepe Le __
36 Speed or pace
38 Edges
40 Slanders
42 Assent asea
43 Elevator alternative
45 Lily-pad sitter
49 Catcher's glove
52 Kindled
53 Like a soufflé
54 It hurts
55 Beerlike brew
56 __ chowder
57 "__-in-the-wool"
58 "I Saw __ Standing There"
59 Slippery swimmers

DOWN

1 Village
2 Brainchild
3 Questionnaire
4 Turn to ice
5 One on the lam
6 "Watch __ step!"
7 __ room (space to move around)
8 Baby
9 Stop living
10 __ at a time (singly)
11 "__ sleeping dogs lie"
20 "__ loves company"
22 Bring from overseas
24 Manage somehow
25 Not __ (at no time)
26 Makes a quilt
27 Halloween flyers
28 "Pardon me!"
29 "I'll have the __" (copycat's order)
30 Capture a convict
34 Tabletop protector from a drink
37 Glued
39 Mar
41 Bible word before "It is done"
44 Heap
46 Enrage
47 Not written
48 Workout rooms
49 Angry
50 Like some wintry roads
51 "Go with __ flow"

Spat

solution on page 307

ACROSS

1 "__ and far between"
4 Pendulum path
7 Abstains from food
12 One of Dumbo's wings
13 "Not for all the __ in China!"
14 Allergy sound
15 Good for nothing
17 Mob
18 Turn down flatly
19 Middle
21 Earth Day verb
23 "That fits you to a __!"
26 The White House has an oval one
29 __ accepted
32 Canyon
33 "Did you __ your hands?"
34 The answer to "Why?"
36 ". . . __ and all the king's men . . ."
37 "Slippery" tree
38 Do penance
40 Pictures
43 Temporary beds
47 "A fool and his __ are soon parted"
49 Height
51 Pond scum
52 "Nine, __, a big fat hen"
53 White pool ball
54 Lowly drudges
55 "__ as a fox"
56 Chick's mom

DOWN

1 Quarrel between families
2 ". . . with the greatest of __ . . ."
3 Small songbird
4 Consumed
5 Damsel in distress event
6 Lawyer's workload
7 "__ or fiction"
8 Parcel of land
9 Abbreviates
10 Stranded motorist's need
11 Pregrown grass
16 Words to the song
20 __ Year's Eve
22 Say it again
24 Threat ender
25 "Mine __ have seen . . ."
26 Bad boss
27 Gas or biodiesel
28 Pink bird with long legs
30 What weightlifters "pump"
31 Tell the actors what to do
35 Be irritating, complaint-wise
36 Youth __ (type of inn)
39 Quizzes
41 Like an ogre
42 Pirate's permissions
44 "That smarts!"
45 "To thine own self be __"
46 "Have you __ enough?"
47 A pirate's might have an X on it
48 "Bravo, bullfighter!"
50 "__ takers?"

___ and far between

solution on page 307

ACROSS

1 Couples
5 Newspaper spots
8 Make a trade
12 "Tell me it __ so!"
13 "What?"
14 "A __ of Two Cities"
15 Mexican moola
16 "Think you're so clever, eh?"
17 Levitate
18 New York __
20 Magazine worker
22 Addams's Family butler
24 "__ into something more comfortable"
25 Mine deposit
26 Has gobbled up
28 Cornfield cry
31 "Try to act your __"
32 Started the day
33 Bowl over
34 Bear's burrow
35 In God We __
36 Place for a Bunsen burner
37 Use a wire whisk
38 Cafeteria carriers
40 "At the point of no __"
43 Look like
44 Shaped like a zero
45 __ rummy (card game)
47 Pageant wear that labels your state
50 "Take a chill __"
51 Generation
52 The Kingston __ ("MTA" signers)
53 Moose relatives
54 Not Dem. or Ind.
55 Place to build

DOWN

1 A __ in the road
2 Utilize
3 Like film scenes that aren't cut
4 Unemotional
5 "__, matey!"
6 "What a dope I am!"
7 __ Joe Jackson
8 "__ down to your undies"
9 "__ and see"
10 As well
11 __ through a telescope
19 __ lobby
21 Eating area
22 Get a __ of (observe)
23 Egg on
24 "I'm a little teapot short and __"
27 One who organizes
28 Fried squid
29 Not at home
30 Spider homes
37 Male cows
39 Vacation purpose
40 You might climb it in gym class
41 Satan's force
42 "Sh, people might __!"
43 Break in two
46 Wrath
48 Have a seat
49 Farming tool

Couples

solution on page 307

ACROSS

1 "Planet of the __"
5 Smack a skeeter
9 "Diamond's __ a Girl's Best Friend"
12 Eye of __ (witch's brew ingredient)
13 Twosome
14 "Without a __ to stand on"
15 ". . . and a partridge in a pear __"
16 Pact pal
17 "It" game
18 __ Grey tea
20 "Based on a true __"
22 Hot food that sounds cold
25 "__ victory!"
27 "If I Only __ a Brain"
28 Neck part
30 Banquet brewers
34 Dots in the ocean
36 Intimidation
38 "Every now and __"
39 "__ as pie"
41 Mineral spring
42 Make a sketch
44 Fall guy
46 Discontinue
49 Lunchtime, often
51 Rowboat accessory
52 "A __ off the old block"
54 Head over heels
58 Be in a play
59 Dad's sis
60 Swelled heads
61 "__ will be done"
62 Coat holders
63 Roller-coaster feature

DOWN

1 Industrious insect
2 Part of MPH
3 Lamb's mom
4 Girder material
5 Practice boxing
6 Clobber
7 Have a cold
8 Romantic rendezvous
9 Low-singing female
10 "Bring up the __"
11 Like flan
19 "It __ Necessarily So"
21 See the sights
22 IOU
23 Corned beef __
24 Thumb-twiddling
26 Butterfly catchers
29 Ocean-borne
31 Sit out for a bit
32 Snoozes
33 "Don't move, Spot"
35 "To what __?"
37 Injector in the ER
40 Storefront shade provider
43 "On last week's show . . . "
45 "I had a date with an __"
46 Winter wear
47 "To __ his own"
48 Ornate
50 Elects
53 Line in a prism display
55 "Four score and seven years __ . . . "
56 Baby's word
57 Serpent with a killer bite

"Planet of the __"

solution on page 307

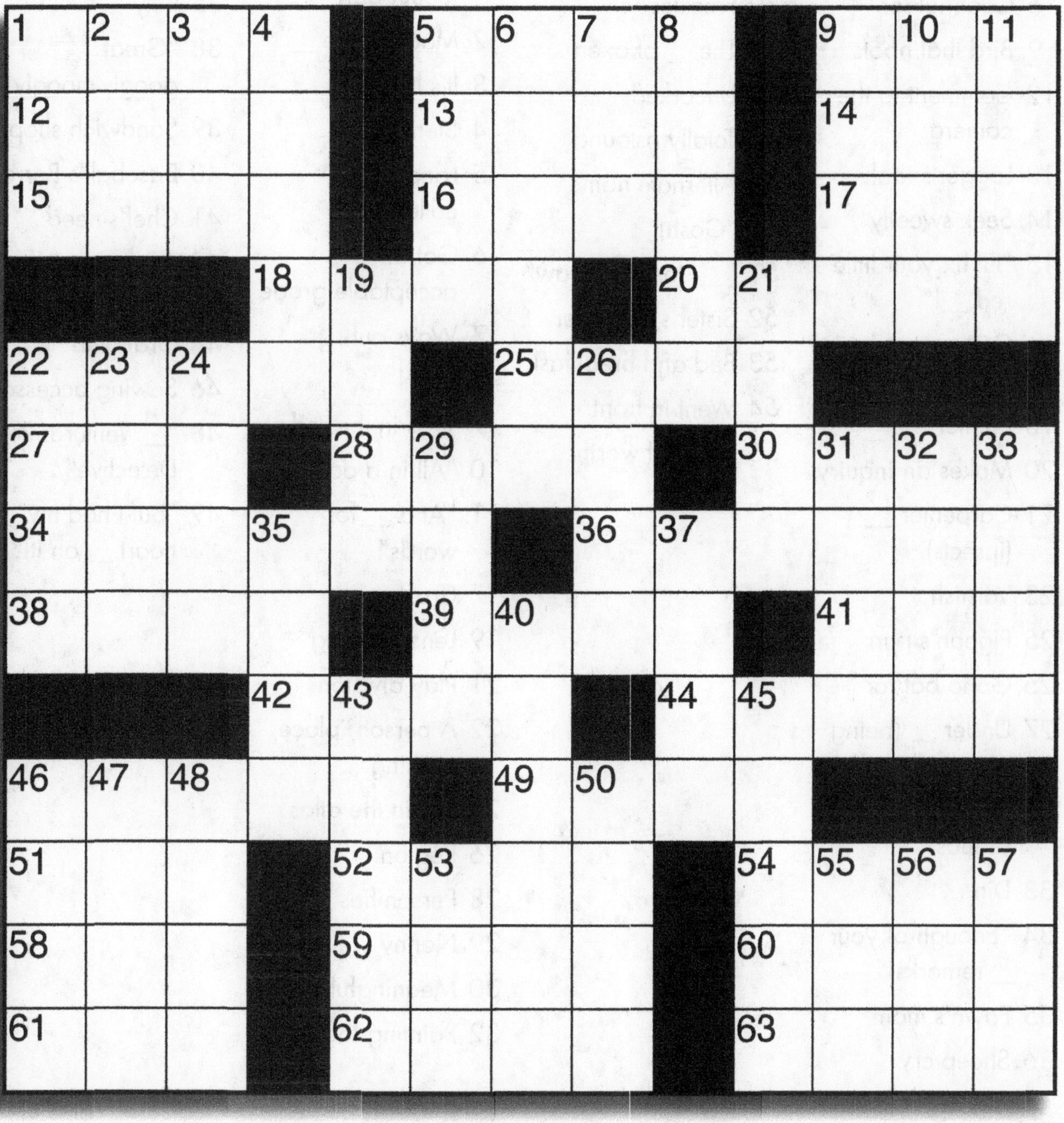

ACROSS

1 1 of 12 in court
6 Coat holder
9 Bird that hoots
12 Comment to the camera
13 Logger's tool
14 Seek sweetly
15 "I'll fix your little red __!"
16 Comes to a boil on the stove
18 Painter
20 Makes an inquiry
21 Carpenter __ (insects)
23 Varnish
25 Pigeon's purr
26 Go to bat for
27 Under __ (being attacked)
31 People who fix pianos
33 Din
34 "Enough of your __ remarks!"
35 Fawn's mom
36 Sheep cry
37 Stared
39 Freckles
40 The __ of oxen
43 Uncorked
45 Totally astound
47 Alternate name
50 "Gosh!"
51 "__, lose, or draw"
52 Sister's daughter
53 Bed and breakfast
54 Went in front
55 Thing of worth

DOWN

1 Upper or lower mouth part
2 Made in the __
3 It's like ziti
4 Stenches
5 Landlord's collection
6 Got an acceptable grade
7 Ways out
8 Jewel
9 Was in the red
10 "All in a day's __"
11 "At a __ for words"
17 Craze
19 Lens opening
21 Play divisions
22 A person, place, or thing
24 Dot in the atlas
26 Region
28 Personifies
29 Nanny __
30 Meaningful times
32 Painting tool
33 Morse __
35 Rely
38 "Great googly-moogly!"
39 Sandwich shops
40 Baseball's Berra
41 Chef's need
42 A __ sense of smell
44 Grandma
46 Sewing accessory
48 "__ Ventura: Pet Detective"
49 "But I had my heart __ on it!"

1 of 12 in court

solution on page 307

ACROSS

1 "__ two peas in a pod"
5 Nat. security police
8 High mountains
12 Holes-in-one
13 Dashed
14 5,280 feet
15 Guy
16 "A fool __ his money . . . "
17 Deadlocked
18 Buddy in Barcelona
20 Not messy
21 Six-shooter
24 Uncommon
26 Weasel-like swimmer
27 Short, stiff hair
31 Caribbean __
32 Tickle pink
34 Embrace
35 Ones in wombs
37 Street talk
39 Fireplace mess
40 Human __ (people)
41 Avoid
44 Grownup
46 Portable shelter
47 Toupee
48 "Have __ no shame?"
52 Staffer
53 Barrel
54 Adore
55 Walked on
56 Slop spot
57 Flock females

DOWN

1 Fall behind
2 Igloo material
3 Hitter Griffey Jr.
4 House and grounds
5 Fragile
6 Fourth of July sound
7 Not outside
8 Make __ (atone)
9 Still in play
10 Comment to the court
11 Had delivered
19 Eels
21 Sit for the camera
22 Object
23 "A __ in the dark"
25 Trucker's fuel
27 "Go by Greyhound"
28 "Better dead __ red"
29 Breathing organ
30 Scrambled __
33 Haircuts like Mr. T's
36 Talked wildly
38 "The Three __ Pigs"
40 Horse and __
41 "Right this second!"
42 Inheritor
43 Dismantle
45 Cut back on the chow
49 "__ now, brown cow?"
50 Preholiday night
51 "Definitely!"

__ two peas in a pod

solution on page 307

ACROSS

1 Cereal type
4 Fall guys
8 "The Old Curiosity __"
12 "__ am I to say?"
13 "Wherefore art __ Romeo?"
14 Annoys
15 "__ 'er rip!"
16 "Butterfingers!"
17 "Good for what __ you"
18 Stinky
20 Pooh pal
22 Diminish
24 Regions
27 Most gross
32 Take the __ (steer)
33 Musical Garfunkel
34 "Where the __ and the antelope play . . ."
35 Friendly
37 Bowling __
38 Start a fuse
40 Disco flashing light
44 Team spirit
48 The Cowardly __ (role in Oz)
49 Dietary fiber
51 Start to __ off (begin to fall asleep)
52 Sacred cow
53 Fly off the handle
54 Henhouse item
55 Contradict orders
56 Like some cheese
57 Trouble

DOWN

1 Screech __
2 "Beg pardon!"
3 Haul
4 Fur shoulder wraps
5 Pirate's greetings
6 Mom's man
7 One taken in by the police
8 Unexpected obstacle
9 Frozen rain
10 Lewd look
11 "Ahem!"
19 Andes pack animal
21 __ blot
23 Fire-truck call
24 Satisfied cry
25 Ump
26 Polar toymaker
28 Couch potato
29 Wiggly swimmer
30 "__ what I mean?"
31 "The old college __"
33 Math class
36 Baby napkin
37 Compensated
39 Mirror __
40 Glided
41 Ocean occurrence
42 "Fiddler on the __"
43 "It's __ a Paper Moon"
45 Once more
46 Corporate symbol
47 Brink
50 Tatter

Cereal type

solution on page 308

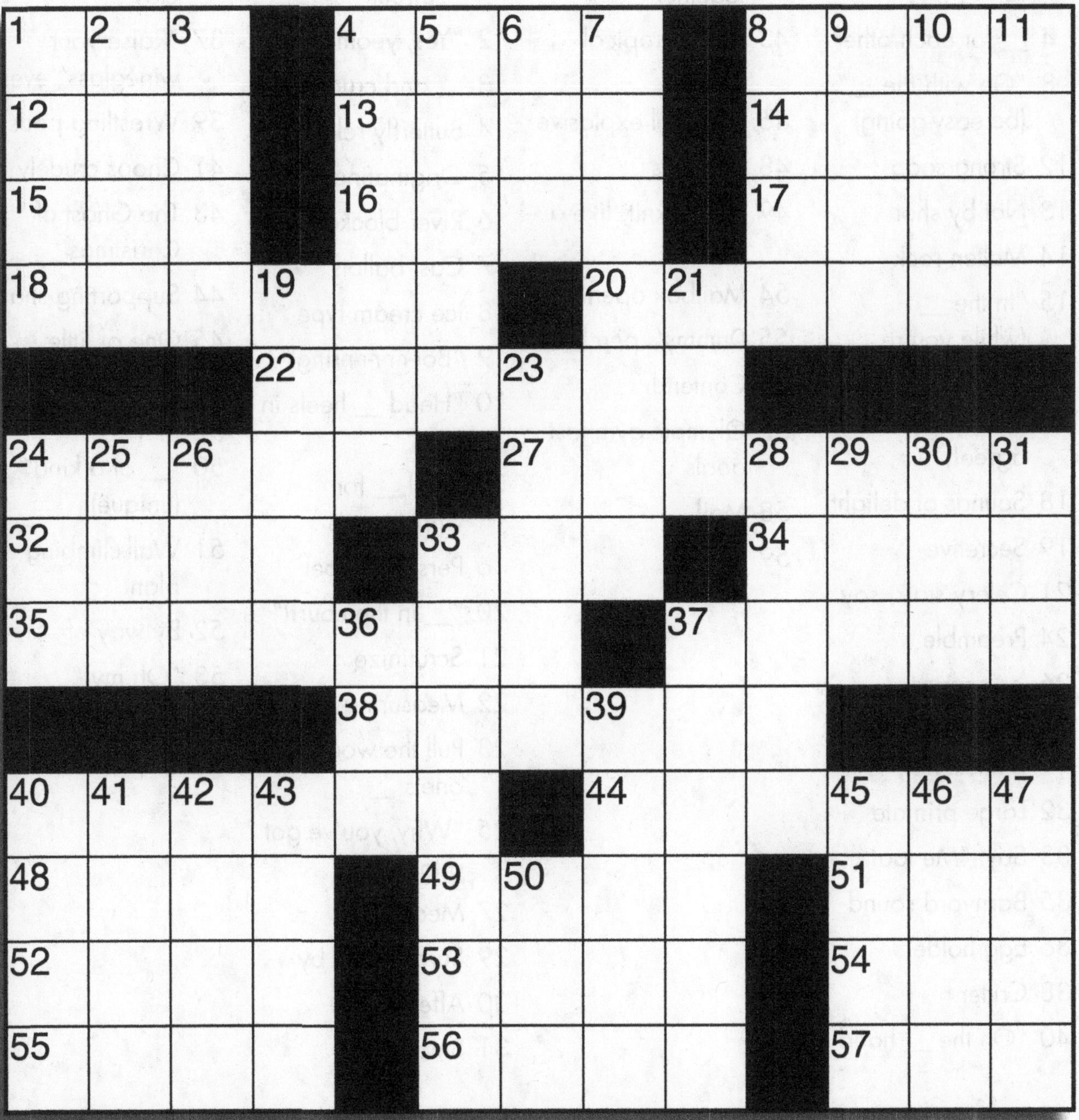

ACROSS

1 "I hate to __ and run . . . "
4 __ for each other
8 "Go with the __" (be easy-going)
12 Strong soap
13 Not by shot
14 Molten rock
15 "In the __ . . . " (while you're waiting)
17 "__ to that!" (I agree!)
18 Sounds of delight
19 Secretive
21 Celery stalk, say
24 Preamble
26 __ pepper
28 Rough __ (early manuscript)
32 Large primate
33 Say, "Me too!"
35 Barnyard sound
36 Egg holders
38 Critter
40 "On the __ hand . . . "
42 Puts two and two together
43 Green tropical fruit
46 Powerful explosive
48 Hatchets
49 Tightly knit, like a group
54 Mailbox opening
55 Dummy's perch
56 Contend
57 Olympic gymnast goals
58 Mail
59 Gab

DOWN

1 "A Nightmare on __ Street"
2 "Yes, yeoman"
3 __ and crumpets
4 Butterfly relative
5 Originating
6 River blocker
7 Cast ballots
8 Ice cream type
9 "Bor-r-r-r-r-ring"
10 "Head __ heels in love"
11 "All I __ for Christmas is . . . "
16 Personal label
20 "__ in the court!"
21 Scrutinize
22 Measuring __
23 Pull the wool over one's __
25 "Why, you've got a lot of __!"
27 Mean
29 Surrounded by
30 Affectionate
31 Small kids
34 Made of baked clay
37 "Raise your wineglass" events
39 Wrestling pads
41 Chops crudely
43 The Ghost of Christmas __
44 Supporting shaft
45 One of little importance
47 Requirement
50 "__ of a kind" (unique)
51 Wall-climbing plant
52 By way of
53 "Oh my!"

I hate to __ and run . . .

solution on page 308

ACROSS

1 "Quiet, please!"
5 A __ in the face (insult)
9 __ Newton (cookie brand)
12 "__ the wild blue yonder"
13 Role model
14 Grand __ Opry
15 Phaser setting
16 Fragile yolk holder
18 Not drunk
20 Car
21 Fool with a cone-shaped hat
23 Punctuation __
27 __ station
30 " . . . makes Jack a dull __"
31 Lawbreaker
32 Supernatural
34 Angry speech that goes on and on
35 Oval or octagon
36 "__ overboard!"
37 Make a seam
38 His-and-__
39 Reef material
41 Give off
43 Store-bought jelly jar's cover
47 Doggie-bag item
51 4-star review
52 Bauxite or galena
53 __ of the Valley
54 Broad smile
55 __ of gum
56 "You're something __!"
57 Shocking swimmers

DOWN

1 Snake sound
2 "__ us a child is born"
3 Ticket __ (movie memento)
4 Fine tuned
5 This lady
6 Inheritance
7 Squabble
8 Starting gate
9 Villain, to the hero
10 __ at ease (uncomfortable)
11 Hair goop
17 Four-bagger
19 Money in Moscow
22 "__ another peep out of you"
24 Sad cry
25 __ off into the sunset
26 "I __ it!" (Aha!)
27 "Amazing!"
28 Need a massage
29 Wound leftover
31 Last
33 Surprise victory
34 Paving substance
36 Places to stay over
39 The __ War (Robert E. Lee & Grant, etc.)
40 Jumbo
42 Undercover spy
44 Nude
45 Immoral
46 Camera part
47 How to go under a limbo stick
48 The Roaring Twenties, for one
49 Served a meal to
50 "A pocket full of __"

Quiet, please!

solution on page 308

4. Jump Start

ACROSS

1 Whitewater __
5 Bawl
8 __ a path to one's door
12 Japan's locale
13 "Stand on your own __ feet"
14 Mean monster
15 __-at-arms
17 Stadium cover
18 __ and cheese sandwich
19 Attractive
21 Corset, today
22 Tiny drop
25 Stupidity
28 Tempt
30 Subway money
31 Caution
32 __ the Snowman
35 Worked with difficulty
37 Appetite
38 Beat at the buffet
40 Office worker
41 __ lodge (winter resort)
44 In addition
47 More pitiful than lame
49 Balance __
50 Resentment
51 Hoist
52 "The ants __ marching one by one . . . "
53 "In one __ and out the other"
54 Like custard

DOWN

1 Diaper __
2 Between ports
3 Sturdy
4 "__—you're it"
5 Like a cloudless night sky
6 Possessed
7 Glass container
8 Crime scene discovery
9 Alter __
10 "Twist my __, why don't you?"
11 Fairway gadget
16 Large-scale work
20 Five-and-__ store
21 Leaves
22 TV knob
23 Land tract
24 Make unstraight
25 Questionable
26 Accept a challenge
27 The __ Curtain
29 British bumbler
33 Kite or pogo stick
34 Materialistic sort
35 Exam proctor
36 Solemn word
39 Miss America prop
40 Weighty book
41 Papa deer
42 Queen's husband
43 Disgusting
44 "It's as easy as __"
45 Actor DiCaprio
46 "Maltese Falcon" detective Spade
48 Electric __ (laser)

Whitewater ___

solution on page 309

ACROSS

1 Prod
5 "And now, on with the __!"
9 Seat at Mass
12 WWII alliance
13 Prickly __ cactus
14 Use a credit card
15 Volcano hole
16 Facts, briefly
17 Eric the __
18 Win the love of
20 __ your fingers
22 Interstate sign
24 __-up (adult)
27 Lipstick or mascara
31 "Ready, aim, __!"
32 "Yer out!" caller
33 Speed __
35 Gender
36 President Clinton
38 Hardworking
40 Blotch
42 "Easier said than __"
43 Coffee alternatives
45 Horse cries
49 Pertinent
51 Tiny
53 Picnic side dish
54 "Oh boy!"
55 Ages
56 Hawaiian dance
57 Slip up
58 Pay one's __ to society
59 Straddling

DOWN

1 Smooth down asphalt
2 Cart pullers
3 Gentle and caring
4 Admiration
5 Lively
6 One who pecks at their food
7 Klutzes
8 Incorrect
9 It's like a dolphin
10 Ram's dam
11 Tie the knot
19 Used a hatchet
21 Rover's response
23 Frightened
25 Little brown songbird
26 Barbershop waiting-room cry
27 Chicago team
28 Delete
29 Paint mess
30 Pilgrim, say
34 Number of cat's lives
37 Be deceitful
39 Japanese female entertainer
41 Called
44 Kingly address
46 Overabundance
47 Heavenly headgear
48 Barter
49 Become mature
50 By means of
52 Bring into the police station

Prod

solution on page 309

ACROSS

1 "Well, __ me down!"
5 Bandstand box
8 Surprise cries
12 Not taped
13 Lamb's remark
14 __ of thumb
15 Premonition
16 Bounce
18 "__ to other matters . . . "
19 Nonreactive
20 Go off the deep __
22 Nibbles
26 They cover boo-boos
31 Inlet
32 "How __ you?"
33 Hits with spitballs
35 "That's a __ one on me!"
36 "Have a __" (take a load off)
38 Boat captains
40 Rabbits
42 Buddy
43 "The __ has landed"
46 Magical glow
50 It's like a banana
53 Boot jingler
54 "Darn it"
55 Showed the way
56 "Let's make the __ of it"
57 Follow instructions
58 Magazine inserts
59 __ in one's pants

DOWN

1 __ out the sun
2 Sour green fruit
3 Easy Bake __ (toy)
4 __ one's way (roamed)
5 Condenses, like a book
6 __ course (what's for dinner)
7 "Pick up the __" (speed up)
8 Polar
9 Puzzled remark
10 Ginger __
11 Erector __ (metal building toy)
17 Globe
21 Short sleep
23 Touch-__ phone
24 Hardly __ (rarely)
25 Does embroidery
26 Wallop
27 Locality
28 Close by
29 Broad-antlered deer
30 Periodic payments
34 Good place for a hot bath
37 Itty-bitty
39 __ TV (screen type)
41 Used a pew
44 Grand affair
45 Told an untruth
47 " . . . rain __ the earth forty days . . . "
48 Corrode
49 Martial __
50 Hardly a beginner
51 Where Igor assists
52 Devoured

"Well, __ me down!"

solution on page 309

ACROSS

1 Place to play darts
4 Pendulum paths
8 "Who's buried in Grant's __?"
12 Gone by
13 Henhouse
14 Awful aroma
15 "There will be a __ investigation"
17 Insignificant
18 "Ode on a Grecian __"
19 Cleaned a tape
21 Get ready to use the garden hose
24 Lab __ (maze solver)
25 The opposite of midnight
26 Bravery
30 Past __ notice
31 Short break
33 "__ a Yellow Ribbon Round the Old Oak Tree"
34 Before a theater audience
36 Snoozing sites
37 Walking on __ (happy as can be)
38 Humiliates
40 Small eatery
43 ". . . in the __ nine days old"
44 Censor
45 Plastic __ (picnic eating items)
50 Put on eBay
51 "__ of the above"
52 "On __ of Old Smoky"
53 "__ Me Out to the Ballgame"
54 "Connect the __"
55 Swine site

DOWN

1 Tap gently
2 "Gross!"
3 Heckler's word
4 Oak nut
5 Circular
6 Gear part
7 Ball shapes
8 Burger topper
9 Poems of praise
10 "__ than meets the eye"
11 __ for speed
16 Make a shambles of
20 Unusual
21 Unfasten
22 Item in speech
23 Misfortunes
26 Color
27 Component
28 "Just to be on the safe __"
29 Sloppiness
31 Couple
32 Run __ (become beached)
35 Spill gossip
36 Baseball hitters
38 More than tired
39 Sharpens
40 Man's __ friend
41 "That gives me an __"
42 Satiny fabric
46 "Not __ shabby"
47 "__ a boy!"
48 Parking __
49 James Bond, for one

Place to play darts

solution on page 309

ACROSS

1 Wise bird
4 Puffed-up hairstyle
8 Marshes
12 Be competitive
13 Farm-field yield
14 Chess castle
15 Warhol work
16 Ceramic __
17 "Welcome" on the waves
18 Subtraction word
20 The Kentucky __
22 Astronomic radio-wave sender
24 Fake the song without the words
27 Take up space
30 Surgeon's sewing
32 Multicolored pattern
33 Slight color
34 Muslim headdress
36 ". . . to __ to buy a fat hen"
37 "Oh, say can you __ . . ."
38 Tex-Mex rollup
40 Started
41 Floppy __
45 Large pond
48 Aussie hello
50 Corn on __ cob
51 "In a one-horse __ sleigh . . ."
52 Verge
53 Officer
54 Man
55 Recolors
56 __ cross buns

DOWN

1 Squashed circle
2 Hidden mike
3 Answer to "Shall we?"
4 "__ your age!"
5 Work-week end, for many
6 Parts in a play
7 Carmen and Aida
8 Burro's cry
9 "How pretty!"
10 Sludge-like stuff
11 "The __'s the limit"
19 Magician wannabe, to Harry Potter
21 Vicious
23 News flash
24 Gorgeous guy
25 Goad
26 Try to __ halfway
27 Makes a choice
28 Whodunit board game
29 "Handle with __"
31 About to fall asleep
35 Was a pest
36 Run a team
39 Like some creeks
40 Angled
42 Scratch provoker
43 "Get lost!"
44 Well-__ secret
45 Like a bump on a __
46 Hairy jungle animal
47 Baseball's Griffey Jr.
49 "__! We Have No Bananas!"

Wise bird

solution on page 309

ACROSS

1 "Can we? Can we? Huh?" person
5 Physically adept
9 Bat wood
12 Vanish __ thin air
13 "How Do I Love __?"
14 Lovebird call
15 Roulette bet
16 America-to-England direction
17 "To each __ own"
18 Pastrami on __
19 Pillow cover
20 Furrier's item
21 Wheel-spinning gambling game
24 The Academy __
26 Categorized
30 Stiff
31 __ protector (power-spike guard)
32 Prepares to pray
34 Give a rating
35 History-class film
37 Time-machine destination
40 Stable food
41 "Keep a __ on it" (maintain secrecy)
44 Top player
45 Booboo's buddy at Jellystone Park
46 __-angle lens
47 "So quiet you could hear a __ drop"
48 Mighty Joe Young and kin
49 What a horseshoe gets attached to
50 Throw in
51 Verbal nudge
52 "This is __ a test . . . "

DOWN

1 "Take a long walk off a short __"
2 Jealousy
3 Economy section, on old liners
4 "Like a __ of bricks"
5 Swipes
6 "It's just a __ he's going through"
7 Changes the clock
8 Until now
9 Sore spot
10 Sully
11 Trebek or Leno
19 Snuggle
20 Study slightly
22 Adapt
23 Starter deciders
24 Noah's craft
25 Come in first
27 What the prefix "tera" means
28 Dyed Easter item
29 Lion's lounge
33 Dives in an arc
34 Escape __ (one like Houdini)
36 Wise men
37 Father
38 Hydrochloric __
39 Passes along
42 Big screen star, generically
43 Disobey
45 Talk a lot
46 "The Man __ Knew Too Much"

"Can we? Can we? Huh?" person

solution on page 309

ACROSS

1 Billy the __
4 Rescuer, to the one being rescued
8 Comics __ (funny section)
12 Bad temper
13 Expel
14 "Go __!" (scat!)
15 Broad-minded
17 Somebody __
18 Scissors sound
19 Standard of excellence
21 Out of sorts
23 Those in charge
27 Accomplish
31 __ academy
32 At __ with (attuned to)
33 One way to have kids
35 Skating on thin __
36 Map book
38 Not to be __ with (uninterruptible)
40 __ skates
42 Shocking swimmer
43 Proofreads
45 Showy
49 Manipulative sort
52 It's more broken than a sprain
54 "Stand on your own two __"
55 Roman robe
56 Basketball hoop's rim string
57 Majestic trees
58 One-dish meal
59 Slope slider

DOWN

1 Model-airplane packages
2 Golf-bag item
3 Lunch spot
4 ". . . sat on __ tuffet . . ."
5 Sent across the Internet
6 Fruit shell
7 Furry fish eater
8 Seafood and rice dish
9 Poking tool
10 Step on the __ (hurry)
11 Seen with the naked __
16 Hero's story
20 Em, to Dorothy
22 Rented
24 Wicked
25 Go fast
26 Snow toy
27 Fly high
28 "__ us a child is born"
29 Jail unit
30 Sentence ender
34 Omen
37 Alarms
39 In nothing __ (very soon)
41 Breaks in relations
44 Quick gait
46 "A River __ Through It"
47 Journey
48 The Bumble in "Rudolph the Red-Nosed Reindeer"
49 Martian craft
50 "A sailor went to __ . . ."
51 "Yikes!"
53 Crow call

Billy the __

solution on page 310

ACROSS

1 Busy insect
4 Weaponry
8 Amount owed
12 Sweet potato
13 ". . . his wife could eat no __ . . ."
14 Grimm monster
15 Paleozoic, for one
16 Tall __ (untrue story)
17 Haunted-house sound
18 Pasta piece
20 "__ that a shame"
21 Pants-on-fire fellow
23 __ out of gas
25 Was in a play
27 Fancy hotels
31 Baby's "little piggy"
32 Make a canyon
34 Devour
35 Provided with all one could need
37 Belief
39 Tie-__ T-shirt
40 Santa checks it twice
41 Went for home plate
44 Eyelid hair
48 Song
49 Yodel reply
50 __ water (sink output)
53 Slow boats
54 Potato __
55 Dolly the clone, for one
56 Break in music
57 Hunt and peck
58 PR concern

DOWN

1 "So long!"
2 "Keep an __ to the ground"
3 Came forth
4 Female singer
5 Enjoy a book
6 Shopping center
7 Scowled
8 Game tile with dots
9 Self conceits
10 __ muffin
11 Pitch a __ (set up camp)
19 Metallic rock
21 "Better __ than never"
22 Touch-screen picture
24 Secondhand
26 Like morning grass
27 Divining __
28 "Please pay at the __"
29 Scottish caps
30 "Right now!"
33 Incumbent's campaign word
36 Most peculiar
38 Flamenco shout
41 Lead actor
42 Fishing __
43 Preps a press
45 In need of a heating pad
46 Send UPS
47 The __ Diamond
51 Reverence
52 Gusto

Busy insect

solution on page 310

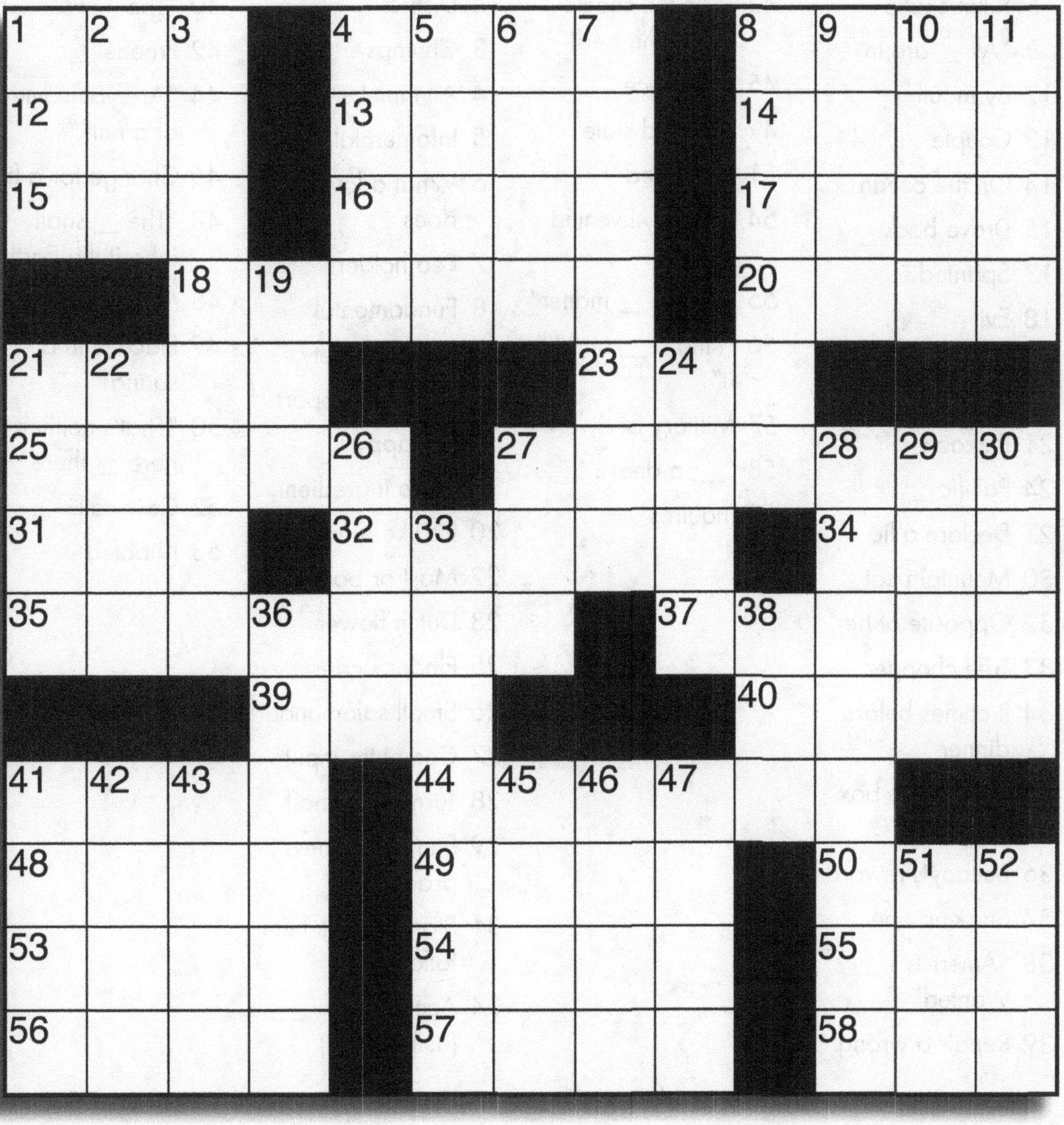

ACROSS

1 Soak up the sun
5 Killer snake
8 "All __ are in"
12 By mouth
13 Couple
14 On the ocean
15 Drove back
17 Sprinted
18 Evil
19 Show signs of waking
21 Pizzazz
24 Pacific __
27 Declare a lie
30 Mountain cat
32 Opposite of he
33 Tree chopper
34 It comes before dinner
35 Magician's box tool
36 Bellboy's reward
37 Stuck-up one
38 "America's __ Wanted"
39 Repair a wrong
41 Gyro bread
43 __ in the sheets (make the bed)
45 Fragrance
49 Agitated state
51 Pretended
54 Saturday Evening __
55 "It does __ matter"
56 "Find a __ and fill it"
57 Military body
58 "__, a deer . . . "
59 Inquires

DOWN

1 __ and bred
2 District
3 Chumps
4 All thumbs
5 Infomercials
6 What a lawyer does
7 Pea holders
8 Fundamental
9 Coffee variety
10 Football support
11 Unhappy
16 Soap ingredient
20 It's like a frog
22 Mast or boom
23 Dutch flower
25 Finder's cries
26 Small salamander
27 Computer input
28 Turnpike turnoff
29 Family business practice
31 Star of Bethlehem followers
34 According to __ (as planned)
38 Home for yachts
40 "The __ Professor"
42 Freeze __
44 "Are you some __ of a nut?"
46 Change for a fiver
47 "The __ shall inherit the Earth"
48 Mixes in
49 Place with a sauna
50 "That's neither here __ there"
52 Cow call
53 Nibbled

Soak up the sun

solution on page 310

ACROSS

1 Boxing punch
4 Dracula's garb
8 Store away
12 "So THAT'S it!"
13 Fragrance
14 Ice-cream holder
15 Make columns
17 Ins and __
18 Short snooze
19 Rabbit food
21 __ student (one who already has a degree)
24 Church's 10%
26 Trademarks
28 Ridiculed
32 Stein filler
33 Chinese bamboo eater
35 "Hurrah!"
36 Really hate
38 Thick
40 Copy-shop task
42 Cut a budget
43 Where to find Skee-ball or pinball
46 Each
48 __ shark (money lender)
49 Detergent
54 Capsized
55 Queen of Hearts munchie
56 "Long, long __..."
57 Poetic works
58 Jacuzzi locales
59 "__, right in the kisser"

DOWN

1 Scribble down
2 "I knew it!"
3 __ for apples
4 Coke or Pepsi
5 Adjust
6 Pooh's has honey
7 Built
8 Got points
9 __ of duty
10 In the know about
11 __ Point Academy
16 Take out a knot
20 "Try not to get __ of yourself"
21 Delighted
22 Be a good __ model
23 "It's been __ since we last saw you!"
25 __ sanctum
27 Noticed
29 Small wildcat
30 Free from worry
31 Became a redhead, say
34 Qualities
37 Hijinks
39 Get through hard work
41 Musical where a diva sings
43 Likewise
44 "Hit the __, jack"
45 Walking stick
47 Grabs a bite
50 Indy-500 unit
51 Tree juice
52 Image of oneself
53 "Michael __ Your Boat Ashore"

Boxing punch

solution on page 310

ACROSS

1 Slippery
4 Give the once-over
8 SAT taker
12 "That's __ bad!"
13 Demolish
14 Went on horseback
15 Tripped
17 Foot or furlong
18 Burn the midnight __
19 Endures
20 Avoid sinking
23 "__ shall I pick you up?"
25 "__ Misbehavin'"
26 Hard to confront
30 __ Holliday
31 Prodded
32 Sticky road stuff
33 Solar and nuclear
35 18-wheeler
36 Matterhorn mountains
37 Sky light with a tail
38 Disreputable
41 Down with the __ (ill)
42 Airport-to-hotel vehicle
43 Thinker
48 Preholiday nights
49 "Off we go, into the __ blue yonder..."
50 "All the President's __"
51 Fit together neatly
52 Selects
53 Teacher's __

DOWN

1 "__ Howdy Doody time!"
2 Foldaway bed
3 "Are __ kidding me?"
4 Path in the sky
5 Sea bird
6 Tell it like it isn't
7 At the __ of one's rope
8 AWOL student
9 Ages and ages
10 Remove questionable language
11 Volleyball dividers
16 Castle surrounder
19 Allow to borrow
20 Lessen
21 Roarer at the circus
22 On one occasion
23 Salary earnings
24 Colors
26 Leak sound
27 Article
28 Identify
29 Gumption
31 Hard to look at
34 Salad veggie
35 Like a lemon
37 Divots
38 Mushroom base
39 "__ a nice day"
40 Tree choppers
41 __-tip pen
43 "It takes __ to tango"
44 It's said twice before "Hooray!"
45 Little devil
46 "On a Clear Day You Can __ Forever"
47 Explosive stick

Slippery

solution on page 310

ACROSS

1 "I don't think so!"
5 "__ the night before Christmas . . ."
9 Blow the lid __
12 Face shape
13 Good enough to eat
14 Really small
15 Transport
16 Without limits
18 Joins a contest
20 Puzzling
21 Sleek gown fabric
23 Away from sunset
27 Made merry
30 Brave but rude
31 "__ your influence"
32 Whinny
34 __ session
35 Devoutness
37 Italian herb
39 Not in danger
40 Pilfered
41 Intention
43 "...with a __ chance of rain"
47 Rubber bands
51 Insult
52 Dust cloth
53 Hint for Holmes
54 Swiss cheese feature
55 Sandwich bread
56 Pay attention to
57 "Ready, willing, and __"

DOWN

1 Pinocchio's stood out
2 Toaster __
3 Gasp
4 Most senior
5 Administrator
6 No-__ situation
7 Smock
8 Poppy __
9 "To each his __"
10 Charge for use
11 Gave grub to
17 Cartoon light bulb
19 __ day fund
22 Moron
24 Distinctive air
25 Read a bar code
26 Proofreader's catch
27 Young dogs
28 Tibet's continent
29 Scuba-diving site, often
30 Seashore find
33 Made at the box office
36 British drinks
38 Tokyo lady with a fan
40 "Say cheese!"
42 Poison-ivy symptom
44 Shapeless lump
45 Ship's shell
46 "I cannot tell a lie; I chopped down that __"
47 Bobble the ball
48 "__ it on thick"
49 Mellow with __
50 Sideline signal

"I don't think so!"

solution on page 310

ACROSS

1 Swan __ (ballet)
5 Mess maker
9 Acquire
12 An __-and-shut case
13 "Arrivederci!"
14 Holiday preceder
15 Manage
16 Coils around
18 Vocal tune
20 Classy chap
21 Suitable
24 Intensify
27 Puff in the sky
29 Doesn't yield to temptation
33 One of two throat hangers
35 Wardrobe
36 Mr. Rogers wore a yellow one
38 Spooky
39 Olden
41 Male child
42 Morally bad
45 Igloo shape
47 Gets
50 "Up, up, and __!"
54 "__ away!" (question)
55 Forgetful actor's request
56 Apple's center
57 Swine's confines
58 "__ Make a Deal"
59 Weeding tools

DOWN

1 Place to park cars
2 King Kong, for one
3 Hockey player Dryden
4 Try to make __ meet
5 "Try not to make a __!"
6 Hang about
7 Pony morsel
8 __ and arrow
9 Actor Hackman
10 __-tempered (rational)
11 "This has been a __ . . ."
17 Set afire
19 Bit of strangeness
21 Bible book
22 Snow-clearing vehicle
23 "At the __, the time will be . . . "
25 Round vegetable
26 Favorable opinion
28 Ready
30 Dear __
31 The Magi, e.g.
32 "Mine eyes have __ the glory . . . "
34 "Shake a __! (hurry up)"
37 Mouse or rat
40 Snouts
42 Memorable periods
43 Bullet-proof __
44 Gross
46 __ and every
48 Infirmed
49 Do battle
51 Pitching __
52 "Blessed __ the meek . . ."
53 "Surely!"

Swan __ (ballet)

solution on page 311

ACROSS

1 Deli sandwich
5 "Gimme five!"
9 "Rub-a-dub-dub three men in a __"
12 Object of devotion
13 Pirate hideout
14 Disco __
15 "The __ must go on!"
16 Rude
18 Place for lost change
19 "It's getting a little __ in here" (brr!)
20 Kingly
22 Building with stores inside
26 Prepare for a test
29 "Would you like to drink bottled or __?"
31 Talk like a dove
32 "Pow, right in the __"
34 Fancy boats
36 Infuriation
37 Mama pig
39 Lover's meeting
40 Semester
42 Like a he-man
44 Gladden
46 What juice strainers strain out
50 Put on seatbelts
53 __ and cons
54 Dry __ (smoke machine need)
55 Square measure
56 Freudian topics
57 "Let it ride" action
58 Janitor's janglers
59 Car scar

DOWN

1 Noise to the villain
2 Canyon callback
3 Stick to the __ of your mouth
4 "Let's continue forward!"
5 Informal lingo
6 Rodeo rope
7 Time on radio or TV
8 Item used onstage
9 "__ for Two"
10 Coffee server
11 Louisville slugger
17 Phys. Ed. place
21 Goo-goo __
23 Throbbing
24 Real estate units
25 ". . . the Minnow would be __"
26 Mini-play
27 Trunk item for when you get a flat
28 Chat-room person
30 "The __ of least resistance"
33 Love story
35 Like cut photos
38 Like thin soup
41 Encountered
43 Surrenders
45 Water-pipe problem
47 Craving
48 "As crazy as a __"
49 "Over here!"
50 Little lie
51 The Red Baron, e.g.
52 "Ready, __, go!"

Deli sandwich

solution on page 311

ACROSS

1 __ Isaac Newton
4 In the thick of
8 Move quickly
12 Where this book was published
13 Lion or horse hair
14 Hoity-toity
15 Benevolent guy
16 Cop a __
17 Collect the crops
18 White-tailed animal
20 Annoy
22 One of the oceans
24 Overcome
27 Crazy __ (card game)
32 "Oh no, not __"
33 Thief
34 Mob
36 Messy
37 Makes happy
39 Deli meat often eaten on rye
43 Type of can you shouldn't shake
47 Give a thumbs-up
48 Green part of the cantaloupe
50 Disappear into thin __
51 Roller derby __
52 Like quiche
53 Battering __
54 Proposer's support
55 Rx detail
56 Sinister

DOWN

1 Brought to court
2 Tiny landmass
3 Tool for making leaf piles
4 Sound booster
5 Ill will
6 Motionless
7 Honey-bun
8 Tiny arrow thrown at a board
9 Acreage
10 "Right this minute!"
11 Empty selling
19 AM or FM device
21 Eavesdropper
23 Sprinter
24 Tended the tots
25 "Ew!"
26 Saloon
28 "Dis-GUSTING!"
29 Hip-__ music
30 On __ of the world
31 Blue yonder
35 Looked at angrily
36 "Ouch, that __!"
38 Cancun compadre
39 A white meat
40 Comparable
41 Not loony
42 Lad
44 Doesn't have both __ in the water
45 Early phone feature
46 West Point team
49 Easter-egg need

__ Isaac Newton

solution on page 311

5. Flying Start

ACROSS

1 Rowing blade
4 Splotch
8 Shrek, for one
12 "Just as I suspected!"
13 Road
14 Eagle's weapon
15 Male cat or turkey
16 Ripened
17 Dunce-cap shape
18 Promoted strongly
20 Cold shoulder
22 Artery's opposite
25 Gush lava
28 Monopoly cubes
31 Robin's home
33 Privy in Parliament
34 Stink
35 Let the __ out of the bag
36 Angelic light
37 House shade tree
38 Via, informally
39 Do a laundry chore
40 Printer's proof
42 Hitch in the plan
44 Bee, to Andy and Opie
46 The terrible twos, for one
50 Appends
52 Astride
55 Guided
56 Remedy
57 Use the phone
58 Droop
59 They sometimes get stubbed
60 "I hear and I __"
61 Item needing smelting

DOWN

1 Hippocratic __
2 "Yoo-hoo!" on the water
3 Motorcycle jump need
4 Razor __
5 Fail to keep up
6 "__ for the money . . ."
7 Places to catch some Zs
8 "Did it ever __ to you that . . ."
9 Ball-shaped
10 Sought office
11 She might have a little lamb
19 "The best thing that __ happened to me"
21 Safety item for trapeze artists
23 Yardstick division
24 Gets closer to
26 Explorer Marco __
27 Tweety or Sylvester
28 One who isn't lazy
29 __ away time
30 Amigo
32 Shock and surprise
36 Like Cousin Itt's voice
38 Unit of weight
41 Clever ploys
43 Submit a resume
45 Sandwich in a shell
47 "The Sun __ Rises"
48 Char
49 Boundary
50 Do a disappearing __
51 Trio minus one
53 "Put it on my __"
54 Yucatan "yay"

Rowing blade

solution on page 312

ACROSS

1 Lunch or dinner
5 Gnaw
9 "__ better to see you with . . ."
12 Toll unit for trucks
13 Listen to
14 One dressed in black and white
15 Gyro bread
16 __ development
18 What a red light means
19 __ pasta
20 Traffic __-up
22 Bacon and __
26 Magazine fillers
29 Chump
31 Bridge guard of fairy tales
32 Oxcart's path
33 Florence Nightingale, for one
35 " . . . two if by __"
36 Prepared to be knighted
38 Orange-colored potato
39 Fix a clothing length
40 Big rig
41 Place where you get cucumbers on your eyes
43 What people do in a parade
47 Decomposes
51 "See ya" in Osaka
54 Leave out
55 Be in the red
56 Breakfast-in-bed need
57 Bulletin board notice
58 Reader's retreat
59 Alters a suit
60 From scratch

DOWN

1 Traveler's needs
2 Highway sign
3 __ sax
4 Jumped
5 "Hat," in France
6 "I've had it up to __!"
7 Get through hard work
8 Little warbler
9 It's like dynamite
10 Tinge
11 To the bitter __
17 Fortuneteller
21 "__ She Lovely"
23 "Gee!"
24 Joy
25 Grand __ (4-run homer)
26 Torah holders
27 Mountain of sand
28 Wineglass part
30 Be nosy
31 Office fill-in
34 Struts
37 Stretch __
42 Sweet smell
44 Chocolate-covered __
45 Few and far between
46 Gullet
48 Writing on the wall
49 "Once upon a __ . . ."
50 Put on cargo
51 Turf
52 Dumbfound
53 Craving

Lunch or dinner

solution on page 312

ACROSS

1 "__, humbug!"
4 Answering-machine sound
8 Physicist's bit
12 Self-image
13 __ of laughter
14 Speeder's penalty
15 Slippery swimmer
16 Not fooled by
17 __ sorry for
18 Spring bloom
20 __ for knowledge
22 Sheet of plywood
24 Way in or way out
25 Taken advantage of
26 Important paper
30 "__ the season to be jolly . . . "
31 High male choir voice
32 Rhyme __ reason
33 Inoffensive
35 Detective's need
36 "Stop!"
37 Teeters on the __
38 Picture taker
41 " . . . let me count the __ . . . "
42 Pros
43 Puppy wagger
45 Beach shade
48 "Of __ I Sing"
49 "Anything __?"
50 Needle part
51 Collections
52 A scout tries to do a good one
53 Droplets at dawn

DOWN

1 Stinging insect
2 Sit at the winery
3 What a halo signifies
4 Barbecue
5 Many millennia
6 "Jack Sprat could __ no fat . . . "
7 Diplomat's concern
8 Give testimony
9 Mezzanine, say
10 "This __ on me!"
11 Unfreeze
19 Walk the __ carpet
21 Sixty minutes
22 Soft golf stroke
23 Mongolia's locale
24 Treat with a hole
26 Like a used balloon
27 __ men (GI's)
28 Sentence's subject
29 Excursion
31 Rip
34 Graduate-school papers
35 Sob
37 Made hay blocks
38 Lions and tigers, but not bears
39 Tylenol target
40 Bump into
41 "__ as an owl"
44 Suds at a saloon
46 Yea vote
47 __ Orleans

"__, humbug!"

solution on page 312

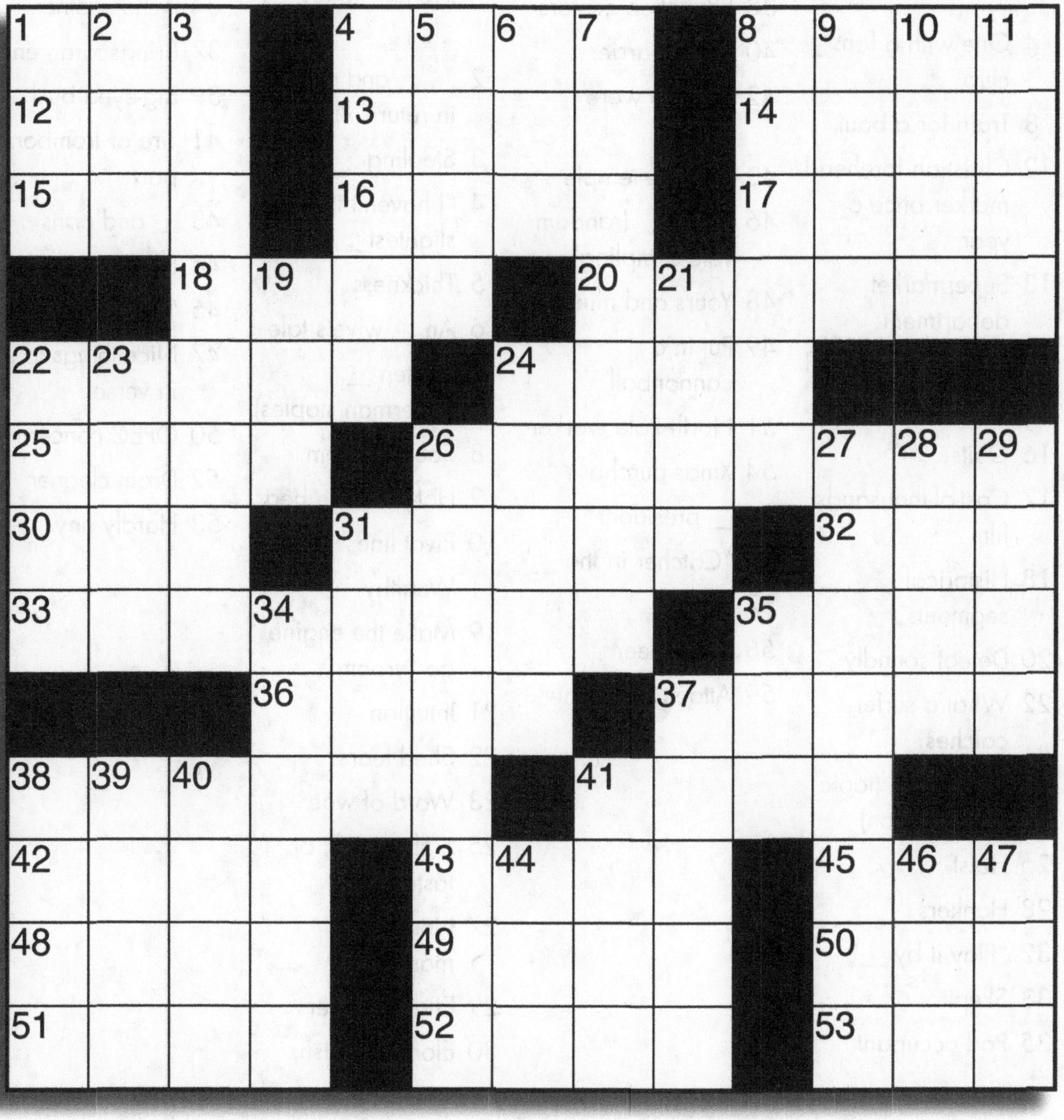

ACROSS

1 "At the drop of a __"
4 One with a fan club
8 Train for a bout
12 Christian forehead marker once a year
13 Supermarket department
14 Prepare for takeoff
15 Downhill slider
16 Quits
17 Cast-of-thousands film
18 Historical segments
20 Defeat soundly
22 What a surfer catches
24 __ at hand (topic of discussion)
26 Hoist
28 Honkers
32 "Play it by __"
33 Skeptic
35 Pod occupant
36 "Gotcha!"
38 Education centers
40 Flood barrier
42 "__ you were here"
43 Chinese temple
46 Straw __ (random vote sampling)
48 Yours and mine
49 Put in a cannonball
51 North Pole worker
54 Xmas purchase
55 __ president
56 "Catcher in the __"
57 Utters
58 Large deer
59 Attach a button

DOWN

1 "Little Bo-Peep __ lost her sheep . . . "
2 " . . . and all I __ in return . . . "
3 Stealing
4 "I haven't the slightest __"
5 Thickness
6 An __ wive's tale
7 Top-ten __ (Letterman staples)
8 Sound system
9 Hot-porridge bear
10 Pivot line
11 Wealthy
19 Make the engine go "vroom"
21 Intuition
22 Shed tears
23 Word of woe
25 Sight, smell, or taste
27 Needed a massage
29 Ending ruiners
30 Elongated fish
31 Soft belt
34 Ache soother
37 Brings to an end
39 Big-eyed bird
41 Tire or trombone part
43 __ and pans
44 Subtle air
45 "The Old __ Mare"
47 Nice things to say, in verse
50 OPEC concern
52 Drain cleaner
53 Hardly any

At the drop of a __

solution on page 312

ACROSS

1 "Do __ give it another thought"
4 Puts a question to
8 Infatuated
12 Simian without a tail
13 Bar tab, say
14 Pinocchio, for one
15 Irritate
16 Beach current
17 Compel
18 "But is it __?"
19 Used knockout gas
21 "Save the best for __"
23 Comedienne Tomlin
24 Bench-press unit
27 Man Friday
29 "__ beyond a shadow of a doubt"
31 Embraces, as a belief
34 Sob story
35 Blend to a pulp
36 Dairy __
37 Ball perch
38 Plaza
40 Dinner and a movie, say
44 Baby goose
47 Water wall
48 Swing to and fro
50 Bluish green
51 "Safe!" caller
52 Pick-up __
53 Wagon tracks
54 "Don't __ it go to your head"
55 Stumble __ (run into)
56 Netting
57 Make an effort

DOWN

1 __ maneuvers (marine practice)
2 Soap __ (daytime TV drama)
3 Pieces of prose
4 "Random __ of kindness"
5 Handheld barriers for knights
6 __ pool (place to wade)
7 Rob
8 Paste
9 Delivery by parachute
10 Muzzle
11 "We __ not alone"
20 "It takes all __"
22 Masking __
25 Adam's wife
26 Apiece
28 Grocery list components
30 Hollow marsh stalk
31 Appropriate
32 "In __ course" (eventually)
33 Pizza sauce spice
34 Brownie ingredients
36 Social group
39 Burglar deterrent
41 Mature audience member
42 Circus employee
43 With nothing in it
45 "You had to __ your big mouth!"
46 Deep cut
48 It might make you sick
49 "Keep a stiff upper __"

Do __ give it another thought

solution on page 312

ACROSS

1 Underhanded
4 Comrades in __
8 Sunbeams
12 Apple __ a la mode
13 Give a __ (care)
14 Object of devotion
15 Six-legged soldier
16 "Lion King" villain
17 "The Gift of the __"
18 Read through quickly
20 Make booties
22 Short swim
23 Grazed
25 "I couldn't __ less"
27 Mariner
30 Like some crosswords
33 Uncle's wives
34 More slippery
35 Says hello to
37 Secretive
38 Gang
39 Concealed
40 Lily __ (frog's hangout)
42 Buck or doe
44 British noble
48 Leader of a pride
50 __ reflux
52 For a nominal __
53 "Do __ others . . ."
54 "__ Might Be Giants"
55 Unedited
56 Goulash
57 Ox-team holder
58 Funny, but not funny ha-ha

DOWN

1 Places with a sauna
2 The Missing __
3 Snowy Sasquatch
4 Massage sounds
5 Porch chair
6 Complain
7 Well disciplined
8 Border
9 Campus studies
10 Yankee Berra
11 Use scissors
19 "Mind over __"
21 Hummus ingredient
24 Examined
26 What water does after high tide
27 Duffel __
28 "__ Gang"
29 Funny little story
31 Shriek that rhymes with "shriek"
32 Lacking water
36 Hot from the sun
37 Scream
40 +
41 "__ that a crying shame?"
43 Off-the-wall response
45 __-Americans
46 "__ my lips"
47 Lascivious
49 "And __ for something completely different"
51 Salon selection

Underhanded

solution on page 312

ACROSS

1 Not given away
5 "Try to __ natural"
8 Lament
12 "__ hands are the devil's . . . "
13 Any ship
14 Ranch unit
15 Conks out
16 It sets in the west
17 Necessity
18 "At once!"
19 All wrapped up
21 Grab
23 More recent
27 "__ a girl!"
30 Hog's home
31 Long for
32 Stable sounds
34 Dinosaur leftover
35 Humming instrument
36 Fish and chips fish, sometimes
37 Work at
38 __ campaign (insult the other candidate)
39 Beasts of burden
41 Be a tutor
43 Eurekas
47 Eatery
50 It's heard in a herd
51 Traveler's permit
52 Rude look
53 Fifth-scale note
54 "On an __ keel"
55 __ for Tots
56 "__ if by land . . . "
57 Security lapse

DOWN

1 Children
2 Rephrase
3 Court statement
4 Irritable
5 Approvals
6 Like some peanut butter
7 Work at a bar
8 Meanders
9 Perfect serve
10 Rage
11 Supervised
20 Make a cryptogram
22 Where landlubbers want to be
24 Stinging insect
25 Black-hearted
26 Confide
27 Pen fillers
28 Packers or Steelers
29 Small, medium, or large
33 Small beards
34 Soldier's pit used for cover
36 Prebutterfly holder
40 Bellybutton
42 Response to "Are not!"
44 Honeycomb locale
45 Offshore
46 The sinking steamer __
47 Makeshift bed
48 Long __ (yore)
49 Peter Pan can do it

Not given away

solution on page 313

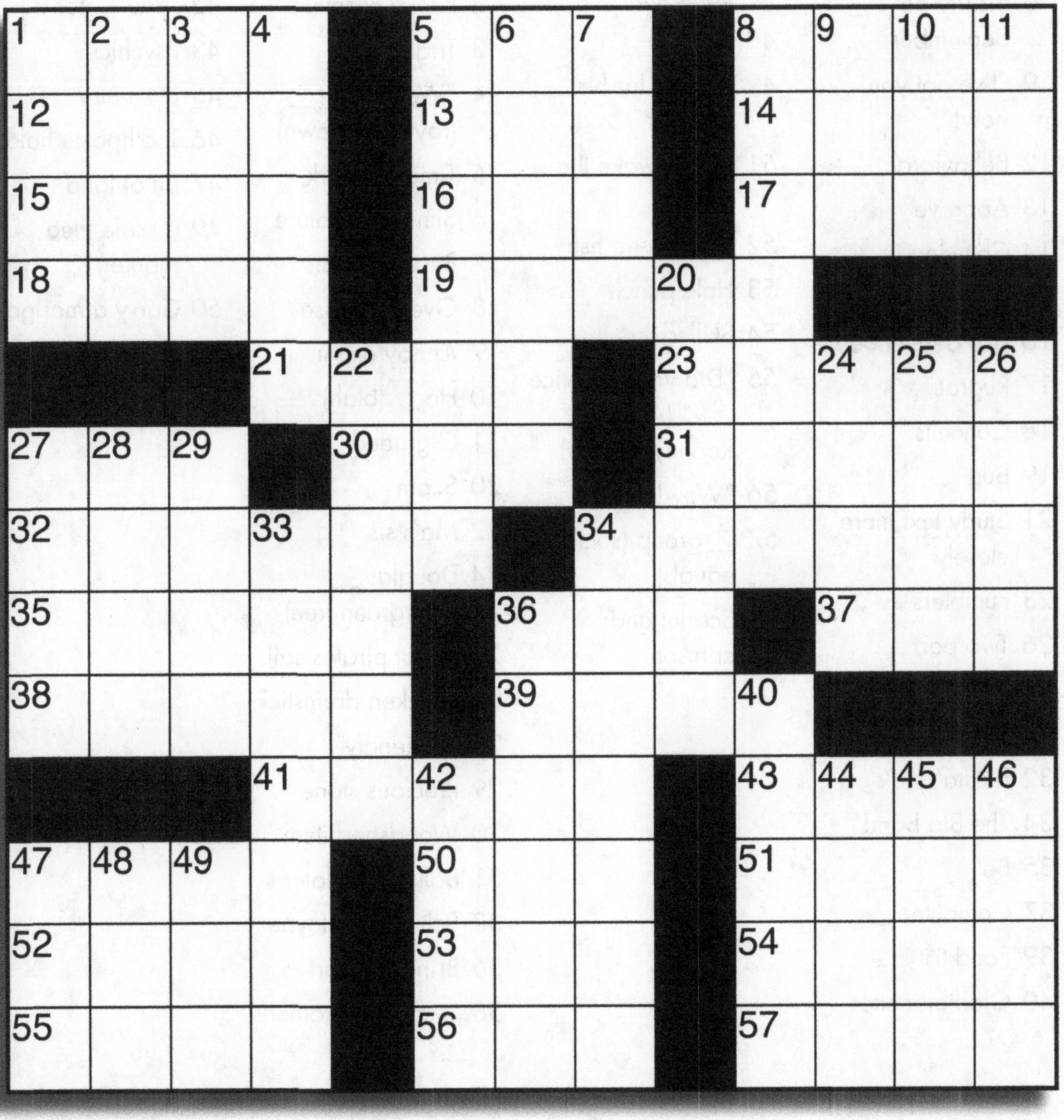

ACROSS

1 Sector
5 "Thirty days __ September . . . "
9 "I've got you now!"
12 Behavioral __
13 Approve
14 Chewing __
15 Authority
16 Like a wet noodle
17 Rugrat
18 Conceits
19 Bug
21 Study text more closely
23 Fumblers
26 Two part
28 Loosen knots
29 Small opening
32 Nikita's no's
34 The Big Band __
35 Be
37 Computer __
39 Food list
40 Gladiator sites
44 Fast-paced and confused
48 Slacken
49 "__ big for his britches"
51 "Don't wake the baby!"
52 Long-nosed fish
53 Hole punch
54 Skilled
55 "Did you __ notice . . ." (Andy Rooney opener)
56 "Wow!"
57 __ group (social equals)
58 Scarlet and crimson

DOWN

1 Rage
2 Facial cosmetic
3 Trial and __
4 "We are not __" (royal put-down)
5 Time off work
6 Similar in nature
7 Beret-like hats
8 Overadvertise
9 Annoy or stir
10 Ho-__ (blah)
11 Gig need
20 Scam
22 Ma's sis
24 Douglas __ (evergreen tree)
25 What pirates sail
27 Chicken drumstick
28 __-friendly
29 Precious stone
30 Woodshed item
31 Balloon deflater
33 School employee
36 Bring to court
38 "Am I my brother's __?"
41 Easily fooled
42 "You __ for it"
43 Psychics
45 Lip injury
46 Toothpaste holder
47 Bit of land
49 __ sale (flea market)
50 Carry a mortgage

Sector

solution on page 313

ACROSS

1 Verve
4 Health club
7 Practices punching
12 Astonishment
13 Got the gold medal
14 Student
15 __ headache
17 Wear away
18 Data
19 Knight's suit
20 Chew out
23 Candied potato
25 Game-show regular
27 "When You Wish Upon a __"
31 Can __ (metal-cutting device)
32 8-legged sea critters
34 Driving __
35 "Domestic or __?"
37 "Surfin' __"
38 Out of style
39 Aroma
43 Sales __ (receipt)
45 Divvy up
46 Gun holder, out West
50 Fake jewelry
51 Self-conceit
52 "Sure thing, cap'n!"
53 Villain's expression
54 Period
55 Place to awake from

DOWN

1 __ on the back (praise)
2 She-sheep
3 __ name (author's handle)
4 Hoodwink
5 Magician's word
6 Aggravates
7 It makes a kettle whistle
8 Happy engine sound
9 Tiny energy source
10 Modify
11 One with second sight
16 Without a sound
20 Polka dot
21 Superman's flapper
22 Bide __ time
24 Above
26 Camera part
27 Watchbands
28 Toddlers
29 Large primates
30 Carnival attraction
33 Cockpit figure
36 __ potatoes
37 Say
39 Weakens
40 Scottish family
41 Choice word
42 Do, re, or mi
44 Emblem
47 Pick up the __ (treat)
48 Birds-__ view
49 "Paint the town __"

Verve

solution on page 313

ACROSS

1 Lamb's dad
4 Swindles
8 Garbage truck of the sea
12 Flamenco cry
13 What a hobo might hop
14 Ran fast
15 Octopus leg
17 White House office shape
18 Felt sore
19 "The Farmer in the __" (song)
20 Jewelry worn down low
23 Use a shovel
25 " . . . but the poor little dog had __"
26 Earth Day verb
30 Big or pinkie digit
31 "__ and Prejudice"
33 "Green Eggs and __"
34 Grimaced
36 Tubular noodle
37 One who goes woof
38 Earth or Mars
40 Comfortable
43 Splatter guard
45 Pay through the __
46 Toddler's ride
50 "My Bonnie Lies __ the Ocean"
51 Pushpin
52 Feel sick
53 __ of cash
54 Yellowbeard's yesses
55 KO counter

DOWN

1 " . . . and all that __"
2 Malted brew
3 "3 __ and a Baby"
4 Premeal prayer
5 Millionaire's boat
6 Stack
7 Went downhill
8 Like an old fogey
9 Sheltered bay
10 Aloud
11 "__, I'll be a monkey's uncle!"
16 Spun story
20 Tiny insects
21 Palindromic time
22 On bended __
24 Titanic sinker
26 Unburden
27 Lower jaw
28 Tardy
29 Spew
31 One paid to play
32 Boater's event
35 Lawn tools
36 Ludicrous
38 "A bargain at any __"
39 Keys open them
40 Skiing surface
41 Bossa __
42 Manipulated
44 "Let us __"
47 Automobile
48 Stretch the truth
49 Arctic assistant

Lamb's dad

solution on page 313

ACROSS

1 Patch of grassy ground
4 Notable times
8 Shredded lettuce
12 Try to court
13 __ file
14 Cab
15 "Tarzan, the __ Man"
16 Greet the dawn
17 Holiday preceders
18 "You there!"
20 Diminish
22 Faster
24 What a majorette twirls
27 Down in the dumps
28 The __ Four (The Beatles)
31 "__ already!" (cut it out!)
33 Accountable, legally
35 Pull a scam
36 Shlep
38 Spry
39 Failure
41 Surround
44 Pull on the ground
48 Dorothy's last name in "The Wizard of Oz"
49 "How unfortunate!"
51 "__ as directed"
52 Tiny biter
53 Model's stance
54 Break a Commandment
55 Gabs
56 Spit out
57 "__ your heart out!"

DOWN

1 Exchange
2 "My mistake!"
3 "__ your dog bite?"
4 Flub
5 Ambushes
6 Things you have
7 Blue-plate __
8 Guide the ride
9 Rock that rolls
10 Logger's aids
11 The Three __ Men
19 Holier-than-__
21 Call again
23 Fisherman
24 "I __ to differ!"
25 "__ day now . . . "
26 __ secret
28 They might have to work with the CIA
29 "__ work and no play . . . "
30 Hive insect
32 Shiny wheel covers
34 Elderly
37 Run like a horse
39 Counts carbs or calories
40 Stop
41 Like Humpty Dumpty
42 Granny
43 Thunder sound
45 Red herring
46 India's continent
47 Dude
50 Do as Betsy Ross did

Patch of grassy ground

solution on page 313

ACROSS

1 Tie the __ (marry)
5 __-blonde hair
8 Lily-pad place
12 Moniker
13 Blown __-high
14 "Howdy, sailor!"
15 "Keep your ears __"
16 Q-__ (cotton-swab name brand)
17 Lug
18 Fender-__
20 "__ Man Flint"
22 Lit sign in a theater
24 Yes-man
28 Thingamajigs
31 Come next
32 "__ none too soon!"
33 Pick up at school
35 Actor Olin of "thirtysomething"
36 Stocky
38 Avoids being tempted
40 "A __ of a different color"
41 Thin
42 Say further
44 Clock-radio features
48 Hunk of meat
51 African snake
53 Target
54 Just above a viscount
55 "My country __ of thee . . . "
56 Ledge
57 Boy
58 Had a bite
59 Pumpkin beginning

DOWN

1 Door feature
2 __ of the neck
3 Prophecy
4 Took care of
5 On horseback
6 Go down the slope
7 Injector, briefly
8 __ of the arts
9 "Now I see!"
10 Forget-me-__
11 Stain anew
19 Revered
21 Peeler or spatula
23 Romanov rulers
25 Answers, "Jeopardy!"-style
26 Song sung by two
27 Hankerings
28 Morse-code signal
29 "I'm __ you!" (watch out!)
30 Bloodhound's clue
34 Come down with again
37 In service
39 Depictions
43 Info
45 Took a ferry
46 Warlock
47 It slides down a slope
48 "Do what you __ out to do"
49 "__ down your weapons!"
50 "Raiders of the Lost __"
52 Use a pew

Tie the __ (marry)

solution on page 313

ACROSS

1 Lost traction
5 Tree cutters
9 __ through the nose
12 With nary a stitch
13 Meanie
14 Swamp gas, say some
15 Look at longingly
16 Go over like a __ balloon
17 __ it on a lark
18 Used a pager
20 Skin art
22 Half of a quarter
24 Cat or mouse item
28 An __ beaver
32 Dance at a luau
33 Daiquiri need
35 Knitted
36 Shouts
38 Goof up
40 Attach papers together
42 Discount price
45 Let out your breath
50 Pass a test with flying colors
51 Roman garment
53 Plow animals
54 "Step on __ gas"
55 Train sound
56 Flex
57 Trinity member
58 "I __ to break up a set"
59 Chances

DOWN

1 Snooty one
2 Olympic sled
3 At a standstill
4 Like Davy Jones's Locker
5 Military person
6 Grow up
7 "The __ of Kahn"
8 Give knockout gas to
9 Gimme golf shot, often
10 '60s hairstyle
11 Toy for "walking the dog"
19 "A mouse!"
21 Defrosts
23 Sourpuss
24 Short question with a long answer
25 Shade of a color
26 Under the weather
27 Taco sauce
29 "He's __ the whole world . . . "
30 Night before holidays
31 GOP member
34 Gas usage rate
37 "A __ in time saves nine"
39 Gender
41 Hawaiian hello
42 "Dagnabbit!"
43 Cave response
44 Prom attendee
46 Rail rider of old
47 Chopped down
48 Give brief use of
49 "At loose __"
52 __ reaction

Lost traction

solution on page 314

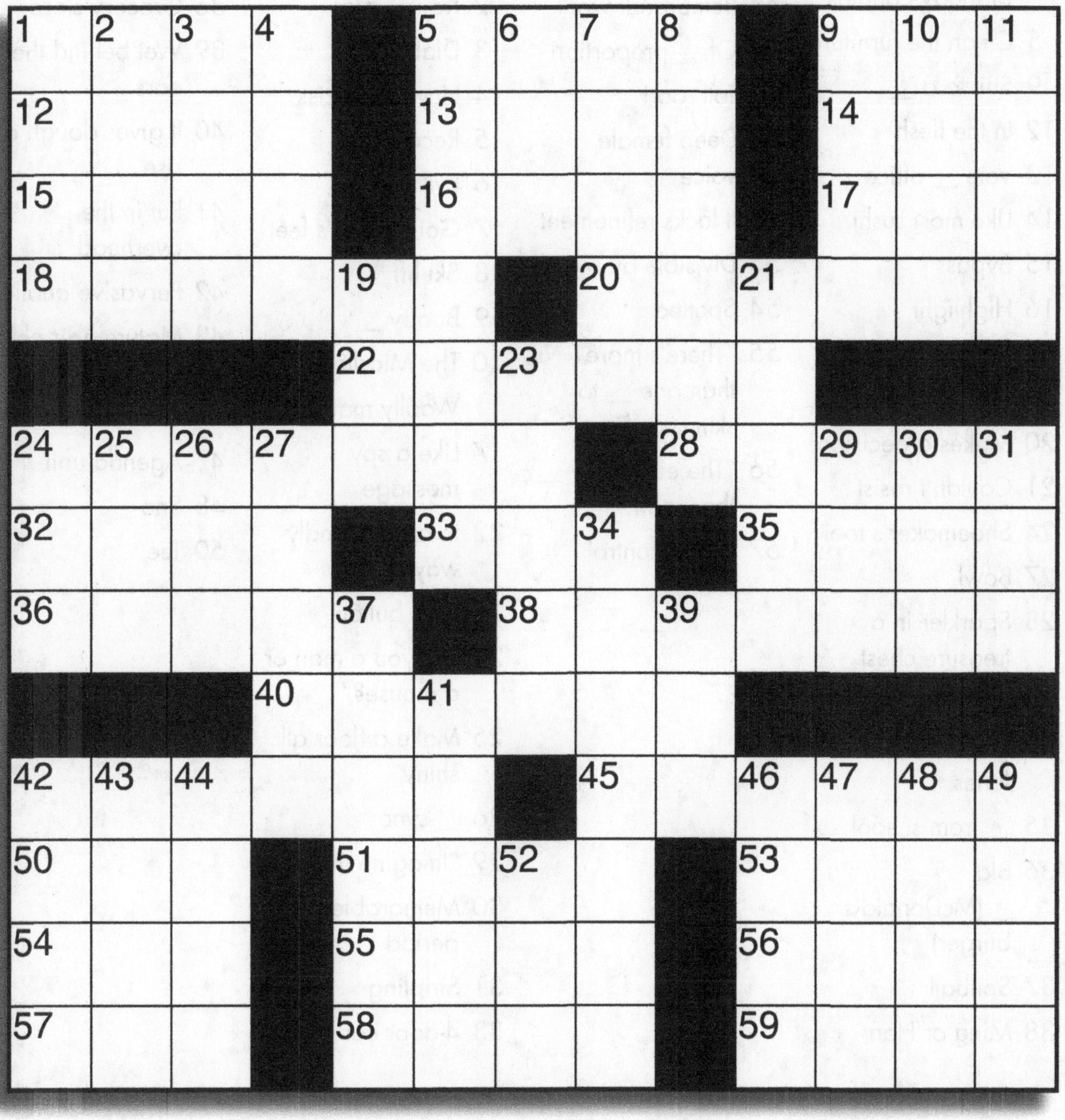

ACROSS

1 Tried to put out the birthday candles
5 Clean the furniture
9 Suit to a __
12 In the flesh
13 Vote __ office
14 Like most sushi
15 Bypass
16 Highlight
18 The Liberty __
19 Talk like a pigeon
20 Makes a decision
21 Couldn't resist
24 Shoemaker's tool
27 Bawl
28 Sparkler in a treasure chest
32 Dried grape
34 Hat for Indiana Jones
35 __ from school
36 Big __ (McDonald's burger)
37 Spitball
38 Ming or Han
41 Lengthy tale
44 Rembrandt work
45 Of __ proportion
49 Toll road
51 Deep female voice
52 It lacks refinement
53 Divisible by two
54 Spotted
55 "There's more than one __ to skin a cat"
56 "The early bird __ the worm"
57 Under control

DOWN

1 Soft lump
2 Key __ pie
3 Diabolical
4 How dogs kiss
5 Recognize
6 Evil
7 Got on one's feet
8 Ski lift
9 Booby __
10 The Middle __
11 Woolly mamas
17 Like a spy message
22 In an unfriendly way
23 VCR button
24 "__ you a man or a mouse?"
25 Make a floor all shiny
26 __-sync
29 "Imagine that!"
30 Memorable period
31 Stripling
33 4-door car
34 Ties tight
36 Grocery store
39 Wet behind the ears
40 It gives dough a rise
41 Put in the overhead
42 Pervasive quality
43 Mature hair color
46 Response to a charge
47 Agenda unit
48 Sno-__
50 Tee

Tried to put out the birthday candles

solution on page 314

ACROSS

1 Scuttlebutt
5 "As I __ saying . . ."
8 Tame
12 Wreck
13 "Come again?"
14 Section
15 In it's __ (uncut)
17 Window __ (lighting adjustment)
18 Boy Scout recitation
19 Old-fashioned
20 Ulysses S. __
23 Was in debt to
25 Goal
26 Convict
30 Staircase shape
33 __ for food
34 Tootsie treatment
36 "Like two peas in a __"
37 Passport stamp
38 Rope a dogie
40 Added employees
43 Sax mouthpiece
45 Make shorter, often
46 Bridges
50 Acting part
51 "__ fleece was white as snow . . ."
52 Hawaiian feast
53 Seeped
54 Private __ (detective)
55 Four years, for a President

DOWN

1 Outrage
2 Person wearing a habit
3 __ as a fiddle
4 French __ soup
5 Stimulate
6 Douglas Fink, for one
7 Timid
8 Bullfighter
9 Crocus kin
10 Eye part
11 Blind __
16 Sinking-ship deserter
19 Cuban cash
20 __ for air
21 "__ for the picking"
22 Between
24 "I now pronounce you husband and __"
26 Put together in math
27 Babies take them
28 Inner selves
29 Decorate anew
31 Eyes fixed upon
32 Amino __
35 Unusual thing
38 Organized
39 Movie ticket type
40 Seasoning
41 Worshiped one
42 Provoke
44 Lessen a burden
46 Try to beat others
47 Prompt on stage
48 Roofing goo
49 Addition total

Scuttlebutt

solution on page 314

6. Start with a Bang

ACROSS

1 Pleads
5 Hard to come by
9 Woof relative
12 Car bar
13 Notion
14 Body of water
15 Electric sign
16 Mists
17 Overnight accommodation
18 Fraidy-__
19 Cafeteria carrier
20 Hibernation location
21 __ a lot of effort into
22 "Well, __ that special?"
23 Wet, as grass
24 List entries
26 Mix with a spoon
28 Rides a bike
30 Out of bed
34 "A friend in __ . . . "
36 "The Phantom of the __"
37 Dextrous
40 Sunrise
42 "Sorcerer's Apprentice" item
43 Swee' __ (Popeye's kid)
44 Command to sled dogs
45 Chomp at the __
46 Ming thing
47 Need a heating pad
48 Apartment __
50 Do away with
51 " . . . and never the twain shall __"
52 Shoe string
53 Sneaky
54 Gets a sum
55 Cereal grain

DOWN

1 Prohibit
2 __ the oath of office
3 Was smug
4 Posted
5 Splits
6 Decorates
7 Yacht race
8 Eggs over __
9 Comment to the audience
10 Subscribe again
11 Tushy
21 Tiny seed
22 Speck on a map
23 Fuddy-duddy
25 "Not in so __ words"
27 __-Man Triathlon
29 Tempted and won over
31 Business workshop
32 Risqué material
33 Something to do in a hammock
35 Ran
37 Cowboy-boot features
38 Danger
39 Newman of music
41 Sharpens
44 Bear with a middle-sized bowl
45 Light __
49 Top-__ list

Pleads

solution on page 315

ACROSS

1 Cost an __ and a leg
4 Ritzy
8 Spill the beans
12 Ghost's cry
13 Angelic crown
14 General helper
15 Storytime spot
16 Kind of vaccine
17 Place for hatchlings
18 Stand with head __
20 Dweeb
22 "Get __!" (scram)
24 Film award
28 Festive celebration
31 Keyboard error
33 "Four score and seven years __ . . ."
34 Navel __ (type of fruit)
36 Earned forgiveness
38 One-__ play
39 "When You Wish __ a Star"
41 Marries
42 " . . . you see the whites of __ eyes"
44 "I've __ Working on the Railroad"
46 "You __ be kidding!"
48 Thing of value
52 Perched upon
55 Foal food
57 Corrida cry
58 "__ eyes have seen . . . "
59 Have a feast
60 Uncle Sam's country
61 Prepare potatoes
62 Aardvark snacks
63 Part of rpm

DOWN

1 Qualified
2 The __ of the crowd
3 Sulk
4 __ album
5 Rowing tool
6 Like Italics
7 Make a __-in-one
8 Musical groups
9 Fabricate
10 TV breaks
11 Double-or-nothing action
19 Hatfields or McCoys
21 " . . . __ for the home team, if they don't win . . . "
23 "And __ on it!" (hurry)
25 Xmas candy shape
26 Matured
27 Fishing gear
28 Billy __ (farm animal)
29 Part of a McDonald's icon
30 "Try not to be __!"
32 Sheet of glass
35 Expert
37 Possesses
40 Acquire
43 Urge forward
45 Smoothes the way
47 Baking __ (flour look-alike)
49 Chicken noodle __
50 "Would you like to try something __?"
51 Shred
52 Sound enhancer
53 Father's Day gift
54 "__ for the road"
56 It gets detonated

Cost an __ and a leg

solution on page 315

ACROSS

1 Owl's call
5 Clickable symbol
9 "Now's as good a time as __"
12 Take apart
13 "Get a __ on!"
14 Bit of tragedy
15 Crock-pot meal
16 Records that were spun
18 Fire-truck needs
20 "What's more . . ."
21 Boxing official
23 Does in, mob-style
27 Spa worker
31 Road __ (night-driving woe)
32 Large deer
33 Went by car
35 Moist
36 Like a snail's trail
38 Occupants
40 Media madness
41 Harbor boat
42 Rye or pumpernickel
46 Puts in the mail
50 Something that gets in the way
54 Any thing
55 Took a bum __
56 __-for-all
57 Idiot
58 Green __ Packers
59 __ of approval
60 From the get-go

DOWN

1 "Be quiet!"
2 Catch __ (start to understand)
3 Feats by Keats
4 Castle features
5 Mischievous munchkin
6 Soft drink
7 Ellipse
8 Fishing boats might drag them behind them
9 Amazement
10 And not
11 "Absolutely!"
17 Utensil
19 Shabby
22 Animal hair
24 Young deer
25 Guitar ridge
26 TV __ (entertainment devices)
27 Sieve
28 Chum
29 Hop, __, and jump
30 Turn into compost
31 Type of species
34 Dog doctor
37 Liquefy
39 To-do list
43 Ones who say "Oops!"
44 Estate unit
45 __ circus
47 Time when both hands are up
48 __ ranch
49 __ flurries
50 Sphere
51 Lamb's call
52 Snoop
53 Electric __

Owl's call

solution on page 315

ACROSS

1 Dwarf with glasses
4 Ming things
8 Friends
12 Shout of discovery
13 "You __ what you sow"
14 On the briny
15 __ one's soul
17 Doorbell sound
18 Wall of shrubs
19 Diminish
20 8 bits on a computer
23 Mixed __
25 Tic-tac-toe win
26 Tease
27 Book-cover words
31 Costume
33 Director's "Go!"
34 "Trick or __!"
35 "Disgusting!"
36 Auction action
37 A new __ on life
39 Runs a scam
40 Alley call
43 "I'm a Yankee Doodle __ . . . "
45 Sushi need
46 Midsections
50 What the nose knows
51 Blueprint
52 "Well, I'll be!"
53 Church benches
54 Stood the __ of time
55 Run a tab

DOWN

1 River barriers
2 "I have you now!"
3 Item in a garage
4 Yen
5 Let back in
6 Pestered
7 __ limit (road sign)
8 Ice cream dessert
9 It's about 30% of the world's land
10 __ an ear (listen)
11 Guru
16 "What's __ big idea?"
20 Cowboy's footwear
21 "I beg __ pardon!"
22 Open-topped bag
24 Yearning
26 Charlie Brown's always got stuck in a tree
28 Itty-bitty
29 Throw for a __
30 Football linemen
32 Stumbles
33 Committee schedules
35 At hand
38 Go with the flow
39 Room for playing dodge ball
40 __ up (support)
41 "Err on the __ of caution"
42 Flat-bottomed boat
44 Parent's warning
47 Arrogance
48 __ Zealand
49 "__ a pin, pick it up . . . "

Dwarf with glasses

solution on page 315

ACROSS

1 __ Scotia
5 Hog heaven
8 Take a __ at (try)
12 Heinous
13 __-tapper (music with a beat)
14 Daddy
15 Sunset direction
16 PreColumbian __
17 Logging tools
18 Columbus's ships, e.g.
19 Get it wrong
20 Game of world domination
21 Russian empresses
24 Twosome
26 __ as a beet
27 What kings over their kingdom do
31 "Who's __ of the big bad wolf?"
33 External eye part
34 Medicine amounts
35 __ and eggs
36 "Said the spider to the __"
37 Ring in a way that echoes
40 Inter-office note
43 "__ the lifeboats!"
44 Upper limbs
47 Experts
48 __ of Reason
49 Deep-__ bends
50 "Hit the road!"
51 __ Arthur Conan Doyle
52 Work to get
53 __ at the moon
54 "__, what's the big idea?"
55 Huskies might pull it

DOWN

1 Colorful salamander
2 "Get __ it!"
3 Ones who come by at hospitals
4 Low-singing females
5 Took the reins
6 Like some affairs
7 Want a lot
8 More skimpy
9 Metered vehicle
10 Associates of Jane Goodall
11 Catch some rays
22 Greet the dawn
23 Bakery byproduct
24 Male parent
25 Roswell sighting
28 "What is that __ racket?"
29 Shaving __
30 Not aye
32 __ spray can
33 Food factory
35 Grinder
38 Tennis whack
39 Attempts to film a scene
40 "Monster __"
41 Reverberate
42 Tabby's talk
45 Petty
46 Transmits

___ Scotia

solution on page 315

ACROSS

1 Pill portion
5 Stick in one's __
9 Chum
12 Matures
13 Owns, in the Bible
14 __ cream
15 Baby sitter's challenge
16 Joined the Marines
18 "Open __!" (entrance password)
20 Noah's boat
21 Blacktop material
22 Weapon's against Goliath
26 Put in danger
30 Bathroom bar
31 Alter a pigment
32 Bizarre
35 Place with a mud bath
36 Small bills
38 Feeling under the __
40 Jacket parts that might hold flowers
43 Enmity
44 Humor
45 Grab
49 Do business
53 Song for one
54 Lend an __
55 __-blue
56 Prima donnas' problems
57 "More than meets the __"
58 Crystal-ball gazer
59 Appointment

DOWN

1 Smidgens
2 Baddie of folklore
3 Sail the Seven __
4 Real-__ company (house-selling group)
5 "Toodle-oo"
6 Tried to get elected
7 World traveler's aid
8 Spin around
9 Peach center
10 Air-battle expert
11 Took by the hand
17 Glides downhill
19 "Tom Sawyer" author Twain
23 Munch
24 Gawk
25 Argue
26 Revered one
27 Talking bird
28 Little Bo-__
29 __-lying areas
33 Rear end
34 Twine
37 Knitted
39 Made fun of
41 Rosters
42 Gawk
46 Frat-party cry
47 Coagulate
48 Vacuum-cleaner attachment
49 Golf-bag item
50 "Hit the Road, Jack" singer Charles
51 "__ you sure?"
52 Billiard stick

Pill portion

solution on page 315

ACROSS

1 Frosty
4 Basketball target
8 Deer dad
12 As well
13 Curly hairstyle
14 Mattress spring
15 Swallowed up
17 Part in a play
18 "I __ to do that"
19 "Does this make __ to you?"
20 Strand
24 "Right this minute!"
27 Make an ID card
31 " . . . and sat down beside __ . . . "
32 Prop for Groucho or George Burns
33 "Under the __" ("Little Mermaid" song)
34 Isolated districts
36 "__ time do you have?"
37 Supervise
39 Birdbath buildup
42 Harvests
46 __ over (peruse)
47 Put your legs on both sides
50 Not wild
51 Ran a tab
52 Lair
53 Got caught by a radar gun
54 Slangy refusal
55 " . . . __ on a tuffet . . . "

DOWN

1 News article
2 Funnel shape
3 Lotus-position discipline
4 Stops the march
5 "A chip __ the old block"
6 Mine yield
7 Escape __ (spaceship lifeboat)
8 What a movie's shown on
9 Daffy Duck or Donald Duck
10 Is feeling under the weather
11 Merriment
16 __ pricing
19 Prepare paint
21 __ Oyl (Popeye's girlfriend)
22 Light-colored beer
23 Stockpile
24 "The old gray mare __ ain't . . . "
25 Countdown start
26 Path of a football pass
28 What an ember becomes
29 Celestial Seasonings product
30 Dog-__-dog
32 Mine opening
35 Rich to the max
36 Garden pest
38 Clear the chalkboard
39 Handicrafts
40 "Look before you __"
41 A __ of chance
43 Puts together
44 __ bargain
45 Mailed
47 Heir, often
48 Noah's limit
49 10-percenter

Frosty

solution on page 316

ACROSS

1 Illuminated
4 Celebrity
8 Negotiator's skill
12 "__ Flew Over the Cuckoo's Nest"
13 Helper
14 Hip-wiggling dance
15 Had a snack
16 Papa's wife
17 Kind of report
18 Finished
20 Disencumber
21 "Name, __, and serial number?"
22 The field of flying
25 Behind bars
27 Do embroidery
28 Relaxation sighs
31 Unsealed
33 Pitiful
35 "As __ your request"
36 Tire filler
38 Charity receivers
39 It might make you sneeze or itch
41 Identifies
44 Andy Capp beverage
45 Beavers build them
48 Ruer's word
49 Shade of color
51 "Casey at the __"
52 Air-taxi destination
53 "Will we __ know?"
54 Polygraph's catch
55 __ and relaxation
56 With little beads of water
57 Common street name

DOWN

1 Burden
2 Fall __ disuse
3 High-school student, usually
4 "I Want You" Uncle
5 Beauty pageant prop
6 Lets in
7 Prepared
8 Rose's spike
9 Angel's emanation
10 Tribal unit
11 Shoot the breeze
19 Smooth out
23 As good as it gets
24 "__ to the fact . . ."
25 Patrolman
26 Perform a parody
28 Receptive
29 "I've __ it up to here!"
30 Cunning
32 Like eyes at the doctor's after drops
34 Plant-to-be
37 Go through again
39 Balance-sheet plus
40 Get a library's permission for more time
41 Duo
42 "When all __ fails . . ."
43 Lasses
46 Postal delivery
47 "From __ to stern"
50 __ out for a part (go to an audition)

Illuminated

solution on page 316

ACROSS

1 Not right
5 Arrived
9 "The long arm of the __"
12 Loafing around
13 Revival meeting cry
14 Meadow mama
15 Ancient
16 Stole the show
18 Phone button
20 Evil eye
21 Disentangle
23 Hunter's weapon
27 Dive, like a submarine
31 Wind catcher at sea
32 "A long, long time __ . . ."
33 "This is the __ thing that's ever happened to me"
35 Squid's squirt
36 Cheerful
38 Television companies
40 Maple __
42 Burn the surface
43 Actor Cruise
45 Payment mixed with the mortgage
49 Den
53 Conceal oneself
54 __ Van Winkle
55 Sign
56 Concept
57 Choose
58 Bunch of cattle
59 Student spot

DOWN

1 Tale teller
2 Fringe
3 Ran away
4 Boredom
5 Witch's stewpot
6 Musical sound booster
7 Interlock
8 Buy a raffle ticket
9 Give a __ up (boost)
10 Stupefy
11 Join in marriage
17 Spindle
19 From the beginning
22 Fairy tale heavies
24 __-weather friend
25 Chain-__ fence
26 Fraternal order members
27 Droops
28 "The __ Duckling"
29 Wild pig
30 Our __ colleague
34 "__ the night before . . ."
37 "In the Line of __"
39 Exotic flower
41 Patio
44 Infiltrator
46 Hitchhiker's goal
47 Praiseful poems
48 Not strong
49 Country-club figure
50 Pay __ service to
51 Prone
52 __ Lady of . . . (start of some church names)

Not right

solution on page 316

ACROSS

1 Sear
5 "__ are you?"
8 __ and such
12 Tryout
14 Grate
15 Sheets and blankets
16 Tract
17 "Golly!"
18 Radio-reception tools
20 "For goodness __!"
23 Shadowboxes
25 "Bravo!" in the bullring
26 Lit
30 __ market (rummage sale)
32 "Now __ here!"
33 One of a car's four
34 Did layout
36 Tiny bit
37 Not in the city
39 Cross-guard's garment
40 Sesame paste
43 Have to pay back
45 On the briny
46 Consecrated
51 Buffalo __
52 English or Spanish
53 Stooges
54 Inside man
55 Frosty's flesh

DOWN

1 Taxi
2 Painter's choice
3 Also say
4 Mountain crest
5 Many are made in Napa Valley
6 Live high off the __
7 In the spotlight
8 Mass __ (buses, subways, etc.)
9 Fabled race loser
10 Web surfer
11 Good places for a massage
13 Even-steven result
19 Banquet brewer
20 Pillowy
21 Pal
22 "__ your shirt on!"
24 Religious painting
27 Ocean motion
28 Timeline segments
29 Cause for Chapter 11
31 Roof things before cable TV
32 "Flash Gordon" and "Phantom Empire"
35 Morning riser
38 Crazy
39 One planet in from Earth
40 Keep __ on (watch)
41 Where the most people live
42 Beatles film
44 Hairpiece
47 Catch some Zs
48 Brownish color
49 Inner self
50 Morning dampness

Sear

solution on page 316

ACROSS

1 Gator kin
5 Female pigs
9 Domino spot
12 Prom-night car
13 Precooking activity
14 "Winner takes __"
15 Trans fat __
16 Suddenly
18 Night-sky streak
20 Go astray
21 Deadly snake
23 Rich cake
27 Talking bird
32 Cat call
33 Holy figurine
34 "Last time I __ you, you were THIS big"
35 Sheet of stamps
36 Walk briskly
37 Train bridges
39 Big trucks
41 " . . . __ freedom ring"
42 Director's call
44 Letter taker
49 Save energy, say
53 "I'll __ be a second"
54 "Eureka!"
55 Bring up
56 "__ to My Lou My Darling"
57 Yoyo or Slinky
58 Tennis-match divisions
59 Promote to the hilt

DOWN

1 "Happy as a __"
2 __ pilaf
3 Skip over
4 ZIP __
5 Least populated
6 Planet
7 "And Then There __ None"
8 Sudden gush
9 __-a-cake
10 Not well
11 Engage in
17 On time
19 Acorn-bearing tree
22 Round gem
24 Actual
25 TV knob
26 Fleecy females
27 La Brea Tar __
28 Realty unit
29 "No __ at the inn"
30 Hijinks
31 Woofers and __
38 "Yuck! This room is a __!"
40 Accusers, in court
43 Sycamore or spruce
45 Luxurious
46 Like a pressman's hands
47 __ of the lip (revelation)
48 Category
49 __ burglar
50 "Eureka!"
51 Veto vote
52 Cauldron

Gator kin

solution on page 316

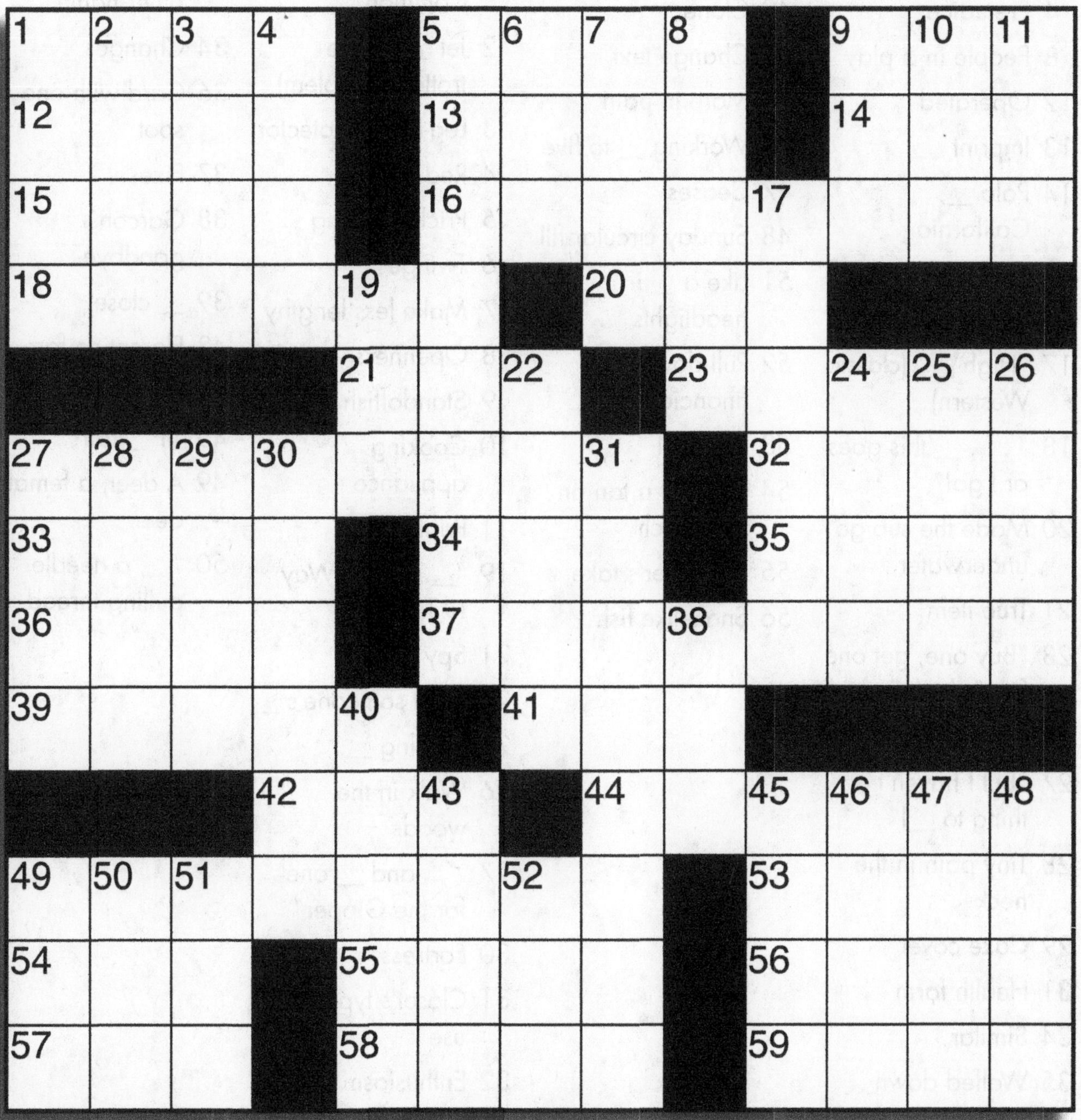

ACROSS

1 Lodge member
4 Prejudice
8 People in a play
12 Operated
13 Imprint
14 Palo __, California
15 "__ before beauty"
16 Sound rebound
17 "High __" (classic Western)
18 ". . . __ this goes or I go!"
20 Made the sub go underwater
21 True item
23 "Buy one, get one free" deal
25 Nervy
27 "But I haven't a thing to __!"
28 Tiny pain in the neck
29 Cake cover
31 Health farm
34 Similar
35 Wolfed down
37 Croquet-ball hitter
40 Clone
41 Change text
42 More in pain
46 Working __ to five
47 Ceases
48 Sunday circular fill
51 Like a __ in headlights
52 Pull down, financially
53 Hair gel
54 Tries for a tan on the beach
55 Plunderer's take
56 Snakelike fish

DOWN

1 Before the Common __
2 Jet __ (globe-trotter's problem)
3 Leg-bend protector
4 Red as a __
5 Prickly feeling
6 Twinge
7 Make less lengthy
8 Openness
9 Standoffish
10 Cooking appliance
11 Printer ink
19 "__ a Long Way to Tiperrary"
21 Spy agcy.
22 Twist someone's __
24 A living __
26 Walk in the woods
27 ." . .and __ one for the Gipper"
30 Fortress
31 Closet's typical use
32 Enthusiasm
33 "A rose by __ other name . . . "
34 Changes
36 Card with one spot
37 Fixes
38 Garcon's goodbye
39 __ closet
43 Florentine farewell
44 Brave person
45 "It __ fair!"
49 A deer, a female deer
50 "__, a needle pulling thread . . . "

Lodge member

solution on page 316

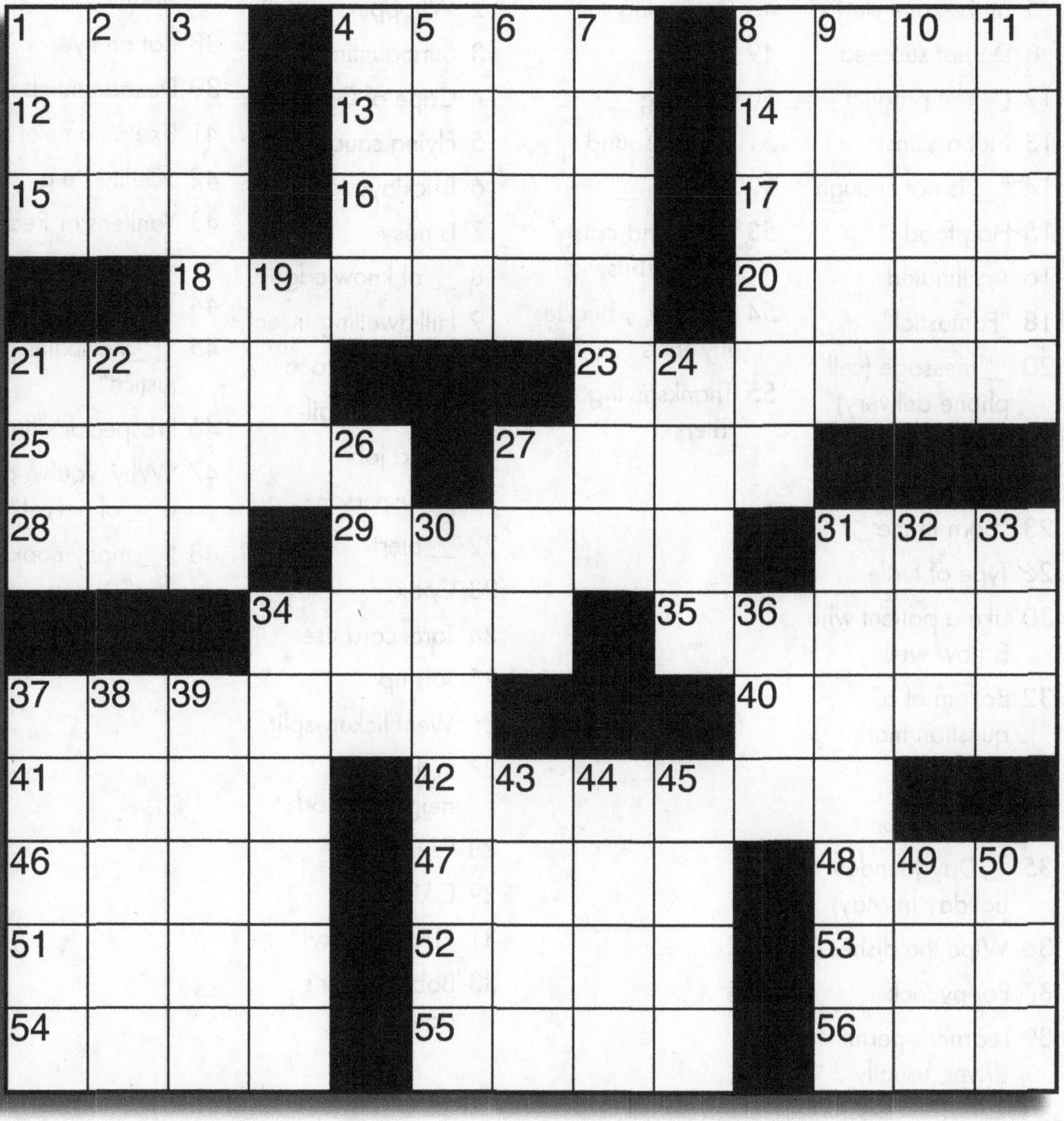

ACROSS

1 Unexciting
5 Strike-zone studier
8 Do not succeed
12 Detroit product
13 Not against
14 "__ is not enough"
15 Hog food
16 Acclimated
18 "Fantastic!"
20 __ message (cell phone delivery)
21 Wipe out pencil marks
23 "Born in the __"
26 Type of turtle
30 Like a patient who is now well
32 Bottom of a question mark
33 Embraced
34 Diner patron
35 __ Day (Sunday holiday in May)
36 Wipe the dishes
37 Poppycock
39 Learner's-permit driver, usually
40 __ perception
45 Easygoing
49 Delight
50 Pumping __
51 Dove's sound
52 Landing __
53 Dogs and cats and gerbils
54 "One, __, buckle my shoe . . ."
55 Thanksgiving taters

DOWN

1 Largemouth __
2 Whopper
3 Surmounting
4 Cape of Good __
5 Flying saucer
6 Bricklayer's need
7 Is nosy
8 __ of knowledge
9 Hill-dwelling insect
10 Skating surface
11 Blazed a trail
17 Did a job
19 Newsperson
22 __ alert
23 Coax
24 Tarot-card user
25 Tots up
26 Went lickety-split
27 In the neighborhood
28 Chichi
29 Eskimo __
31 "That's yucky!"
33 Bobby-soxer's dance
35 "Gilligan's Island" boat
38 Bat an eye
39 Decade numbers
41 Like an omelet
42 "Guilty," e.g.
43 Yankees or Red Sox
44 Word on a towel
45 "__ the scales of justice"
46 Prospector's find
47 "Why, you've got a __ of nerve!"
48 "__ many cooks . . ."

Unexciting

solution on page 317

ACROSS

1 Cry at the villain
4 Kayaker's need
7 Glass that bends light
12 Cops __ robbers
13 "That's all __ wrote!"
14 Wheel spokes
15 Figured out
17 Stinks
18 Matching
19 Stories
20 Bakery need
23 "When, if __?"
25 Vesuvius output
26 Visible air
27 Have __ last laugh
30 Breakfast dish
32 The Foreign __ (faroff militia)
34 Part of wpm
35 "__ but not least . . . "
37 "The Donna __ Show"
38 Infant
39 Feathered friends
40 Win without a loss
43 Payphone part
45 Some have ivy on them
46 They're visible when you go "ah"
50 Bride's walkway
51 "The goose that lays the golden __"
52 Through
53 Need a bandage
54 Meadow sound
55 "As of __ . . . " (so far)

DOWN

1 Naughty
2 "__ of these days, Alice . . . "
3 __ man out
4 "Sesame Street" grouch
5 Buttinsky's word
6 Cash in
7 Fancy business word for groomed pupil
8 Airport controller's tool
9 Adored one
10 Title of respect
11 Hit or __
16 Customary
20 Box office bomb
21 Feeble
22 Eggs __ easy
24 It's shocking
26 Pierce
27 Bleacher feature
28 Tended the garden
29 "The __ justify the means "
31 Went by
33 Southern side dish
36 Planetary __
38 Southern __
39 What a beatnik beats
40 "__ the deck, matey!"
41 Moan
42 "So what __ is new?"
44 Trademark
47 College-campus climber
48 State a falsehood
49 Found a lap

Cry at the villain

solution on page 317

ACROSS

1 Fill-in worker
5 Peter __ (foe of Captain Hook)
8 Stick around
12 Aroma
13 Anger
14 __ Canaveral
15 Gawk at
16 Bubble-sheet smudges
18 Driving-range need
19 __ pole
20 Underwhelmed
22 Pale grey
25 Gumshoe
28 Street fight
30 Got in one's sights
31 :
32 Type of card or union
34 Extends a subscription
35 Actor Olin of "L.A. Doctors"
36 Tears to pieces
38 Almost straight up
39 Mummy's home
43 Like sandpaper
46 Cruel
47 Christmas __
48 Winning streak
49 Scoundrel
50 Retained
51 Movie-making site
52 Toboggan, more generically

DOWN

1 Trumpet sound
2 Hem
3 Lawn tunneler
4 __ innocent until found guilty
5 Holy pictures
6 "You are here" map feature
7 Less messy
8 "The __ of the Earth" (lowest of the low)
9 __ and feather
10 Do an impression
11 "Uh-huh!"
17 "I've been __ by the Dark Side of the Force"
21 Ones who need not do laundry
22 "Ready, willing, and __"
23 Like a turtle
24 Coop mamas
25 Santa's bag
26 Employ
27 Sermon response
29 Scary creatures
33 His and hers
34 Preacher's advice
37 Song and dance show
38 __ and pepper
40 Stadium shape
41 "Is this thing on?" device
42 Oozed
43 "Don't __ me, I just work here"
44 Pollen spreader
45 Modern music

Fill-in worker

solution on page 317

7. Make a Fresh Start

ACROSS

1 Write a bit
4 __ and ah
7 Plus-column item
12 Impress mightily
13 Dined
14 Baton __, Louisiana
15 Rich
17 Idiot
18 "Put to good __"
19 "Have you heard the __?"
20 Up and __
23 Police action
25 __ rug
26 "What is the __ of this?"
31 The softest stone
32 Do wrong
33 Not docked
34 Siding with
36 Goo
37 Corner chess piece
39 Hereditary unit
40 "The Legend of Sleepy __"
44 Drink on draft
46 ". . . in order to form a more perfect __ . . . "
47 Restrained
51 Large pebble
52 Roadie's load
53 Ahab's affirmative
54 Sharpened
55 "Every dog __ his day"
56 Big bench

DOWN

1 Chin
2 Part of IOU
3 Mad Hatter's __ party
4 Stable staple
5 "A rose by any __ name . . . "
6 "You there!"
7 Navy fleet
8 Chimney stuff
9 "Certainly!"
10 Head swellers
11 Camping need
16 Craziness
19 Mortgage
20 Facts and figures
21 Type of surgeon
22 "Lassie, Timmy fell into the __!"
24 Chum in Chile
27 Bugged
28 Emerald __ (Ireland)
29 Night-sign gas
30 Stare open-mouthed
32 "Neither __ nor rain nor dark of night . . . "
35 Made wrinkle-free
38 Fate
40 "Silence!"
41 Wise about
42 Leo the __
43 Single
45 Place for a kiss
47 Cry from Scrooge
48 Drink like a dog
49 It can wink
50 Beads at sunup

Write a bit

solution on page 318

ACROSS

1 Bulls-eye flyer
5 Comfy shirt
8 It might be next to the egg salad
12 Customer
13 Scarecrow stuffing
14 Cleanser scent
15 Contrary
17 Food cooker
18 Furrows
19 Clever
21 Complain
23 Circular pool with crocodiles
24 Gotten up
25 Large vase
26 "__ for the course"
29 Bullring cry
30 Showed concern
32 "Long, long __..."
33 Marry
34 Black's better than red, in finance
35 Assessed
37 "All work and no __ . . . "
38 Respond to the snooze alarm
39 Avow
42 __ hydrant
43 Crazy bird
44 Showy wealth
48 In a little while
49 "Twelve Angry __"
50 Look over quickly
51 "__ the Lonely"
52 Babble
53 Cultivate

DOWN

1 Couple
2 Nile biter
3 Did again, as a role
4 Acting company
5 The one here
6 Wolf down
7 It's not a pretty picture
8 Baseball or soccer
9 "Words to __ by"
10 Once again
11 __ one's way (wander)
16 Tracing guides
20 Banister
21 Enlarge
22 Agitate
23 Like clouded water
26 "__ is a virtue"
27 Becomes older
28 Took a plane
31 Study of the body
36 Bring into custody
37 Cent
39 Furthermore
40 Saturday-morning TV viewing
41 __ and die
42 In a __ (sad)
45 __ shooter
46 ". . . which nobody __ deny"
47 Dead-__ street

Bulls-eye flyer

solution on page 318

ACROSS

1 Plaster dressing
5 Reading rooms
9 Sunbather's quest
12 Wagon need
13 Off ramp
14 "Looky here!"
15 Stagger
16 Little
17 Small opening
18 Least young
20 Alleviate
21 Get up and go
23 "Let us now sing our national __"
25 First woman in the Bible
26 "__ now or never"
27 Agendas
31 Calm
33 Parody
34 Beginning
35 __ tent
36 Cotton __ (Eli Whitney invention)
37 Song's words
39 __ chocolate
40 Amazes
43 Foreigner's speech standout
45 Diva's possession
46 Toll road, briefly
47 Large land mass
50 Goof up
51 Applications
52 Scream
53 Ballpoint __
54 Wagers
55 "Buy low, __ high"

DOWN

1 Train unit
2 Have an __ to grind
3 Infant's garments
4 "__ me what you want"
5 Peace after the Cold War
6 Is
7 Last inning, if no overtime
8 Hog's home
9 Greek garb
10 Cries of discovery
11 "Nah!"
19 Delicate
20 Discharge
21 Durango dough
22 Balanced
24 Slip away
28 What tourists do
29 Triplets
30 Transported
32 Sushi fish
33 Victory
35 White __ fence
38 "You __ a good point"
40 Cry
41 Foul fellow
42 "A little __ around the edges"
44 Votes against
46 British saloon
48 Unhealthy
49 "__ in a day's work"

Plaster dressing

solution on page 318

ACROSS

1 Capitol top
5 Conspiracy
9 Health club
12 Comparable
13 __ mower
14 Dance like Gregory Hines
15 Sensible
16 Liter or meter
17 " . . . comin' through the __"
18 __ peroxide
20 Fewer
21 Musician's job
22 "__ and bear it"
24 Some socks, color-wise
28 Borders
31 "Neither hide __ hair . . ."
32 Expression
34 "A Tale of __ Cities"
35 Kite string
37 Ruined, like a room
39 __-cheap
41 Coal case
42 Cut out, like a coupon
44 Your __ (kingly address)
49 "__ Father . . . " (the Lord's Prayer)
50 Biting bug
51 Not stifling
52 __ football
53 Move like molasses
54 "__-high to a grasshopper"
55 Yearning
56 Raised dogs
57 Fixes a hem

DOWN

1 Short race
2 All right
3 Never __ (forget it)
4 Renewable __
5 Placed a stopper in a drain
6 "Life in the fast __"
7 Indebted
8 Explosive stick
9 Might and power
10 Picks up the check
11 Tarzan's friends
19 More slippery
20 Pot top
23 Not go away
24 Picnic pest
25 Skid __
26 Football field
27 Command to a dog
29 Shepherd's charge
30 Greens-keeper's patch
33 Went around, in space
36 "__ it in the bud"
38 Checks out secretly
40 High male voice
42 Imitate
43 Tempt
45 Find-the-path puzzle
46 "Floating on cloud __"
47 Staff
48 Hurricane centers
50 Wad

Capitol top

solution on page 318

ACROSS

1 Start of FBI
4 Humanities
8 Compact __ player
12 "You __ what you eat"
13 Pirate's plunder
14 Sing in canon, say
15 __ chicken (dish from India)
17 Winter shoe
18 Deduce
19 Picnic pests
20 Potbellied __
23 Go to seed
25 Gofer
26 Dark-hair coloring
31 "I didn't know that!"
32 Two-door car
33 "So THAT'S your game!"
34 Attacks
36 Wound reminder
37 Conducted
38 Physical comic at the circus
39 Prissy
42 Mountain of cheese and chips
45 Alter
46 . . .
50 Get __ goat
51 Amaze
52 Poker card
53 "Right away!"
54 Wails
55 Make a bleached blonde, say

DOWN

1 "Chew the __"
2 Time period
3 "A __ of thieves"
4 Go it __ (fly solo)
5 Heliport place
6 Shredded
7 Saddle parts
8 War of words
9 Saint's image
10 "Not by a long __!"
11 Army beds
16 Submarine command
20 Epic story
21 Does up a sneaker
22 Wordsworth works
24 "__ from the Heart"
26 Bravery
27 Tire track
28 Tex-Mex sandwich
29 Defrost
30 Bring home the bacon
32 Stage signal
35 "__, but not quite"
36 Splatter
38 Beards hide them
39 Experts
40 __-a-cop (security guard)
41 Scheme
43 Chorus member
44 Item for a caveman or golfer
47 Depressed
48 Like hail
49 "As far as the eyes can __"

Start of FBI

solution on page 318

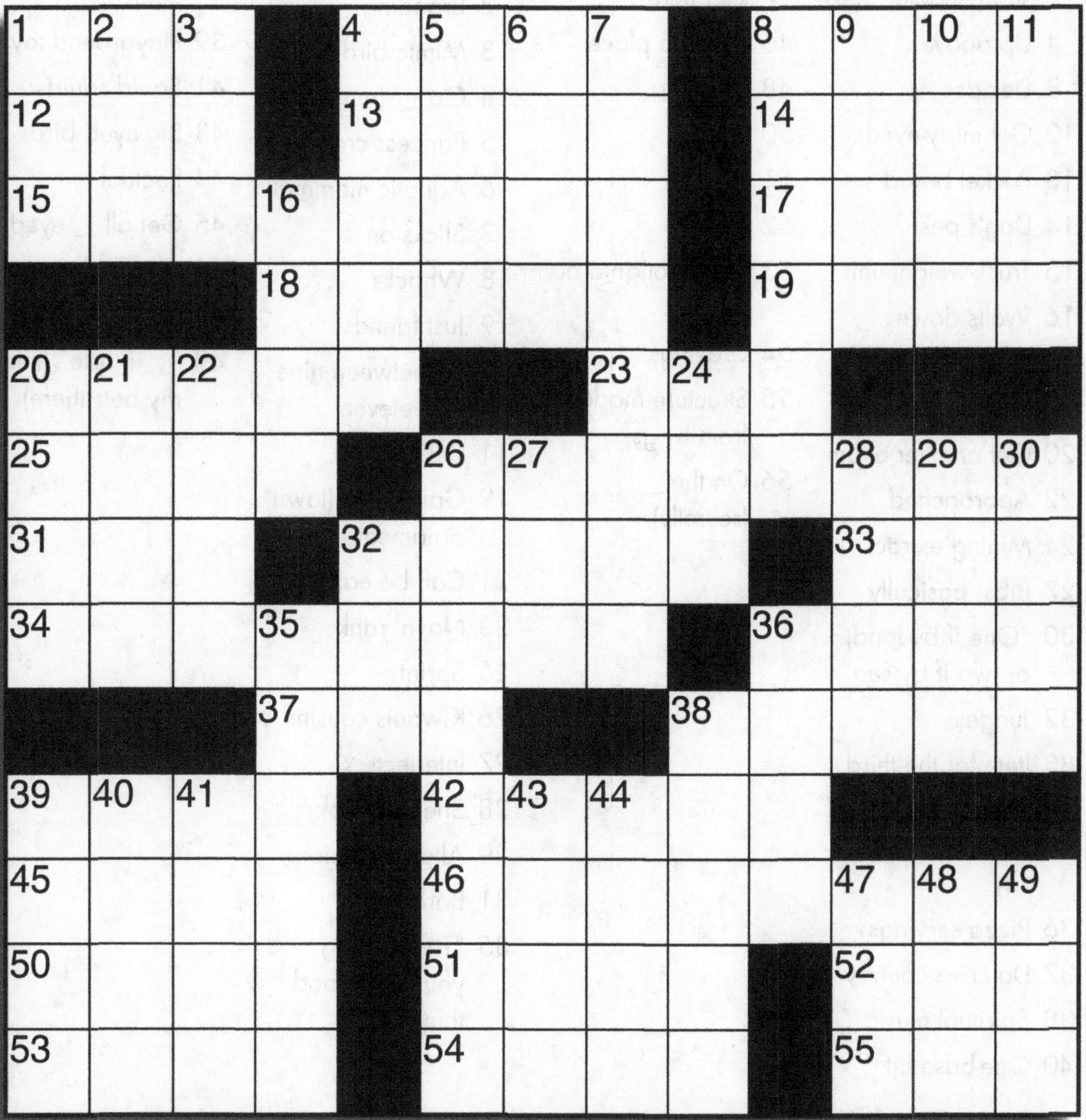

ACROSS

1 What a sharpshooter does
4 Up above
8 Decides
12 Get misty-eyed
13 Pocket bread
14 Dog's pest
15 Truck-weight unit
16 Wolfs down
17 Vampire tooth
18 Entanglement
20 Get another exam
22 Approached
24 Mining extract
27 Bibs, basically
30 "One if by land, or two if by sea"
32 Judges
33 Item for the third pig's house
34 Prepare shrimp, say
36 Pizza servings
37 Do cross-country
38 Spiritual music
40 One-base hit
42 "The __ is my shepherd . . . "
46 Boot-top place
48 Fish lung
50 Teeny
51 Weirdo
52 Inactive
53 "There oughta be a __"
54 Cravings
55 Structure made from twigs
56 On the __ (secretly)

DOWN

1 Takes measures
2 Branding __
3 Mimic bird
4 Go __ (run amok)
5 Princess crowns
6 Aquatic mammal
7 Sticks on
8 Whacks
9 Just friends
10 It's between nine and eleven
11 Deflate
19 Garden __ (lawn ornament)
21 Can be eaten
23 Naval rank
25 Sprint
26 Kiwanis cousins
27 Interjects
28 Sneak a look
29 Altered version
31 Barbecue
35 "That's using your __" (good thinking!)
36 Magicians cast them
39 Playground toy
41 Squid squirts
43 Big-eyed birds
44 Factual
45 Get all __-eyed
46 Cloud's home
47 Do garden work
49 "__ it ride" (keep my bets there)

What a sharpshooter does

solution on page 318

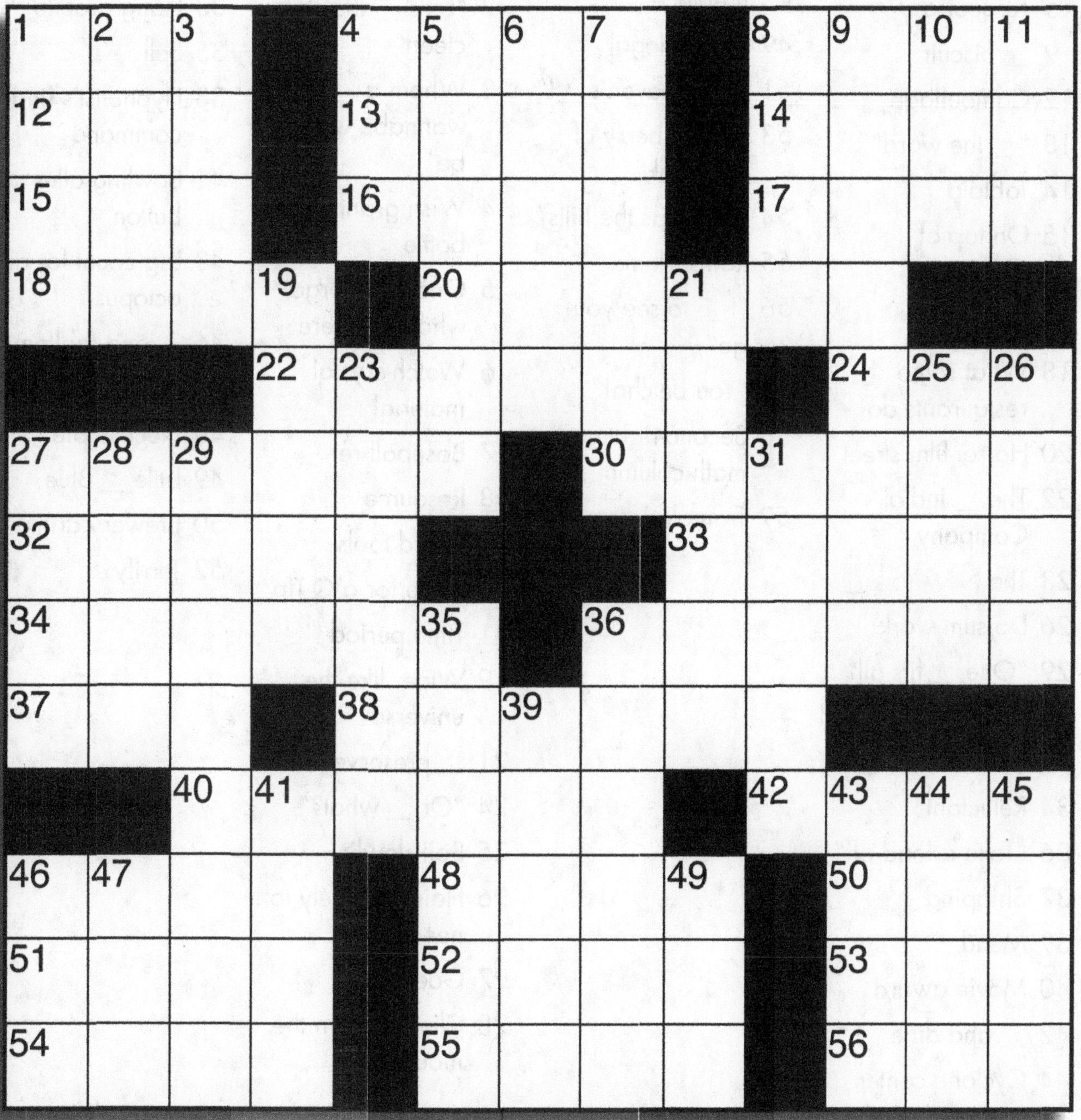

ACROSS

1 Small branch
5 Turquoise
9 __ biscuit
12 Camouflage
13 "__ the word"
14 Tabloid
15 On top of
16 Siestas
17 Enmity
18 What some restaurants do
20 Horror-film street
22 The __ India Company
23 The New York __
26 Do sum work
29 "One __ fits all"
31 Pool-table material
32 Mexican party
34 Reluctant
36 "Take a load off"
37 Shipping __
39 Mend
40 Movie award
42 __ and dine
44 Cyclone center
45 Log holder in the fireplace
49 Make illegal
51 "For Heaven's __!"
53 Roddenberry of "Star Trek"
54 "As __ as the hills"
55 Rams' dams
56 "I __ to see you go"
57 "You betcha!"
58 Second-rightmost math column
59 Trampled

DOWN

1 Dry splat
2 "Let's __ the slate clean"
3 Whom a wannabe wants to be
4 Wish granter in a bottle
5 One who forgot who they were
6 Watch-crystal material
7 Baseball ref
8 Resource
9 Beard tools
10 Place for a Q-Tip
11 Time period
19 Wide, like the universe
21 __ preserver
24 "Or __ what?"
25 Boil slowly
26 Hairstyle likely to need a pick
27 Goes kaput
28 Climbs down the mountain
30 Lack of difficulty
33 Hang around
35 Sell
38 Hypnotist's final command
41 Bowling alley button
43 Leg count for an octopus
46 __ end (bottom)
47 Aware of
48 Necessitate
49 Little __ Blue
50 Brewery drink
52 Terrify

Small branch

solution on page 319

ACROSS

1 Sits for a portrait
6 Yellow Pages fillers
9 "Oh yeah, sez __?"
12 Forbidden trade item from Africa
13 Bubble __
14 Safflower __
15 __ a successor
16 Embodiment
18 Vote into office
19 Aquarium scoops
20 Watch over
22 "Kick the __" (just say no)
26 "Four score and seven years __ . . ."
29 Ring around the cellar
31 Devil-may-care
32 Most intrusive
34 Inconvenience
36 Dimwit
37 Legendary tale
39 Backspace or tab
40 Parsley piece
42 "__ in a while"
44 Clump of hair
46 Ill-suited
50 Last Supper participant
53 Look at intently
54 Traffic-light color
55 __-dried tomato
56 Creepy
57 It's all the rage, briefly
58 However
59 __ rehearsal

DOWN

1 Tree with needles
2 Roundish
3 "You've got __ nerve!"
4 Upright
5 Methods
6 Roster
7 Pull a scam
8 Granny __ apple
9 Try to romance
10 "Leave __ alone, you big bully!"
11 Yucatan "yay"
17 Russian rulers, once
21 Sticky __
23 Soak up the sun
24 __ of Wight
25 "See how __ run . . ."
26 Trajectories
27 Swallowing sound
28 Kitchen emanation
30 Lean
33 Corrects text
35 Said "He did it!"
38 Powerful
41 Brave
43 Infiltrate
45 Chimney part
47 Taxi rider
48 Purple flower
49 Kicker's stands
50 Short bark
51 Black-eyed __
52 Strange

Sits for a portrait

solution on page 319

ACROSS

1 Consider
6 "Oh, what's the __?"
9 Weatherman's display
12 Dome Nome home
13 Star Trek weapons
15 Raggedy Ann and Andy
16 Spoofs
17 High temperature
19 "Groovy!"
20 On vacation
23 Element
25 Pen names
28 An open-__ question
33 __ the Leader
34 "Nothing up my __" (magician's line)
35 "Terrific!"
36 "Few and far __"
37 Brutish sort
39 Nose around
40 Prepare potatoes
44 Reddish
47 Headache reliever
49 Sworn statements
53 4 o'clock in England
54 "Home __ home"
55 "__ it been that long?"
56 "When Harry __ Sally"
57 Rival

DOWN

1 Accomplished
2 Swelled head
3 Unwell
4 Game where you try to get the ball in the hole
5 Snowman's carrot
6 Annoys
7 Advice to kids who say "Mine!"
8 "Let them __ cake!"
9 Measly
10 Neck of the woods
11 "Hey, Mac!"
14 Sermon subject
18 Pay-Per-__
20 Bumblers
21 Move like lava
22 Single __ (all in a row)
24 Disappear like the Wicked Witch
26 "Give it your __"
27 Han __ (Star Wars role)
29 "Not much, what's __ with you?"
30 Bottomless
31 "If I __ catch you doing that again . . ."
32 Just say no
34 Bird food
36 Dark-haired one
38 Dirt and soot
40 It has its plusses and minuses
41 On a voyage
42 Jacuzzi locales
43 Wallop
45 Two aspirins, say
46 Sign of sleepiness
48 __ shot (drum sound or basketball throw)
50 Pigskin perch
51 Clothing seam
52 Swine site

Consider

solution on page 319

ACROSS

1 Item ridden by Huckleberry Finn
5 "Get in on the __"
8 Junk hauler
12 Piece of land
13 "Are you up to __ task?"
14 Oft-quoted catcher
15 "__ what happened?"
16 Cure leather hides
17 Umpire's decision
18 Pioneers who went out West
20 Lopped off
21 Reverence
23 "There has been a __ development"
27 Campfire treat
31 Wrinkle removers
32 "Well done!"
33 Shows to be 100% true
35 Honked one's horn
36 Got rid of typos
38 __ citizenship
41 Like nonpermanent markers
46 Rode off __ the sunset
47 Detective Spade
48 Mule's cry
49 "Halt!"
50 Railroad __
51 Highway path
52 Plate after third
53 Peanut butter __ jelly
54 "To the __ of the Earth"

DOWN

1 Charlie Brown's cry
2 Aspirin target
3 Worry
4 Pup __
5 Swear
6 Graph
7 Past, present, and future
8 Shade tree with patchy bark
9 Prod or urge
10 Eye at the beach
11 "Where the __ Things Are"
19 Captured on film
22 Reporters with the troops
23 Parachute cord
24 Transgress
25 Speak lovingly
26 What you mail a letter in
28 Knock
29 "The Three Faces of __"
30 Lay down the lawn
34 Mexican nap
35 Smiled ear to ear
37 Locomotive
38 Alternative to a cone
39 Sermon preposition
40 Molecule component
42 Talented
43 Oat __
44 "__ ho!" (crow's nest cry)
45 Peepers

Item ridden by Huckleberry Finn

solution on page 319

ACROSS

1 Classic "Star Trek" episode
6 "It all makes sense now!"
9 Shirt sleeve
12 In the know
13 Operate
14 __ anemone
15 Fringe benefits
16 Dictionaries have lots of them
18 Popping the question
20 Put on the brakes
21 Winter woe
23 Linger
25 Half a circle's width
28 Wag one's tongue
32 Hot spots
33 Hollow rock with crystals in it
34 Deep-red jewel
36 Designate
37 Revered ones
39 Combo
40 Half the clues in this puzzle
43 Small child
46 Mysteries
48 Be humorous
51 December temp job
52 Chowed down
53 Ambulance sound
54 Bread for a Reuben, often
55 "Neither fish __ fowl . . . "
56 Spirited horse

DOWN

1 Something to do in a crib
2 Have an obligation
3 One who pillages
4 Sacred chests
5 Computer spot
6 Coliseum
7 Wanting food
8 Tiny colonist
9 The Urals border it
10 Projectionist's item
11 Sail support
17 Song lyrics, usually
19 "__ a date!"
21 Pond hopper
22 Magma flow
24 Cleaning cloths
26 Baseball-game division
27 "Not now, but I __ to"
29 Dampness
30 Advantage
31 Sublet
35 Sun-dried __
36 Cleopatra's snake
38 One who is a failure
40 Bambi's mom
41 "We've __ Just Begun"
42 Bride's title
44 Throw the football
45 Exude
47 "I never met a __ I didn't like"
49 "__ you later!"
50 Off the deep __

Classic "Star Trek" episode

solution on page 319

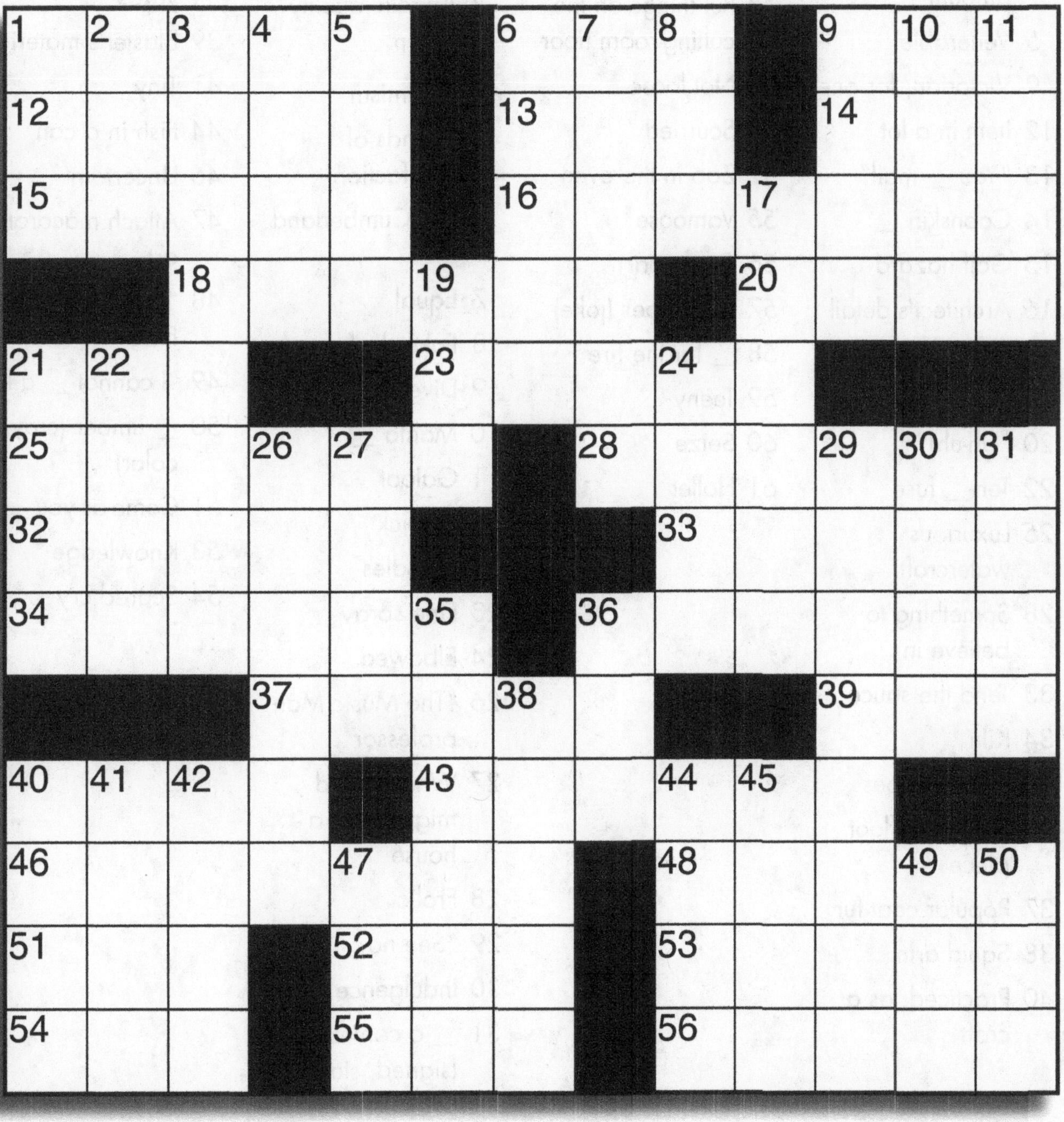

ACROSS

1 Tiny cooking amount
5 Venerable
9 Victorian, for one
12 Item in a lot
13 "You __ mail"
14 Coonskin __
15 Golf hazard
16 Architect's detail
17 Caustic cleaner
18 Devoured
20 "Uh-uh!"
22 Ten-__ fuse
25 Luxurious watercraft
28 Something to believe in
33 Tend the sauce
34 Kiln
35 Hit the slopes
36 Bathroom floor piece
37 Popular coat fur
38 Squid arm
40 Practiced, as a craft
42 Cub Scout unit
43 Put things on the cutting-room floor
45 Not loose
50 Scurried
52 Zap in the oven
55 Vamoose
56 Circle part
57 __-slapper (joke)
58 __ for the fire
59 Teeny
60 Seize
61 Holler

DOWN

1 March 17, say
2 Angelic quality
3 ASAP
4 Optimism
5 Sounds of satisfaction
6 The Cumberland __
7 Equal
8 Fake duck
9 Diverse
10 Manta __
11 Galoot
19 Nitpick
21 Noodles
23 Fine spray
24 Elbowed
26 "The Music Man" professor
27 Where a kid might build a house
28 Frolic
29 "See no __ . . ."
30 Indulgence
31 __ a contract (signed, slangily)
32 "The whole __ yards"
39 Blaster's material
41 Tiny
44 Fish in a can
46 Uncertain
47 Attach macaroni art
48 "Don't sic 'em," to Fido
49 "I cannot __ a lie"
50 __ umber (crayon color)
51 Come-as-you-__
53 Knowledge
54 Scared cry

Tiny cooking amount

solution on page 319

1	2	3	4		5	6	7	8		9	10	11
12					13					14		
15					16					17		
18				19			20		21			
				22	23	24		25			26	27
28	29	30	31				32		33			
34					35				36			
37					38			39				
40				41		42						
		43			44			45	46	47	48	49
50	51			52		53	54		55			
56				57					58			
59				60					61			

ACROSS

1 "Insert __ A in slot B"
4 Lowlife
8 "We __ You a Merry Christmas"
12 Pro
13 Snack shop
14 __ banter
15 Prom supervisor
17 Jazz or Magic
18 Mean leader
19 Melts
20 Put back to the original condition
23 __ put (it's like a medicine ball in sports)
26 Presented, as a trophy
30 "On __ Majesty's Secret Service"
31 Faintly
33 Propel a canoe
34 Public disgrace
36 "Why, the __ idea!"
37 Occur before

40 Doom and __
43 __ quencher
47 Maui meal
48 Uselessness
50 Antlered ones
51 Prison at sea
52 Spunk
53 Ultimatum word
54 Snowfall measure
55 Barnyard mama

DOWN

1 Way with words
2 Painful
3 Polar __
4 Script unit
5 Supermarket carriages
6 "Close Encounters . . ." craft
7 Gents
8 Dry up
9 Hunch
10 Picnic side dish
11 __ and haws
16 Piece
19 Caterer's item
21 Domesticated
22 "The __ and the Pussycat"
23 This girl
24 "Yoo-hoo!"
25 Iron __
27 Forest female
28 An __ for music
29 "Like watching paint __"
31 College room

32 Resentment
35 Husband or wife
36 Bride's headgear
38 Top floor
39 Poultry portion choice
40 Happiness
41 Break in the action
42 Acorns, as adults
44 Ready to eat
45 Hearty meal
46 Class
48 Wiretap group
49 Coffee server

Insert __ A in slot B

solution on page 320

1	2	3	■	4	5	6	7	■	8	9	10	11
12			■	13				■	14			
15			16					■	17			
18						■		19				
■	■	■	20			21	22			■	■	■
23	24	25		■		26				27	28	29
30			■	31	32				■	33		
34			35				■		36			
■	■	■	37				38	39		■	■	■
40	41	42			■		43			44	45	46
47				■	48	49						
50				■	51				■	52		
53				■	54				■	55		

ACROSS

1 Star that goes boom
5 __ and con
8 Ash
12 Woodshed items
13 Eye cover
14 Duet plus one
15 Untidiness
16 Awfully cute
18 Creature
20 Dull routine
21 Explore the Internet
23 Cajun soup
27 Shiny
31 Yield, as bank interest
32 "__ nation, indivisible . . . "
33 Strong point
35 PC alternative
36 "Just in the nick of __"
38 House loan
40 Bee "bite"
42 Indy event
43 Swindle
45 Nouns, in essence
49 __ frisbee
53 __ opera (daytime TV fare)
54 Increase
55 Sty guy
56 Golf goal
57 Hoopla
58 "At __ time" (whenever)
59 Again

DOWN

1 First, middle, or last
2 Plow pullers
3 Hunter's top
4 Help out
5 Pool-table place
6 Relieve
7 Nose wrinkler
8 Freeze-tag imitation
9 Ball
10 Snake-__ salesman
11 Sock's closed end
17 Carpet
19 Gang territory
22 Excitement
24 Baby's first word, often
25 "I don't mean to __, but . . . "
26 "__ upon a time . . . "
27 Heaps
28 Troop division
29 Truck made for hauling
30 Tactic
34 Inscribe
37 "The Little __ That Could"
39 Japanese entertainer
41 Trainer's place
44 Mama's man
46 Witching hour's opposite
47 __-force winds
48 Erupt
49 "Nasty!"
50 Deposit eggs
51 __ the balance
52 "Cat on a Hot __ Roof"

Star that goes boom

solution on page 320

ACROSS

1 Health __
4 What a burglar does
7 Around, timewise
12 __ and caboodle
13 Astonish
14 Atlantic __
15 "Are we having fun __?"
16 Cribbage pin
17 Center
18 Parenthetical remark
20 Nuisances
21 Curved through the air
23 Wedding-cake feature
25 "__ it or leave it"
26 "Hey, you!"
27 "You're out!" caller
30 "Try not to __ it!"
32 Bees collect it
34 Parts __ billion
35 Overlook
37 Indiana Jones or the Rocketeer
38 Jumps like a frog
39 "She gets what she __"
40 Waited impatiently
43 Places of refuge
45 "The __ Suspects"
46 Picasso piece
47 Prankish pipsqueak
50 Tennis start
51 High-wire act safety need
52 Baseballer Gehrig
53 Didn't like
54 Sunlight time
55 "__ of a gun!"

DOWN

1 The limit
2 Deep-dish __
3 Assailant
4 Fast
5 Was obligated to
6 Has kids, Biblically
7 Try to win at sports
8 Less friendly
9 Colors from blushing
10 Theater folk
11 Hill-dwelling insects
19 Psychic
21 Over
22 Thumbs-way-up review
24 "Money __ everything"
26 "__ and Circumstance"
27 Forks and spoons
28 Wal-__
29 They know what they're doing
31 Scribbled and squiggled
33 Toast
36 Rhode __ (state)
38 "__ ho!" (seaman's cry)
39 Humorous
40 "When __ comes to shove"
41 Like mariners
42 Brusque
44 Vicinity
48 __ goo gai pan
49 "Wurst" form of humor

Health

solution on page 320

8. Start the Ball Rolling

ACROSS

1 "__ she sweet?"
5 A worm on a hook, say
9 Spot's statement
12 On the house
13 __ one's back
14 Velcro inspirationClingy
15 They go across
16 Lady Jane __
17 Whopper
18 Before a crowd
20 Passed along
21 Public-address __
24 Accumulate
28 Harangues
32 Baseball team's place by the field
34 Drool
35 Sullied one's name
37 Winter weather
38 Go back on one's word
40 Ones in a card deck
43 Glowing
48 Toothed wheel
49 Dunderhead
51 "There once was a lady who lived in a __"
52 __ along with (accompany)
53 Used a loom
54 "Win, __, or draw"
55 Shrewd
56 Has bills
57 Needle parts

DOWN

1 __-Americans
2 Certain golf club
3 Anchorman's concern
4 "This is a __ of the emergency broadcast system"
5 Like oversized pants
6 Take into the station
7 Frost
8 "__ kingdom come . . . "
9 Skilled
10 Render useless
11 Be distressed
19 Make a guarantee
20 Tiny
22 "Whether __ nobler to take arms . . . "
23 Wiped clean
24 Profits for the press
25 "Try to keep __!" (sh!)
26 Ripen, as cheese
27 Flies high
29 Game cube
30 Eden dweller
31 " . . . and __ down beside her . . . "
33 Gymnast's goal
36 Get by reasoning
39 Fence doors
40 Does something
41 Santa's "Sorry!"
42 Like cake batter, often
44 Gilligan's home
45 Crows-nest cry
46 Win by a __
47 __ off (annoys)
49 "Shave and a haircut—__ bits"
50 "Amazing!"

"__ She Sweet?"

solution on page 321

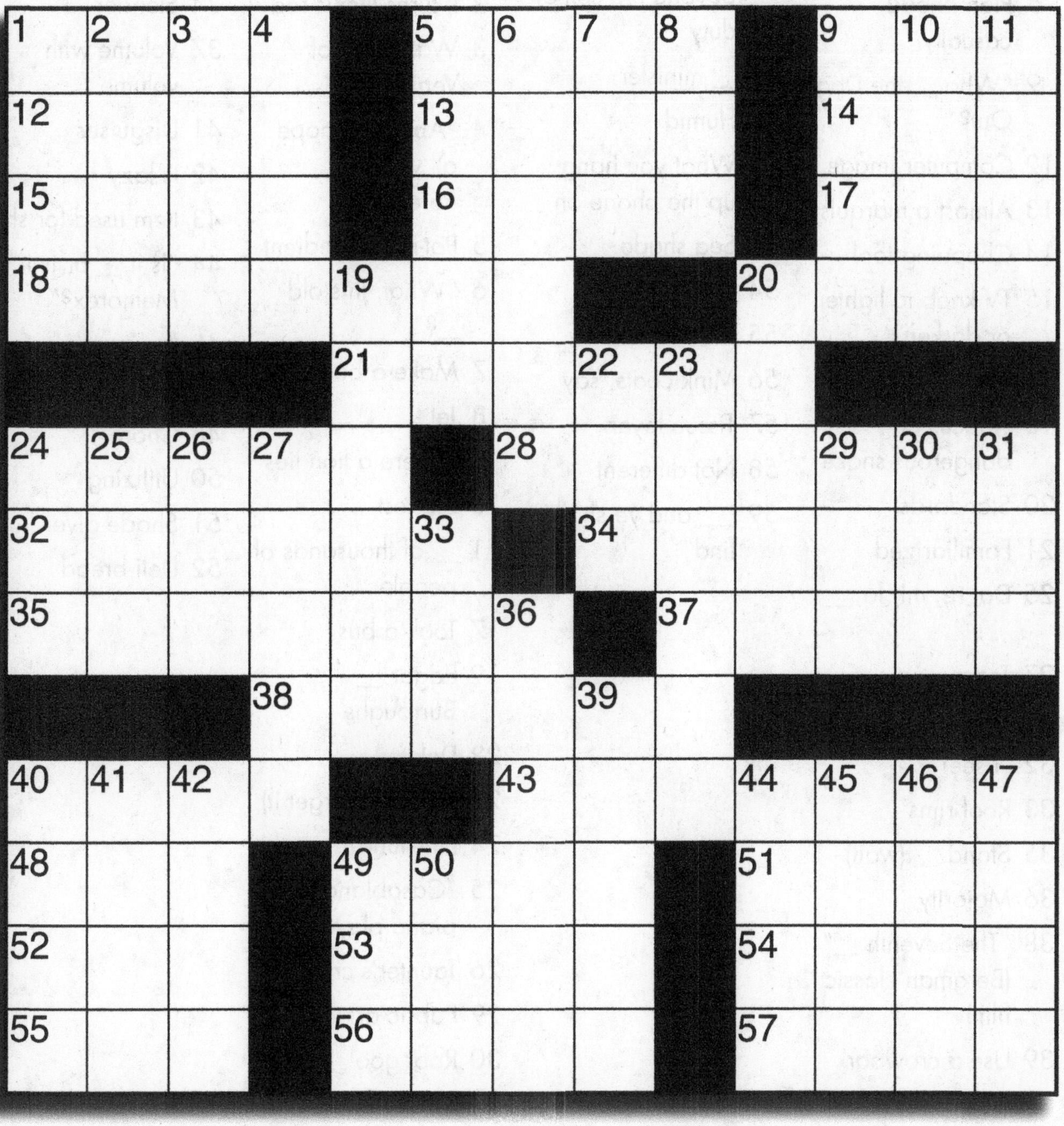

ACROSS

1 Use a beeper
5 Plan ahead, casually
9 "Who __ the Dogs Out?"
12 Computer image
13 Almost a marquis
14 Chopping tool
15 TV knob to lighten or darken
16 Farm-based
18 Abacus or dangerous snake
20 Standards
21 Familiarized
25 Do, re, mi, fa, __ . . .
27 Team
28 Has a snack
32 "I see!"
33 Roof rims
35 Stand __ (wait)
36 Majority
38 "The Seventh __" (Bergman classic film)
39 Use a crowbar
40 It's above and beyond the call of duty
43 __ minister
46 Humid
49 What you hang up the phone on
53 Sea shade
54 Cask wood
55 Munster mom
56 Mink coats, say
57 Tissue layer
58 Not different
59 "__ and ye shall find"

DOWN

1 Falafel bread
2 It turns litmus red
3 Watercraft of Venice
4 "Abandon hope all ye who __ here"
5 Pot-pie ingredient
6 "What, this old __?"
7 Make a boo-boo
8 Jet
9 Where a lion lies
10 Big test
11 __ of thousands of people
17 Took a bus
19 Edgar __ Burroughs
22 Delete
23 __ mind (forget it)
24 Fine-tune
25 "Casablanca" piano player
26 Taunter's cry
29 Fabric art
30 Roof goo
31 Boar's abode
34 Slender
37 Volume with volume
41 Disguises
42 Is lazy
43 Item used for show
44 "Is it __ or is it Memorex?"
45 "__-poo!"
47 Confident
48 Chore
50 Utilizing
51 Shade giver
52 Deli bread

Use a beeper

solution on page 321

ACROSS

1 A retainer fixes the upper one
4 Key mistake
8 Belfry birds
12 Grand __ Opry
13 "The __ Less Taken"
14 Broadcast
15 Double-crossed
17 "__ fishin'"
18 False god
19 Sudden thrust
20 Mistake
23 Idled
25 Spoken
26 Leave port
27 Deprived
29 Elbowed
34 Dishwasher shelf
36 "__, medium, or well-done?"
37 Woolly __ (Ice Age creature)
41 Statute
42 Phrase-book entry
43 Auditioner's goal
45 Tall, round farm building
46 Insurance provides it
50 Long fish
51 Prayer ender
52 Piece of wood for Woods
53 Subterfuge
54 Look after
55 Tundra wanderer

DOWN

1 Occupation
2 Drink on draft
3 Drenched
4 Swap
5 Toy that makes a comeback
6 Spanish mixture dish
7 Offbeat
8 Activated
9 "Honor __ thieves"
10 Smattering
11 Hero's mount
16 __ through one's drawers
19 "The first step is a __"
20 Clump
21 "You __ So Beautiful"
22 "As __ as I can tell . . ."
24 Pigpen pronouncement
26 "Pronto!"
28 "Where are you __?"
30 Washing-machine follower
31 Guy's date
32 Important time span
33 Droplets at dawn
35 Fender finish
37 Hoarder
38 Sartre's "see ya"
39 Factories
40 Bullwinkle, for one
41 Mix well
44 Bread cooker
46 Meower
47 Did lunch
48 Slowly firm up
49 "That scares me!"

A retainer fixes the upper one

solution on page 321

ACROSS

1 Sounded a bell
5 Trajectory
8 Heroic tale
12 Consumer
13 "__ I help you?"
14 Wide-__ spaces
15 "No more Mr. __ guy!"
16 "See a __, pick it up . . . "
17 Clarinet need
18 Stolen
20 Locale
22 Loose garments
24 "The Man Who Knew __ Much"
27 Deep-beaked seabird
30 Barbecue chef's attire
32 "They appear to be __ matched"
33 __ tag
34 Scorch
35 Fancy parties
36 "How __ are you now?"
37 Climb
39 Waitress burden
40 TV sound
44 Repeat verbatim
47 "__ about time!"
49 Make over
50 Mad Libs category
51 "As __ crow flies"
52 Roadrunner cry
53 Rounded roof
54 Mean witch's spell
55 Health farms

DOWN

1 "The __ of the litter"
2 It covers a lot of ground
3 Stick one's __ out (risk)
4 "Hello" or "Hi"
5 Sound device
6 Wrinkled fruit
7 Pessimist
8 __ throat
9 Goon
10 "Aw, shucks!"
11 Cowboys __ Indians
19 Atomic
21 Romanov royal
23 Thumbs-down vote
24 Ash or oak
25 Move like the Blob
26 Place next to the decimal point
27 Mexican money
28 Nastiness
29 Make a loan
31 Bothers
33 Challenger
35 Wheat-harvesting tool
38 " . . . __ the Lord" (Bible phrase)
39 Inflection
41 Profound
42 Brainstorming contribution
43 "Uh-oh!"
44 At wit's __
45 Murmur
46 Fine-motor sound
48 Gender

Sounded a bell

solution on page 321

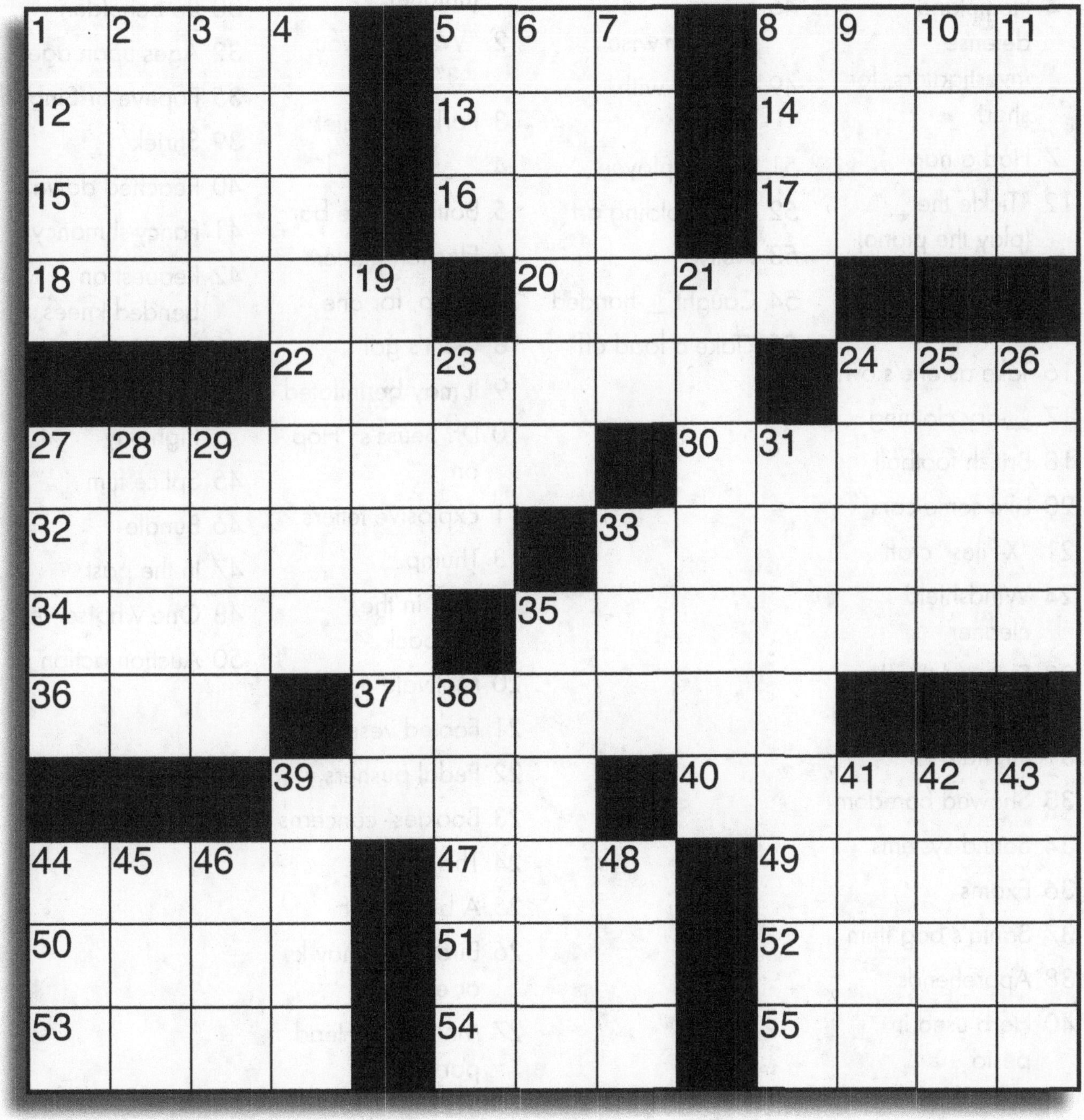

ACROSS

1 __ Largo
4 Homeland defense investigators, for short
7 Had a nap
12 "Tickle the __" (play the piano)
14 Conestoga __
15 Counteracts
16 Take as one's own
17 __-dry clothing
18 British football
20 Like some cars
21 "X-Files" craft
24 Windshield cleaner
28 Enjoyed the flavor of
31 Infuriate
33 Showed boredom
34 Sound systems
36 Exams
37 Santa's bag item
38 Apprehends
40 Herb used in pesto
42 Army post
46 Sway, decision-wise
49 Named with stickers
51 CIA employee
52 Paper-folding art
53 Nutty
54 Caught __-handed
55 "Take a load off"

DOWN

1 "One of a __" (unique)
2 "Well, did you __?"
3 Park food thief
4 "__ to be tied"
5 Bottles at the bar
6 Election matters
7 Q-Tip, for one
8 Gent's gal
9 It may be inflated
10 Dr. Seuss's "Hop on __"
11 Explosive letters
13 Thump
19 "Hi" in the Outback
20 Motivate
21 Footed vessels
22 Pedal pushers
23 Bookies' concerns
24 The Wild __
25 A big fan of
26 Bird of __ (hawk or eagle)
27 Mr. Potato Head part
29 Cauldrons
30 Be beholden
32 Ages upon ages
35 Popeye or Sinbad
39 Shriek
40 Reached down
41 Fancy-shmancy
42 Request on bended knees
43 "Oh dear!"
44 Hauler on the highway
45 Splice film
46 Bundle
47 In the past
48 One who served
50 Auction action

___ Largo

solution on page 321

ACROSS

1 Ridicule
5 Winnie the __
9 __ and order
12 Yearning
13 Perimeter
14 Dazzle
15 Leap __
16 True-blue
18 Farm building
19 Netizens
20 Goes on stage
22 "__ does it!"
26 Raked item
28 Hooded winter coat
29 Kool-__
32 Evade
34 Gratuity
35 Hardware for making holes
37 Not sloppy
39 Audition tape
40 Draw a picture
44 Petty quarrels
48 Graceful
49 Under __ (stressed)
52 Choreography unit
53 Sugar __ Leonard
54 Use a swizzle stick
55 "You're something __!"
56 __ in a million
57 Tugboat sound
58 Synchronizes

DOWN

1 On-the-fence response
2 "My bonnie lies over the __ . . . "
3 Diagram
4 Popcorn popper
5 Casual study
6 Rhymed verses
7 Make eyes at
8 Will recipient
9 Jekyll's workroom
10 Leather-working tool
11 Itsy-bitsy
17 Braving the waves
21 Movie spool
23 "Wherefore __ thou Romeo"
24 Water __
25 Gab
27 Enjoyable
28 Mountain __
29 Tack on
30 Wrath
31 Barely lit
33 After-dinner treat
36 Weight-__ plan
38 Mocks
41 Lord or Lady
42 Aim rival
43 Showily promotes
45 "Hey, you!"
46 Jalopy
47 Ernie Kovacs' "The Nairobi __"
49 Turn __ (start making money)
50 Turned chicken
51 With a jaundiced __

Ridicule

solution on page 321

ACROSS

1 Warmongers
6 Briquette remnant
9 Flyers
12 Sports site
13 "__ Done Him Wrong"
14 __ gloss
15 Antique
16 A sprig of __
18 Meager
20 Lion in the sky
21 Dawn direction
23 Has
27 Dad's dad
31 "__ shalt not kill"
32 Relay __
33 Do evil
35 Swarm's home
36 Billy Goats Gruff enemy
37 Secretary's small tablet
39 Unwelcome plant
40 Pack away
41 Developer's need
43 Fruit-juice blend
48 Compared
52 All by oneself
53 __ up one's sleeve
54 Iced __
55 Floated, like a bad check
56 Take down a __
57 Sphere
58 What a volcano does

DOWN

1 Angel's instrument
2 Province
3 "That may be __ and good for you . . . "
4 A warm __ sweater
5 Holy
6 Deadly snake that's not of the U.S.
7 Word in many Commandments
8 Marked place on a mall map
9 Crawling on __ fours
10 "The __ is cast"
11 Espionage agent
17 Give comfort to
19 Yammers
22 __ Bernard (Alps dog)
24 Lion tamer's item
25 Exploding star
26 Litigated
27 " . . . and a pinch to __ an inch"
28 "Why, it's all the __"
29 Realty unit
30 "Like finding a __ in a haystack"
34 High time
38 Adjusts slightly
40 Maneuver the wheel
42 "__ something else . . . " (change the subject)
44 Paper __
45 __ bag (carryall)
46 From square one
47 Beatty film
48 Drink like a cat
49 Rock-salt target
50 Cask
51 Apply lightly

Warmongers

solution on page 322

ACROSS

1 Signs of things to come
6 Dead __ Scrolls
9 Mineral spring
12 Wreak __
13 Miscalculate
14 Water spigot
15 Aida or Carmen
16 Scavenge
18 Cut of steak
20 "Old Blue __"
21 __ party (husband-to-be event)
25 "It shall be duly __"
27 __ curve (tight U)
29 Essential
33 Yank a weed
34 Extremely safe
35 Bird beds
36 Renters
37 Indian home
39 Young girl
40 Female singer
43 Leaf collector
45 Disasters
47 Gather together
52 Collide
53 "It's of no __!" (why even try?)
54 Scoundrel
55 Tram filler
56 It might be unmade
57 Used a broom

DOWN

1 "You think you're so clever?"
2 Road guide
3 Christmas __
4 And not
5 Harry Potter has one
6 Church lecture
7 Let loose
8 Richard Kimble's pursuee's lack
9 "We hope you enjoy your __ with us"
10 Errand boy
11 Parodies
17 The M in MD
19 Minute or hour
21 Steer clear of
22 Cassette __
23 Put on __ (be a snob)
24 Small caves
26 Tied
28 __ a question
30 Star-Kist __
31 __ and crafts
32 Minus
34 __ shelter
36 Ridiculed
38 Text
40 Curly hairstyle
41 Truth avoider
42 Easy to manage
44 "Do Your __ Hang Low"
46 Li'l lion
48 Trim
49 Driver's-license info
50 Have dinner
51 __ in motion (make start)

Signs of things to come

solution on page 322

ACROSS

1 Prepare to drag race
4 It comes in mint condition
8 "Ready, willing, and __"
12 Log splitter
13 Aggravate
14 "As the __ flies"
15 Traps
17 "I can name that __ in two notes"
18 Dark ale
19 Skimpy beachwear
21 "All You __ Is Love" (Beatles song)
24 "Roses __ red . . . "
25 Political favor in a bill
28 "__ We Got Fun?"
30 Noah's number
33 Andy Capp beverage
34 __ a blank check
35 Haul
36 "You can't teach an old dog __ tricks"
37 Swab the __
38 "As __ on TV"
39 Hunter who hoots
41 Put in stitches
43 Saw eye-to-eye
46 Hardship
50 In the buff
51 Height
54 "Star __: The Next Generation"
55 Stains a shirt, say
56 Note after fa
57 Laundry lather
58 Placed in the mail
59 "__ it on for size"

DOWN

1 Séance sounds
2 Leave the stage
3 Line-item __
4 Shipping case
5 Tin Man's request
6 Sickly
7 Ant colony
8 Cast member
9 Dark-haired
10 "So __!" (goodbye)
11 Baa maids
16 Grand __ Railroad
20 Despise
22 Comfort
23 Platters
25 Place to fry an egg
26 Bullfight cry
27 Changed the phrasing
29 Cold War weapon threat
31 Misfortune
32 Toot one's __ horn
34 Run in neutral
38 Mean mood
40 They make up months
42 Hand joint
43 Army __ (insects)
44 Spiritual guide
45 Many Little League coaches
47 Strong wind
48 Annoying smell
49 Have some trust
52 Caustic cleaner
53 " . . . __ lords a-leaping . . . "

Prepare to drag race

solution on page 322

ACROSS

1 Story with a punch line
5 Bank vault
9 Prison inmate
12 Globe center
13 Cat's scratcher
14 Go __ over (fall for)
15 Gambles
16 __-Bopp Comet
17 Synagogue seat
18 Tennis shoes
20 "Say it __ so!"
21 Gabs
23 "__ with their 'eads!"
26 "Affirmative!"
27 Legal "out"
31 Outer space radio-wave sender
33 Primitive fellows
34 Pickup __
35 "There's a __ in the air"
36 Fountain __
37 Took for granted
40 Quahog
43 Sacred
47 Reaction to fireworks
48 Vaudeville yanker
49 Did a zigzag
50 "You're __ late"
51 Bat paths
52 "By the __ of our teeth"
53 Babe's abode
54 Plumbing joints
55 Wiggly swimmers

DOWN

1 Pokes in the boxing ring
2 Cattle
3 High-flying toy
4 Literary work
5 Plotter
6 Emergency sounds
7 "True or __"
8 Flock mom
9 Toy gun ammo
10 "This is __ for discussion"
11 Congressman Gingrich
19 Portable canoes
20 Puddle-hopper destination
22 Move down a cliff
23 Pick
24 Canine's coat
25 Bug
28 Unruly kid
29 Honey producer
30 Vacationer's stopover
32 Con job
33 Adrift
35 Hint
38 Portion
39 Plunge into liquid
40 Hotel's extra beds
41 Stolen spoils
42 Pirate's word of greeting
44 Roused from slumber
45 Maliciousness
46 Lion's lairs
48 Garfield of the comics

Story with a punch line

solution on page 322

ACROSS

1 The __ (information superhighway)
4 Chums
8 "Poor me!"
12 Long __ (yore)
13 Wrack and __
14 Chauffeured car
15 Pea holder
16 "The very __!"
17 Heat water until it bubbles
18 Asleep
20 Word-processor command
21 Graceful dance
23 Weightlifter's room
25 __ car lot
26 "Roger Rabbit" henchmen
30 "To __ with Love"
31 __ little eyes
33 Do a floor chore
34 __ Choice (coffee brand)
36 __ or MasterCard
37 Munched
38 __ and turns
40 Impale
43 Tasks
45 Mournful cry
46 Ilk
47 Read the riot __ to
50 Wheel spindle
51 Monumental
52 Jog fast
53 Light fog
54 Pier
55 Thus far

DOWN

1 Preschool rest time
2 Immodesty
3 Most one year olds
4 Nobel Peace __
5 Accountant's review
6 Debtor's load
7 Caught
8 Musical purchases
9 Big cat
10 Within
11 Singer's chance to shine
19 To a ripe __ age
21 __ one's chops
22 Korea's site
24 "Whoopee!"
26 "Who __ that masked man?"
27 Diplomat
28 "Raiders of the __ Ark"
29 Health resorts
31 Ante up
32 Constructed
35 Pill shape
36 Go head-to-head
38 "What is the __ of conversation?"
39 Deep-sea dive site, often
40 Did the backstroke
41 Wet-weather transportation scarcity
42 Is sick
44 Needle-y doctor's tool
48 Game ball
49 It's like dynamite

The __ (information superhighway)

solution on page 322

ACROSS

1 "The __ is up!"
4 Like most colleges
8 Abolishes
12 Prohibition __
13 Right __ (shortly)
14 Well-kept
15 Send out to the networks
17 Ingredient in a float
18 Let off some steam
19 __ eclipse
20 Leg up
23 One granting three wishes
25 Dawdle
27 Liquor in grog
28 Dog's dialogue
31 Kid's drawing item
33 Sneezer's need
35 Tailor's task
36 "i" topper
38 The ones over here
39 Doc
41 Devours
42 Relating to the unborn
45 Made footprints
47 Picture on your monitor
48 "It would be my __!"
52 Pump or clog
53 Yachting hazard
54 __ sauce
55 Tykes
56 Betting ratios
57 Knock the socks off

DOWN

1 Airplane
2 Fury
3 Young woman
4 Place with stalactites
5 Not yet paid
6 Egg-hunt time
7 Easter-egg need
8 Follow
9 Broadway blinker
10 Baby's father
11 "__ Trek"
16 __ nook and cranny
19 Speed __ (highway sign)
20 Whittle
21 Take a chance
22 Dieter's measure
24 Macadamia or almond
26 Alpine cry
28 Gone fishing
29 Oxidize
30 Dues that are paid
32 Blynken's shipmate
34 Tool shelters
37 Named
39 Hair on lions and horses
40 Byword
42 Knuckle sandwich
43 Repeat
44 Horn sound
46 Clumsy folk
48 Major-leaguer
49 Country that makes freedom fries
50 Steinbeck's "Cannery __"
51 "Queer __ for the Straight Guy"

The __ is up!

solution on page 322

ACROSS

1 Scrabble tile holder
5 "__ as a kite"
9 Drain, as energy
12 PhD test type
13 Property unit
14 Bolo __
15 Bill of fare
16 In the vicinity of
17 Strike caller
18 Used rubber cement
20 Null and __
22 Flavorful
24 Waiter's wages
27 "Murder, __ Wrote"
30 Run afoul of the __
31 Air-conditioned
32 Price
34 At __'s end
36 Grass-skirt dance
37 Highway traveler
38 Spare __ (BBQ offering)
40 Blubber showily
41 __ function (sine, tangent, and other functions)
42 Not fancy
44 Givers of myrrh, gold, and frankincense
46 Awakened
50 Ram's cry
52 Greenish blue
54 Double agent
55 Carpenter __ (insect)
56 100%
57 Place to hold up in baseball
58 Hearty bread
59 Dispatches
60 Drove too fast

DOWN

1 Easy victory
2 Territory
3 Recyclable metal, often
4 Clumsy one
5 Manual wood cutter
6 Rocky-road __ cream
7 Brown turkey sauce
8 Hercules or Tarzan
9 Bookish
10 Objective
11 Spirit
19 Electrified fish
21 Restless desire
23 Perform with a baton
25 __ shirt
26 Piece of marble
27 Ella's and Cab's musical style
28 Miles per __
29 Approximation
33 "Animal House" party garb
35 Like a beauty-pageant winner
39 Life story
42 Irritate
43 Causes a loss of sensation
45 Hangs open
47 Shower need
48 If not
49 Ownership paper
50 Salad __
51 "In __ case . . . "
53 Big jar

Scrabble tile holder

solution on page 323

ACROSS

1 Less modern
6 "__ been a pleasure!"
9 __ the question
12 Bluish purple
13 Have chits out
14 Hearing organ
15 Signed, in slang
16 Food-regimen related
18 Driving-range need
19 Egg beaters
21 "At the __ of no return"
22 Physicist's unit
26 Beseech
29 " . . . ere he __ out of sight . . . "
30 Mislead
31 Big hotel rooms
32 Warnings
33 Marathon people
34 Put on cargo
35 Latin American line dance
36 Make mad
38 One's __ in life
41 Fight locale in many a Western
44 __ drab
46 "Caught ya!"
47 Ocean-temperature tester
48 __ base (where warships dock)
49 Bankroll
50 "It's the __ of an era!"
51 What you should do in a bee

DOWN

1 Fail to mention
2 Swimming-pool division
3 "Let's __ it out!"
4 "All About __"
5 Old California trees
6 Popular antiseptic
7 Chubby Checkers dance
8 Hide and go __
9 Goober __
10 You can't get upstream without it
11 "I don't mean to __, but . . . "
17 Russian empress
20 Put on the payroll
21 Pirate's verb or noun
23 Bring along
24 "Roll __ Beethoven"
25 The Captain's __ (private dining room)
26 Matinee __
27 Brief work for a secretary
28 Sincere appeal
29 Castle prisons
31 Chanted
33 Wandered
35 Warble
37 Promissory __
38 "Saturday Night __"
39 Racetrack shape
40 Kiss and __
41 Gift ribbon
42 Cry to the cookie-jar raider
43 Gangster's gun
45 Track unit

Less modern

solution on page 323

ACROSS

1 Run easily
4 Tarzan swing
8 Propels a boat
12 Cakes and __
13 Wrought __
14 Fix a typo
15 Impulse
16 Perform a song
17 Ballpark refreshment
18 Chalkboard __
20 Grandiose
21 Farm units
23 "__ or nothing"
25 Take it easy
26 Arrogant
31 Daycare attendee
32 Burdened
33 Pasture sound
34 Conducted
36 Storage places
37 Curved line
38 Daring
39 __ pump
42 Flotilla
45 Mouse catcher
46 Quantum __
47 Soda, or soda-can opener
50 Bugbear
51 Hang out in the hammock
52 Blast-furnace food
53 Jury member
54 Downhill racer
55 The American __ Cross

DOWN

1 Blue __ (type of bird)
2 Corrida cry
3 Produce
4 Passport stamps
5 Eye part
6 "__ of your business!"
7 With a design cut into it
8 Remember
9 Perfume
10 Go limp
11 "__ tuned" (keep watching)
19 Hockey official
21 Choir part
22 Hen's pen
24 Tyke
26 Boos
27 Bunyan's tool
28 Rich Little, for one
29 It's like forever
30 Promising
32 Paver's material
35 Urban musician
36 Baby bloom
38 Held one's mouth wide open
39 "Whoa!"
40 Whim
41 Colt's mom
43 __ estate
44 Labyrinth
48 "We __ not amused" (royal putdown)
49 Trundle __

Run easily

solution on page 323

9. Start from Scratch

ACROSS

1 Joseph's had many colors
5 Place for a mud bath
8 And
12 __ and for all
13 Botch
14 "__ it the truth!"
15 Adult-to-be
16 Finish
18 Big shake
20 Mother in the mud
21 Torah holder
24 Worshipped
26 Dog
28 Like rotini
32 Pony pace
33 Grandmother
34 Workplaces for Ed Norton
37 Gold __
39 Sayings
41 Baa belle
42 Doggie's hand
45 Train's bellhop
47 University life
49 Wise birds
53 Traffic-sign word
54 Golfer's goal
55 Food restriction
56 Ballyhoo
57 Cagey
58 Like meringue

DOWN

1 Triage bed
2 "__ a penny . . . hot cross buns"
3 Get an "A" on
4 Circus shelter
5 Drop out of a group
6 Teaser ad
7 Knight wardrobe selections
8 Crony
9 "My bonnie __ over the ocean . . . "
10 "A law __ itself"
11 Thick soup
17 Warm-up, for short
19 Hightailed it
21 Performs on stage
22 Far from common
23 "I don't __ what you see in him!"
25 Li'l dent
27 "__ of note"
29 Fury
30 Freshly
31 __-night TV (early morning fare)
35 At the end of one's __
36 Jazz dances
37 Document certifier
38 "__ it or lose it"
40 "__ and error"
42 Beat a __ to your door
43 Twinging
44 Star Trek speed
46 Took a cab
48 Postage __
50 Halloween need for being the Bride of Frankenstein
51 Part of a journey
52 It's fit for pigs

Joseph's had many colors

solution on page 324

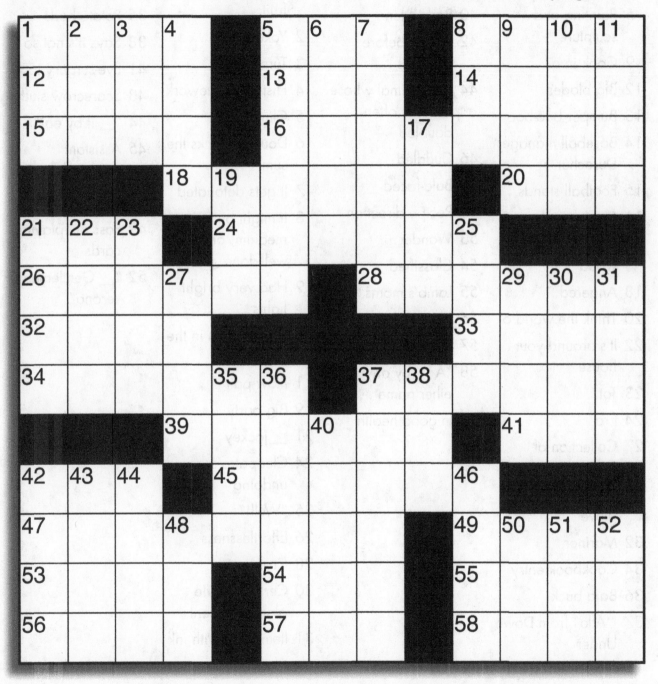

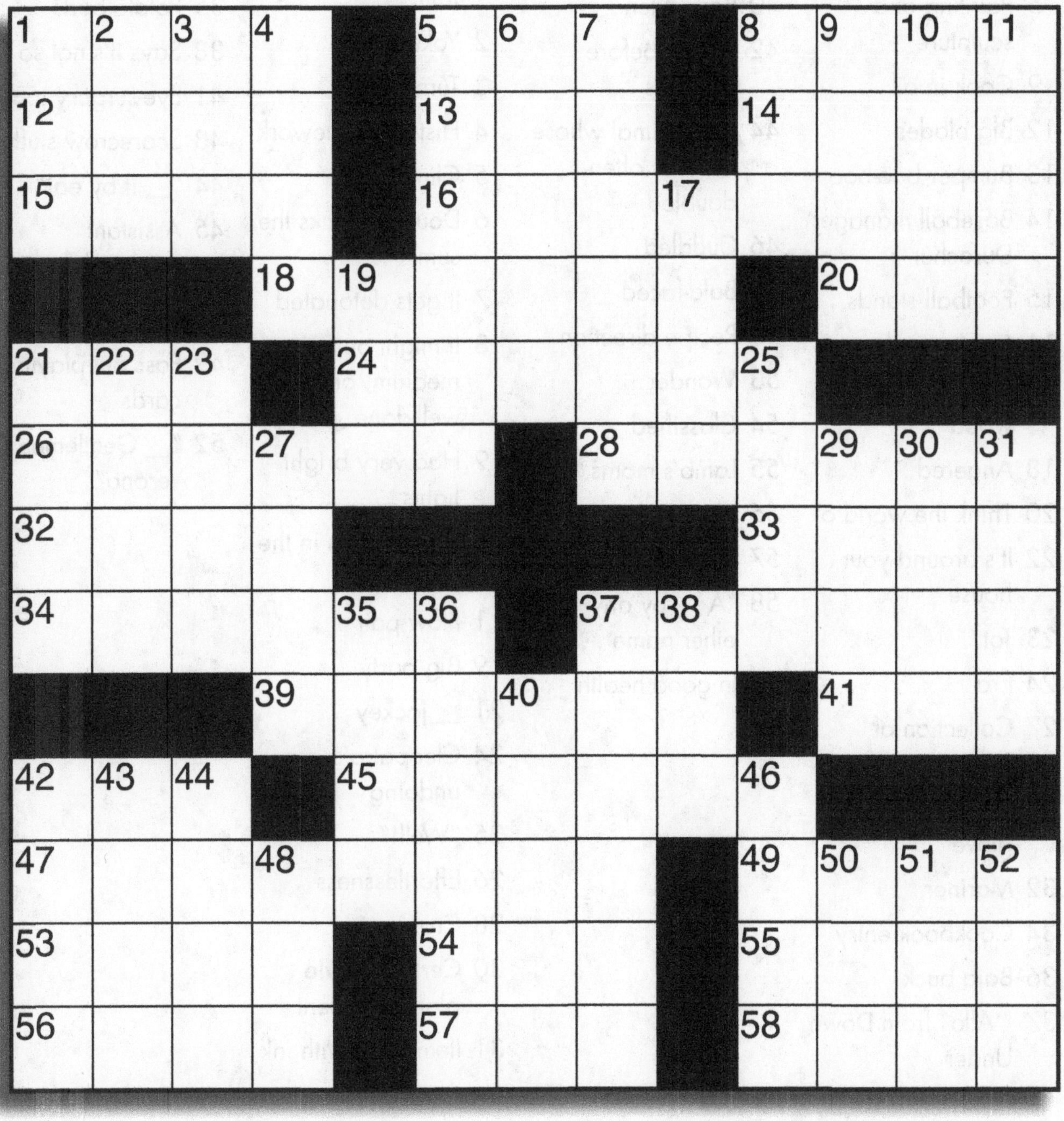

ACROSS

1 Symbol of peace
5 Painting and sculpture
9 Cook in oil
12 Big blades
13 Bumper boo-boo
14 Baseball manager Durocher
15 Football stands
16 Can't stand
17 Butcher-block wood
18 Angered
20 Think the world of
22 It's around your house
23 Tot
24 Era
27 Collection of names
29 Thwack with a glove
32 Mariner
34 Cookbook entry
36 Baja buck
37 "'Allo" from Down Under
39 __-gallon hat
40 Bedridden
42 Nights before holidays
44 Zoo animal whose name is often doubled
46 Cuddled
50 Bald-faced __
51 Recipe direction
53 Wander
54 Classified __
55 Lamb's moms
56 Nepal's locale
57 "Okey-dokey!"
58 "A __ by any other name . . . "
59 In good health

DOWN

1 Middle Eastern fruit
2 Yoke of __
3 Turn hard
4 History homework
5 Clinging
6 Double checks the sum
7 It gets detonated
8 It might be rare, medium, or well-done
9 Had very bright lights
10 "Entrance is in the __"
11 Plow pair
19 Big party
21 __ jockey
24 Cleopatra's undoing
25 "Well!"
26 Effortlessness
28 Cross over
30 Certain movie planet resident
31 Item filled with ink
33 Shaper for Jell-O
35 Potato buds
38 Says it's not so
41 Eye-surgery tool
43 Scarecrow stuffing
44 "__ it by ear"
45 Assistant
47 Come in last
48 Axis of __
49 Pass out playing cards
52 "__ Gentlemen of Verona"

Symbol of peace

solution on page 324

ACROSS

1 Toss and turn
5 "Excuse me!"
9 Hailed vehicle
12 Like Tiny Tim's leg
13 Achy
14 Spectrum part
15 Analogous
16 Plane-flight slower
18 Flower part
20 "Oh when the __, come marching in . . ."
21 5-cent pieces
24 Assistant on the go
27 "__ the Magic Dragon"
31 Barn __
32 Adversary
35 Mystery author Grafton
36 Split __ (hair problem)
38 Big cat that's been spotted
40 Carve wood
43 Achieve
46 Destiny
50 Roofing items
53 Perjurer
54 Author Kesey
55 "I'm outta __!"
56 Colossal
57 "__ Spot Run"
58 ASAP
59 Family rooms

DOWN

1 Door for a cat or dog
2 Croupier's tool
3 Yield
4 Apartment dweller
5 Ski wood
6 Tool that's like a spade
7 Wipe clean
8 Military award
9 Dimple site
10 Harriet, to Bruce Wayne
11 Sleep spots
17 Puff of smoke
19 __ rickey
22 "You __ do it with Play-Doh"
23 Prepared to propose
24 Adversary
25 Hoist by one's __ petard
26 "The __ Man and the Sea"
28 "___ Today"
29 What cats shed
30 Provided meals to
33 Congregated
34 Sunny-side up center
37 Graceful lake bird
39 Rang
41 __ and lows
42 Cove
43 Sets a price
44 "I do not love __ Doctor Fell"
45 Pitchfork feature
47 No longer green
48 __ Street USA (part of Disney)
49 Multi-episode storylines
51 Distinct period
52 __ in one's ways

Toss and turn

solution on page 324

ACROSS

1 Log slicer
4 "Come over here!"
8 Wrestling surfaces
12 Pumpkin __
13 Place for poi
14 Locality
15 Rage
16 "Up in __" (indignant)
17 Expedition
18 WPM skill
20 Sun's shape
22 "__ to say . . . "
24 Pilot's escape button
27 Jumping-jacks unit
28 Herbal __
31 "Golly!"
32 They're after las but before dos
33 Encounter
34 Bilk
35 Kennel sound
36 Do a crabwalk
37 Sailing race
40 Superstar
42 Kind of potato
46 Big __ (football conference)
47 Sad look
49 Install, as carpet
50 In addition
51 "In the __ of duty"
52 "Don't __, don't tell"
53 "__ Richard's Almanac"
54 The E in BPOE
55 "Toodle-oo!"

DOWN

1 Hock a loogey
2 Atmospheric
3 Bawl
4 The Daily __ (Clark Kent's employer)
5 Sudden __ in sales
6 Malone of "Cheers"
7 Skirmishes
8 Nature trails
9 Hauled in to the station
10 Bucks and does
11 "For old time's __"
19 Foot part
21 Pizzazz
23 Float aimlessly
24 Silly Putty holder
25 Pleasure
26 After-dinner drink
29 Elongated fish
30 Gobbled
32 Step on
33 A swing and a __
35 In the past
36 Stir-fries
38 Key in, as data
39 Elephant's snout
40 Baby bird sound
41 Circle of light
43 Quincy's table
44 __ Bake Oven
45 Stripling
48 Black gold

Log slicer

solution on page 324

ACROSS

1 __ the riot act
5 Small blob
8 Weep
12 Rolling bar
13 Project Bluebook concern
14 Sailor's salutation
15 "Open sesame," for one
17 All there
18 Sign of fire
19 Senate votes
21 Weigh-station user
23 Eye shield
27 Price label
30 Type of tape
32 Like half of all crossword clues
35 It might come with a side dish
36 Magnetic personality
38 __ of the line
39 Entice
40 Capping
43 Help cure
45 Rough
49 Oompah instrument
52 Those who are a small percentage
54 Foreboding
55 Sleet, basically
56 Clean erasers
57 Picks
58 Lawn beads
59 Medal of Honor recipient

DOWN

1 Knocks
2 Final or midterm
3 Additionally
4 Reporter's station
5 Pair
6 Scared
7 __ language
8 Musician who's good with low notes
9 Cry of triumph
10 "How the West Was __"
11 Pipe cleaner
16 Minuscule
20 __-steven
22 Sunday service
24 "Yes, your __" (something a royal servant might say)
25 Rotisserie __
26 Film critic Rex __
27 Verbal refinement
28 Weekend warrior's woe
29 Metric weight
31 Warmth
33 Ones like Little Annie
34 Location
37 Spite
41 "I've got you now!"
42 Dry out
44 During
46 Tick off
47 Hollywood heavy
48 Shot, for short
49 "You're never __ old to learn"
50 "Kill the __!"
51 Casino event
53 Brand-spanking __

___ the riot act

solution on page 324

ACROSS

1 5-__ farm
5 __ of Capri
9 Disorderly crowd
12 April __'s Day
13 It's cooked in a kiln
14 Overwhelm
15 Insurance concern
16 Toy with a tail
17 Thicken
18 Cheer for the bullfighter
19 "Take a __ out of crime"
20 Vapor
21 Mouse house
23 FBI agent
25 Bistro server
27 "Fantasy Island" role
31 First Greek letter
32 Bronze medal position
33 The Sahara __
35 Labeled for purchase
36 "Catcher in the __"
37 __ and roll
38 Therefore
41 Hit the __ on the head
43 Flip one's __ (get mad)
46 "It __ been a pleasure"
47 Stubborn as a __
48 "West __ Story"
49 "__ you serious?"
50 Historic times
51 Floating
52 Get hitched
53 "One Flew Over the Cuckoo's __"
54 "What could be easier __ that?"

DOWN

1 Puffed-up hairstyle
2 Spiral
3 They're in some teabags
4 Antlered one
5 More disgusting
6 Thin opening
7 Most recent
8 "__ of the Tiger"
9 The Three Wise Men
10 Carries a mortgage
11 It ties pants at the top
19 __-eyed
20 Legendary
22 "Do unto __ as you would have them do unto you"
24 What a neighborhood watch does
25 Bit of chewing tobacco
26 Brewery drink
28 Sensitive, like Elmo
29 Unrefined deposit
30 Quirky
34 Teacher's perk
35 Reverend
38 Melt
39 Jack rabbit
40 __ to be (was)
42 Word of regret
44 "You have no __!"
45 College official
47 "A Few Good __"
48 Took a load off

"God's Little ___"

solution on page 324

ACROSS

1 Guinea __
4 "I'll __ ya—last one there is a rotten egg!"
8 Miniature __
12 Cain and Abel's mom
13 Holy figure
14 Vocal
15 Freight weight
16 Soil
17 Dreaded person
18 Sports official
20 Sump pumps do it
22 __ extinguisher
23 Gas-station freebie
24 Take-home
25 Rhythm
26 Apportion
28 Cuba or Hawaii
30 Fascinated
34 "The Spy Who __ Me" (Bond film)
36 Sonar's principle
37 Good place for a hot bath
40 Former M&M color
41 "Don't leave!"
42 Money
45 __ Walter Scott
46 Press
47 Chicken cage
49 Bran source
51 Bitter dispute
52 Threshold
53 Postal creed word
54 Contractor's charges
55 "__ Santa . . . "
56 Bashful

DOWN

1 __ peeve
2 Piano keys, in slang
3 Robert E. Lee, for one
4 Eliminate
5 Not a base
6 Livestock pen
7 Necessitated
8 Thug
9 Church instrument
10 Like an elephant
11 Armada
19 __ position (wrapped up in a ball)
21 Rule with an __ hand
22 The PATRIOT Act gave them special powers
26 __ to the next level
27 Rapunzel feature
29 End on a happy __
31 They speak louder than words
32 "Let my people go" was said to him
33 Barbie or GI Joe
35 Make hard to read
37 What shoe heels might do to a floor
38 Liquefy in a food processor
39 Quibble
43 Cincinnati team
44 Hindu exercise
48 __ capita
50 "__ not to make a scene"

Guinea __

solution on page 325

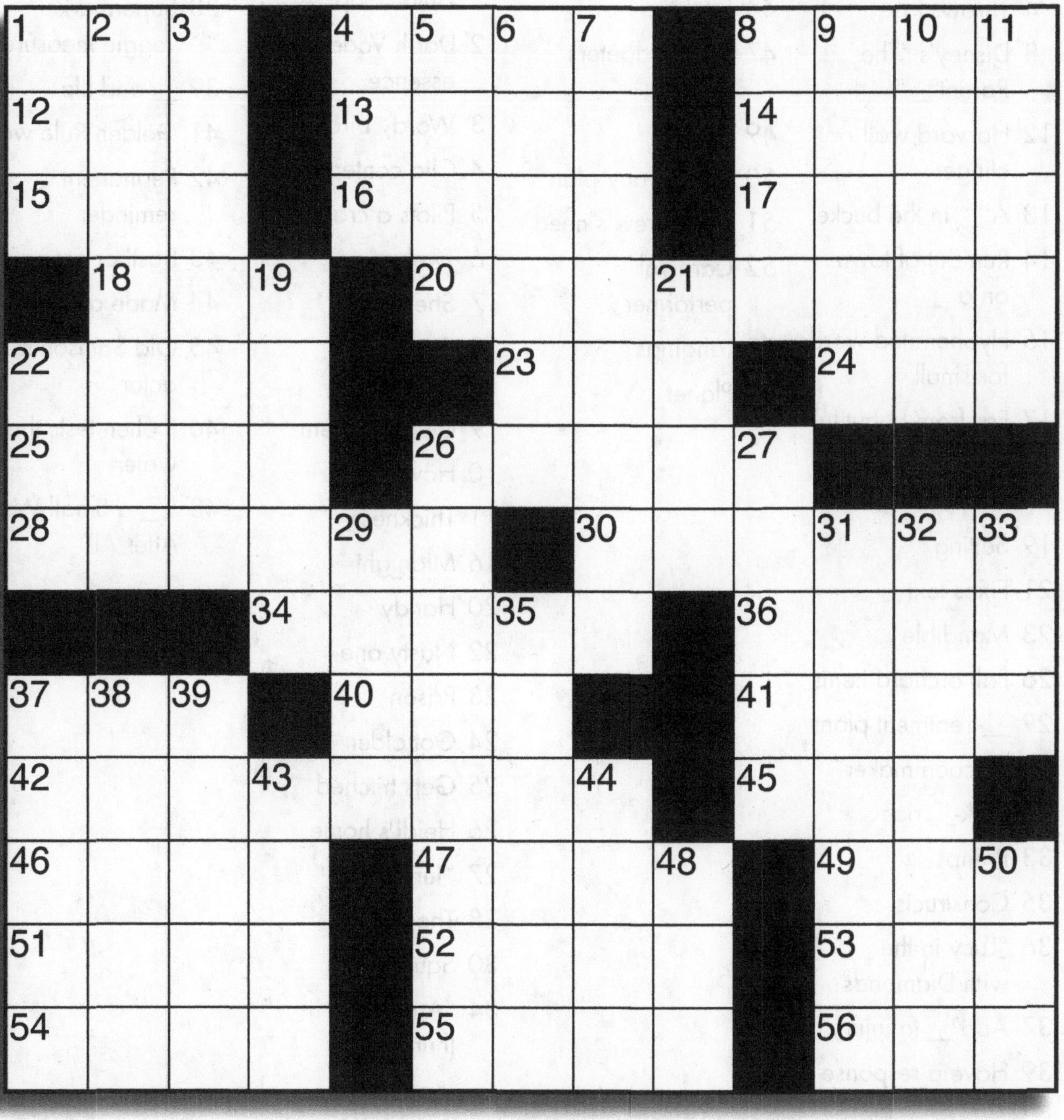

ACROSS

1 __ and haw
4 Throws in
8 Disney's "The Parent __"
12 Harvard wall clinger
13 A __ in the bucket
14 Run out of town on a __
15 Hyphenated word for small
17 Far from beautiful
18 It might be next to the potato salad
19 Setting
21 Fixes text
23 Mandible
26 Fall orchard items
29 __-treatment plant
31 Cocoon maker
32 Pork-__ rice
33 Primps
35 Constructs
36 "Lucy in the __ with Diamonds"
37 Add __ to injury
39 Have a response
40 Librarian's request
44 Statistics
47 What fidgeters lack
49 Atop
50 Conspiracy plan
51 Road crew's need
52 Carnival performer
53 Longings
54 Planet

DOWN

1 Place for a Hula-Hoop
2 Darth Vader's essence
3 Wordy birdie
4 Clio contenders
5 Pilots a craft
6 Twelve
7 Shells out
8 One of two answers
9 Cleaning item
10 Have the flu
11 Thickness
16 Midnight
20 Handy
22 Nasty one
23 Prison
24 Got older
25 Gets hitched
26 Heidi's home
27 "Jurassic __"
28 The hunted
30 Squirm
34 "And make it __" (hurry it up)
35 VCR item
38 Supermarket veggie measurer
39 __ and file
41 Golden Rule word
42 Permanent reminder
43 Basil or oregano
44 Made a hole
45 Old Samsonite ad actor
46 It often tests the water
48 "__ a Small World After All"

__ and haw

solution on page 325

ACROSS

1 Face cover for Halloween
5 Blubber
8 Messy one
12 Draft animals
13 Golfer's concern
14 "Yes! We __ No Bananas"
15 Long for
16 Dreamed of
18 Respect
20 Alludes
21 Closet
23 Tranquilized
26 Wood used for paneling
29 "Are we there yet?" event
30 Tease
32 "__, Brittania"
33 Talk up a storm
34 Methodical
36 High-octane gas
39 Catered event
42 They come as a surprise
46 Boastful one
48 "When all is said and __ . . ."
49 Solitary
50 Note before la
51 Eject
52 "Green __ and Ham"
53 Woolly mama
54 Gives permission to

DOWN

1 Pout
2 Pole-to-pole line
3 Shipped
4 Baby bouncer
5 One who wants to peek at a peak
6 Edge
7 Desire
8 9-to-5, say
9 Carpool __
10 "Went __ like a lead balloon"
11 Motel room items
17 "My word!"
19 "Dig in!"
22 Nonliteral phrase
23 Swine's home
24 The Gay Nineties, for one
25 Party bowlful
26 "__ Town"
27 "__ kidding aside . . ."
28 Essential
31 Beard fiber
32 Change a room
35 "But of course!"
36 This book has over 300 of them
37 18-wheeler
38 Correct a mistake
39 Talented
40 Kermit the __
41 Snake tooth
43 "O __ All Ye Faithful"
44 __ one's brow
45 __ sail (goes on an ocean voyage)
47 Tic-tac-toe win reading across

Face cover for Halloween

solution on page 325

ACROSS

1 It reeks
5 Tend the tots
8 Sound of a punch
12 Au naturel
13 Hole-in-__
14 Condoleeza __
15 Scoundrels
16 Census question
17 Region
18 "Let's play something __!"
19 "A chicken in every __"
20 Exterminator's target
21 Base beats
24 Make cloth
27 "I Can __ Clearly Now"
28 Saloon
31 Brokered a deal
33 Like a clear night sky
35 "What have you __ there?"
36 __ reader (one who listens by watching)
38 Make amends
39 Attack
41 Pour forth
44 Likely
45 "The Seven Year __"
49 PBS science series
50 Slugger's stick
51 Uncommon
52 Blog author
53 Soap ingredient
54 Blue book event
55 Twist
56 Muff site
57 Lowers the lights

DOWN

1 "__ bitten, twice shy"
2 __ personality
3 Probability
4 Schedule a rental car, say
5 Like bath water
6 Gold bars
7 What a baby does that increases drooling
8 Preps the presents
9 Take on workers
10 King toppers
11 __ and potatoes
22 Head over __ in love
23 "Put the pedal to the __"
24 Shake, like a dog's tail
25 Freudian topic
26 Museum display
28 Old hand
29 Footed vessel
30 "Ta-ta!"
32 Make nonworking, like an alarm
34 Decked out
37 Tropical fruit
39 Prize
40 Pronounce
41 Social slight
42 A model might strike one
43 Fairly matched
46 "Somebody, call me a __"
47 Pack tightly
48 __ in (confines)

It reeks

solution on page 325

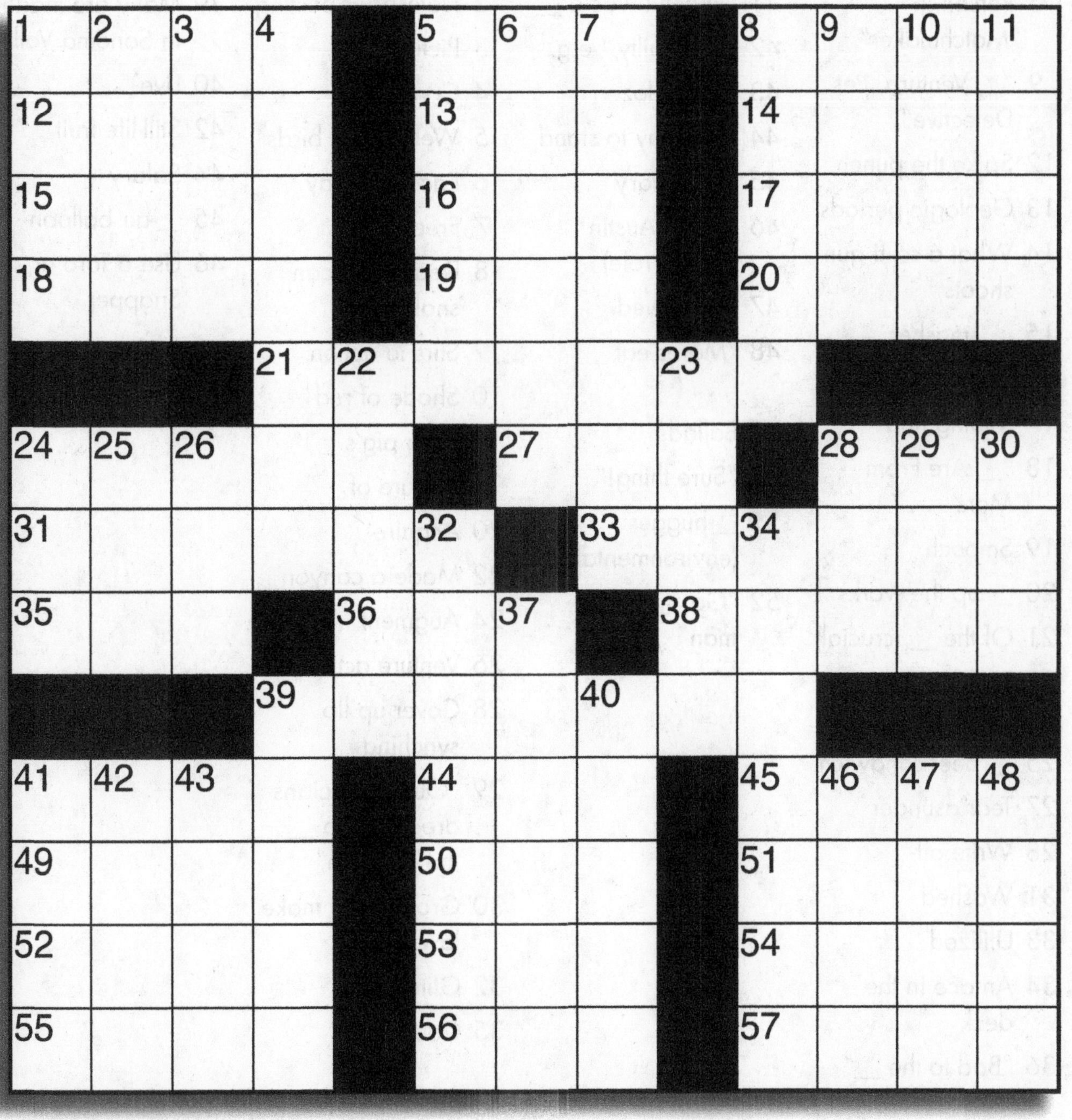

ACROSS

1 Ocean jail
5 Person in "Matchmaker"
9 "__ Ventura, Pet Detective"
12 Spike the punch
13 Geologic periods
14 What a sci-fi gun shoots
15 __ smasher
16 Thpeak like thith
17 Mining find
18 "__ Are From Mars . . . "
19 Smooch
20 __ up the works
21 Of the __ (crucial)
23 Earth's largest continent
25 __ beef sandwich
27 Tear asunder
28 Write off
31 Washed
33 Utilized
34 An ace in the deck
36 "Bad to the __"
37 Amaze
41 "When I was a __"
42 "Not guilty," e.g.
43 Half a dozen
44 One way to stand
45 Beneficiary
46 __-Me (Austin Powers role)
47 Swallowed
48 "Mares eat __ . . . "
49 Ballads
50 "Sure thing!"
51 __-hugger (environmentalist)
52 "Go __, young man"

DOWN

1 "Who's to __?"
2 Hotel-door posting
3 Pictures
4 Crystal
5 Web-footed birds
6 Faces the day
7 Free ticket
8 Deadly African snake
9 Stirs to action
10 Shade of red
11 "In a pig's __!"
19 Be sure of
20 Acquire
22 Made a canyon
24 Augment
26 Venture across
28 Cover up lip synching
29 "Our technicians are trying to __ the problem"
30 Groups that make laws
32 Glimmer
35 Courteous
38 Put __ (reserve)
39 Many are made in Sonoma Valley
40 Live
42 Still-life fruit
44 Salary
45 __-air balloon
46 Use a Toro or Snapper

Ocean Jail

solution on page 325

ACROSS

1 Leaf collection for jumping into
5 Unruly __
8 Newborn
12 Cathedral relic
13 Shock
14 Kirlian photography phenomena
15 They're just below jacks
16 Sailing events
18 "No __, no glory"
20 Haunted-house haunter
21 "In one ear and out the __"
23 Whistle sound
25 "So that's your game!"
26 Knitting material
28 Coffee servers
32 Any __ in a storm
34 Well-worn path
35 __ camp
36 Gets some color in the summer
37 Drain problem
39 Dream Team jersey letters
40 Sore
42 Raring to go
44 Copy, at a magazine
47 Carve
48 Obscured
51 Comet part
54 Give the cold shoulder to
55 Tent stake
56 Cruel person
57 Forum frock
58 Pub pint
59 Coarse grass

DOWN

1 Cherry stone
2 __ tongs
3 Cowboy's charge
4 Come after
5 The Red Planet
6 Use credit
7 __, borrow, or steal
8 Place for a soak
9 Sedan or coupe
10 Bikini parts
11 Away from the setting sun
17 Gone by
19 Take a crack at
21 Klutz's cry
22 You, Biblically
23 Yours __ (letter closer)
24 Not fooled by
27 Eyebrow shape or foot part
29 Fiber
30 Sneezer
31 "A __ Is Born"
33 Romanov royal
38 Nab
41 Policeman
43 Thespian
44 Take it easy
45 Flight guide for a bat
46 Spark __ (car part)
47 Skirt
49 Good place for a massage
50 Bioelectric fish
52 Bile
53 Spearheaded

Leaf collection for jumping into

solution on page 325

ACROSS

1 "All You Need Is __" (Beatles song)
5 Open just a bit
9 Little rascal
12 Skillet material
13 Dog in "Peter Pan"
14 __'easter
15 Housekeeper
16 Hard trip
17 CIA agent
18 More ancient
20 Perspiration
22 Purpose
24 Lugs
27 Winter wear
32 __-jerk reaction
33 Vincent __ Gogh
34 Shaggy
36 Crow call
37 Liberal __
39 Policemen
41 Sheet-music line
43 Owed
44 Cook's garment
47 __ race (baton event)
51 Bled in the laundry
53 They can be bruised or inflated
55 The cover of __ Magazine
56 Joan of __ (French heroine)
57 Female singer
58 Jazz great __ "Fatha" Hines
59 Lil'
60 "Peachy __!"
61 "Good to the last __"

DOWN

1 VIP's wheels
2 Evangelist Roberts
3 Hollow space in a wall
4 Make beloved
5 Crumb carrier
6 Jelly containers
7 Once again
8 Made leaf piles
9 For __ (as an example)
10 Unruly hair
11 Be a nudnik
19 Calorie-laden
21 Floating zoo
23 Castle defense
25 __ shift
26 Makes a sweater
27 Egg-shaped
28 Differ
29 Way in
30 __ one's dirty laundry
31 Trudged
35 "Here's mud in __ eye!"
38 Taste tea
40 "Keep your eyes __"
42 Haunted house door sound
45 Stare at rudely
46 "Johnny One-__"
48 Snake-oil salesman
49 '60s hairstyle
50 Kennel cry
51 Like uncut diamonds
52 "__ we having fun yet?"
54 Beaver, to Ward

"All You Need Is __" (Beatles song)

solution on page 326

ACROSS

1 Cay
5 Sales pitches
8 Orderly
12 __ polish
13 Kook
14 Dessert __
15 Like laced laces
16 "Shop til __ drop"
17 In no __ (right away)
18 Least modern
20 Multi-emergencies
22 "Ain't I a __?"
24 Halloween need
27 Annoying ones
31 "Tie a Yellow Ribbon Round the Old __ Tree"
32 Flu symptom
34 "Surprise!"
35 "Good __!" (Charlie Brown saying)
37 Lived
39 Invigorate
41 Video __
44 __ up on its hind legs
48 Cow sounds
49 Make a move
51 Talking doll word
52 Spinning one's wheels
53 Where a sock puppet's face is
54 Folic __
55 Cherished
56 Divot material
57 Earns after taxes

DOWN

1 "__ each life, some rain must fall"
2 It hangs from a mast
3 Told a whopper
4 First-born
5 Whenever
6 Tango team
7 Unable to budge
8 Clothing
9 Flower of one's eye
10 "The Hunchback of Notre __"
11 "For Your __ Only"
19 __ cabbage
21 Get back at
23 "It'll __ work!"
24 Minor worker
25 Low-tech propeller
26 Enjoy Vail or Okemo
28 Stayed with Junior
29 "A chip off __ old block"
30 Feeling blue
33 Put effort in
36 Pencil topper
38 Mystical healer
40 Impressive deeds
41 Among
42 Went by taxi
43 Drink in a can or bottle
45 Track-meet event
46 Send out
47 Fathers
50 Happy baby sound

Cay

solution on page 326

ACROSS

1 Had feelings
5 Not operating
8 Cushions
12 Lion's den
13 Jack Horner's fare
14 __ poll
15 Not moored
16 Cherish as sacred
18 Writers for pro crossword solvers
19 "At any __ . . ." (however)
20 Do a tailor's job
21 Faith __ (doctor of a sort)
23 Narrow back street
26 Make a faux pas
27 Spin like a __
30 Like a parka on top
32 Stoplight, say
34 Temp teacher
35 Dinette __
37 Wacky
38 Citrus fruit
40 Chats
43 Peeve
44 Shadowbox
48 Accomplished one
50 "For Pete's __!"
51 Put an edge on
52 __ zone (football place)
53 "What __ lurks in the hearts of men?"
54 Reporter's concern
55 Pig's digs
56 Contradict

DOWN

1 Ruckus
2 Lighten up
3 Property right
4 Slandered
5 Show at the Met
6 "Time for the grand __"
7 Becomes more problematic
8 According to
9 "Turn it on it's __"
10 Eat well
11 Fret
17 Red __ (false clue)
22 Urban blight
23 "That hits the spot!" sounds
24 Little Cindy __ Who
25 Plopped tennis shot
27 Blaster's material
28 Feedbag morsel
29 Wield
31 Infers
33 Took a stab in the dark
36 __ competition (beauty pageant part)
39 Socially inept
40 "I'm about ready for bed" preceder
41 Throbbing pain
42 "That was a close one!"
45 __ the way
46 Alike
47 Have faith
49 "__ the economy, stupid"

Had feelings

solution on page 326

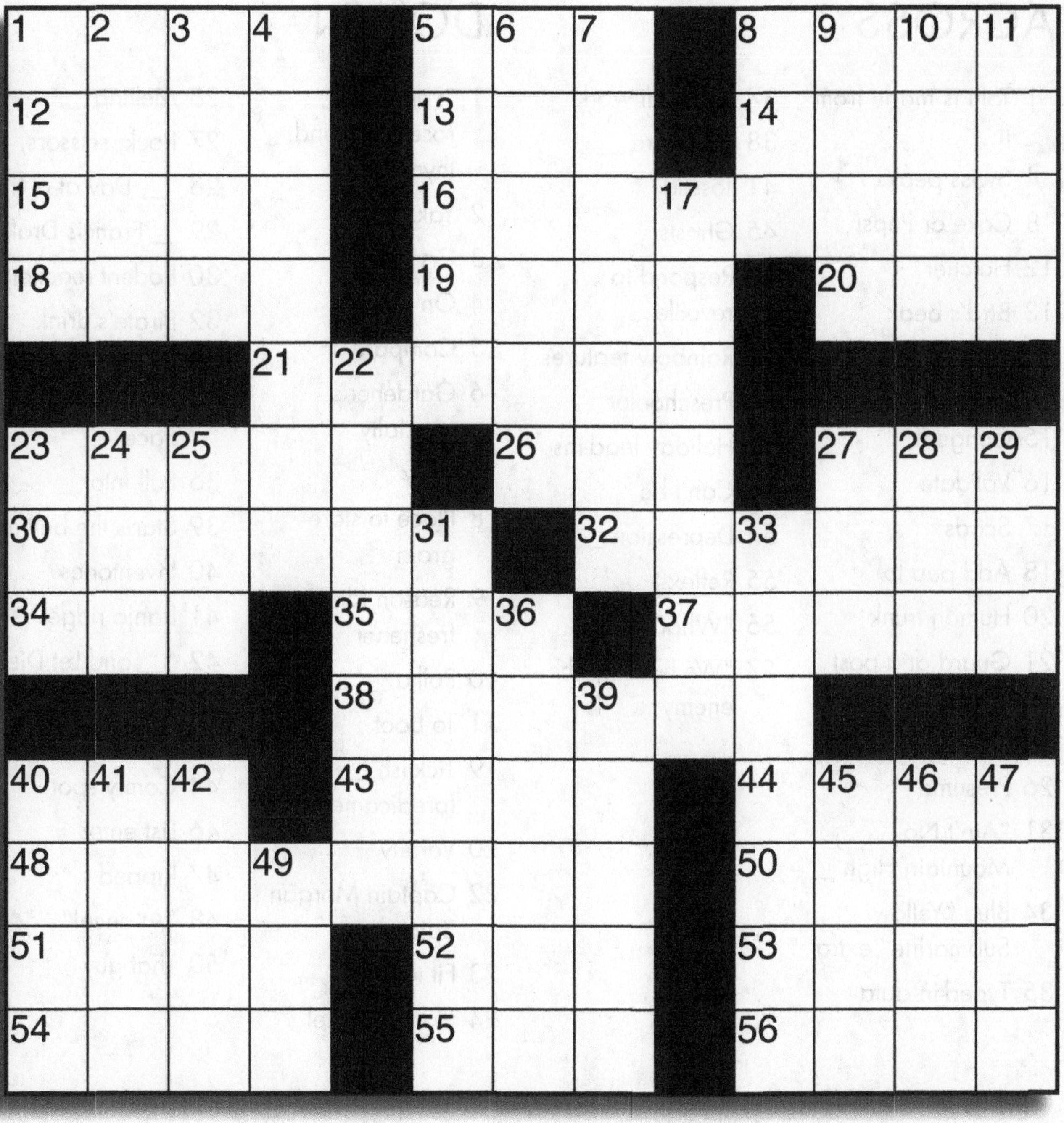

10. Start Over

ACROSS

1 Tofu is made from it
4 Swiss peaks
8 Coke or Pepsi
12 Hatchet
13 Bird's beak
14 "American __" (TV talent show)
15 Congeal
16 Validate
17 Scads
18 Add pep to
20 Human trunk
21 Guard at a post
23 __ the scales of justice
26 Presume
31 "Ain't No Mountain High __"
34 Blue "Yellow Submarine" extra
35 Typed-in data
37 Bonus at work
38 Baltimore __
41 Tossed
45 Ghosts
49 Respond to reveille
50 Rainbow features
51 Preschooler
52 Holiday lead-ins
53 Can't be
54 Depression __
55 Reflex __
56 "What a __!"
57 "We have __ the enemy . . ."

DOWN

1 "Parsley, __, rosemary, and thyme"
2 Yaks
3 Cry out
4 On top of
5 Compare
6 Gardener's specialty
7 Wily
8 Place to store grain
9 Reason for air freshener
10 Polka __
11 To boot
19 Ticklish __ (predicament)
20 Variety
22 Captain Morgan's Spiced __
23 Fit to a __
24 Country hotel
25 Melting __
27 Rock, scissors, __
28 "__ Day at a Time"
29 __ Francis Drake
30 Rodent reaction
32 Pirate's drink
33 "I've Grown Accustomed to __ Face"
36 Fall into __
39 Starts the betting
40 Inventories
41 Banjo ridge
42 "__ and Let Die" (Bond film)
43 "1,001 __!"
44 Comfy spot
46 List entry
47 Ripped
48 "At once!"
50 That guy

Tofu is made from it

solution on page 327

ACROSS

1 Lay low
4 Accord
8 " . . . or to take __ against a sea of troubles . . . "
12 Bravo in the bullring
13 Agile
14 Turned __ red
15 Magical being
16 Flow slowly
17 Metallic fabric with an accent mark
18 Gobble up
20 Process, as film
22 Burn a bit
24 Tourist ID
25 Cafeteria of vending machines
27 Snoop around
32 Any of six car-radio buttons
33 Gala
34 Village __ (tribal leader)
35 Bringing home the bacon
36 Optimistic
38 Related groups
39 Psychiatrist
43 Playroom
44 High–__ act
45 Walking stick
47 Earl Grey __
50 Air heroes
51 Cyclotron item
52 Pantyhose holder
53 Thumbs-up votes
54 Modernize
55 Lady deer

DOWN

1 Weed digger
2 Ailing
3 Beaten
4 Sideways whisper
5 "The Naked __"
6 College-class unit
7 Uses a keyboard
8 Skilled
9 Bona fide
10 __ pad
11 Procedure part
19 Obeyed reveille
21 Steam
22 Magician's wear
23 Toss
24 Witch's pot
26 "__ Christmas!"
28 Laundry cycle
29 Got one's bearings
30 "__ over like a lead balloon"
31 Octopus's eight
33 "Who am I to __?"
35 Fancy digs
37 Boxing's __ De La Hoya
39 "Bombs __!"
40 "__ guys finish last"
41 Painter's calculation
42 "__ is more"
43 Promo tape
46 Land east of Eden
48 It may be bruised
49 Victorian __

Lie low

solution on page 327

ACROSS

1 __ thumbs (clumsy)
4 What Dorian Gray's picture did
8 Linger
12 Tint
13 Sandwich shop
14 "The buck stops __"
15 Canine comment
16 Writing fluids
17 Mare's meal
18 Parlor piece
20 Paid players
22 Sound of windblown leaves
24 Hole goal
27 Santa __
30 Stuffed pasta
32 "__ to the Chief"
33 "April showers bring __ flowers"
34 "Mr. __'s Wild Ride"
35 Permanent paint
37 All keyed up
38 It might be a kneeler
39 Regard
41 Makes sums
43 Renter
47 Kind of lox
49 Symbol
51 Roulette bet
52 Verbal elbowing
53 Brief slumbers
54 Type of dried fruit
55 Perry White, to Clark Kent
56 Earl __ tea
57 Downed

DOWN

1 Gleeful cries
2 Attract
3 "Out in __ field" (way off base)
4 Bistro bye-byes
5 Bits of DNA
6 Forest critter
7 Exhibition
8 "Vamoose!"
9 Small cooking amount
10 __ deco
11 "Of course!"
19 Indeed
21 Give it some gas
23 __ of land
25 Hamlet's lament
26 Rollercoaster or Tilt-A-Whirl
27 Gent
28 "Arsenic and Old __"
29 Things to broadcast across
31 Agenda entries
33 "What's __ from this picture?"
36 Put out the first card
37 Tiny
40 Rush to wed
42 Floodgate
44 Futon
45 Make a second draft
46 Barely defeat
47 Take into custody
48 "I now hold the upper hand!"
50 Auto

__ thumbs (clumsy)

solution on page 327

ACROSS

1 Understanding
4 " . . . or take arms against a __ of troubles"
7 Polliwog or caterpillar
12 Hitching quickly
14 One more time
15 Fragrance
16 Like commercial and residential areas
17 Soft cry
18 "You __ Live Twice"
20 "La-di-da"
21 Vaccination
25 Globe shape
29 What Houdini routinely did
31 Siren
32 Safe place
33 Long fish
35 Squad-car squealers
36 Meadow moms
37 Preacher's word
39 Drove above the limit
40 "__ a minute now . . . "
44 Debate
48 Grassy plain
50 __ and desist
51 Hollywood hopeful's hope
52 Double-__ sword
53 Hankering
54 Have bills

DOWN

1 "__ a stiff upper lip"
2 Alternatively
3 Cockpit front
4 Go astray
5 "Bravo!"
6 Salesman
7 __ Susan (table that turns)
8 In the past
9 Did a lap
10 Struggle
11 "Up __ at 'em!"
13 __ talk (confidence builder)
19 Strong soap
20 "You and what __?"
21 Injury mark
22 King's "I __ a Dream"
23 Major sporting event
24 Hamilton bills
25 Equivalent
26 Farm-soil tiller
27 __ Krishna
28 Jurassic and Paleozoic
30 Calf's front
34 Weaken
35 Tranquilize
38 Sloppy
39 Ranked contestant
40 Caught with a hand in the cookie __
41 Negate
42 Slope powder
43 Gentle
44 World War I flying __
45 "The __ Badge of Courage"
46 One-liner
47 In __ (occupied)
49 Dick __ Dyke

Understanding

solution on page 327

ACROSS

1 "Blind as a __"
4 Goad
8 Idiots
12 Stein filler
13 Lovers' __
14 Popeye, after eating spinach
15 Sample soup
16 Springtime flower
17 Spinach and meat have lots of it
18 Preholiday time
19 Step quickly
20 Gladys Knight backup singer
21 Boy Scout's daily duty
23 Newsboy's wad
25 "So, it's YOU!"
27 Ordinarily disposed
29 Numbed
31 Shoulder wrap
34 Tarnishes, as iron does
35 Wage __
37 "Please, I __ of you!"
38 Dutch __ disease
39 Light as a feather
41 America's Atlantic side, say
45 Enemy
47 Fens
49 Little white __ (fib)
50 Clone
51 At the summit
52 It needs refinement
53 "You drive a __ bargain"
54 Unaccompanied
55 Rock Cornish game __
56 "Bette Davis __"
57 Scribbled
58 "__ luck?"

DOWN

1 "__ on a true story"
2 "__ and kicking"
3 Prairie home
4 Narrow opening
5 Tropical talking bird
6 State of the __ address
7 Took a breather
8 Nina, Pinta, or Santa Maria
9 Rabbit ears on the roof
10 Any Biblical seer
11 "Sanford and __"
22 Daybreak
24 Without a doubt
26 Movie preceders
28 "No contest," e.g.
30 Downhill racer
31 __ eye-to-eye
32 Midpoint
33 Dresser
36 Raunchy, like humor
37 Age-old
40 Helicopter part
42 Island greeting
43 Alarm
44 Little
46 Loose __
48 Shoot out
50 "Don't spill __ beans"

Blind as a ___

solution on page 327

ACROSS

1 Item by Scott Joplin
4 Speakeasy risk
8 Room-service prop
12 Fleecy female
13 Try to persuade
14 Anger
15 __ and ink
16 TV rooms
17 Neck and neck
18 Conclude
20 Unfeeling quality
22 Wander off
24 Oversee
25 Lint __ (dryer part)
26 Exported
27 Moo goo gai __
30 Surpass in stuffing oneself
32 Cowboy-game tile
34 Microscopic
35 Response to hooks in the ring
37 __ and sciences
38 Boldly attempt
39 Secret supply
40 New lease on life
43 Half a score
44 Zoning measure
45 __ lamp ('60s item)
47 "Rumor __ it . . . "
50 Casual conversation
51 Rotten
52 Killer snake
53 Forever and a day
54 Bargain
55 Where to see a constellation

DOWN

1 Agent, for short
2 Bewilder
3 Beget
4 Not pale
5 "The Times They __ A-Changing"
6 Light on fire
7 Moves downward
8 "It seems to be a growing __"
9 Babble wildly
10 "Rock of __"
11 Desires
19 Neck part
21 "Guess who I ran __ today?"
22 Load cargo
23 "Too good to be __"
26 Scared and surprised
27 Vicious fish
28 Aardvark munchies
29 Nibble
31 Not quite shut
33 Chess win
36 Mind your manners
38 Eats less
39 Shower __
40 Regatta
41 Repeated sound
42 Fiber source
46 Passing through
48 "__ me no questions, I'll tell you no lies"
49 Secret agent

Item by Scott Joplin

solution on page 327

ACROSS

1 Lymph __
6 "Isn't __ Lovely?"
9 Identify
12 Spirit-world game
13 Phrasing
15 Nest places
16 Peachlike fruit
17 Monkey
19 Jumble
20 "Right now!"
23 Competed
25 Soothe
27 Go over again
32 "Gesundheit" preceder
33 Vile
34 Office items
36 Brook
37 Circle
39 Mend socks
40 Head toppers
44 Ascend
46 Different
48 Desert __ (watering hole)
52 One way to help save the environment
53 Feather
54 "A bicycle built for __"
55 Squeamish response
56 Nodded off

DOWN

1 "Death Be __ Proud"
2 "__ Miss Brooks"
3 Do or __
4 __ seat (spy car feature)
5 Cummerbund
6 Hindu teacher
7 Storage bin
8 Blunder
9 Tempo
10 Psyche parts
11 "As good as it __"
14 __ sum
18 __ League school
20 Mineral springs
21 Social grace
22 Feel pain
24 Parking-lot ding
26 It's what's for dinner
28 Powder-puff alternative
29 Cruising
30 Constellation dot
31 Sacred song
35 Hammer and __ (Russian icon)
36 Make use of a lift ticket
38 Glossy
40 Injured
41 All over again
42 Mexican munchie
43 Clever
45 Janitor tools
47 Zamboni target
49 File a complaint
50 Rapscallion
51 All __ (ready)

Lymph __

solution on page 328

ACROSS

1 Clump of earth
5 School __
8 Stepped heavily
12 Taxi alternative
13 Firewood, later
14 Worked-for income
15 Related
16 "Amazing!"
17 __ of Man
18 Doled
20 "Birds of a __ flock together"
22 Burst forth
24 It's sprayed from a can
28 Having prongs
33 De-creased
34 The B in FBI
35 "Sooner or __"
36 Kitchen alcove
37 Brink
39 __ paint (poster medium)
43 Eccentric
48 Line of rotation
49 Prima donna problem
51 Dragon's breath
52 Thumbs-down review
53 Flatfoot
54 Hopping bug
55 Cast forth
56 It makes a blast
57 Visionary

DOWN

1 Dig for mollusks
2 Work __ a dog
3 Pass over
4 Completed
5 Grocery holder
6 Functional
7 Animal that goes "baa"
8 Nincompoop
9 Impetuous
10 Come-hither look
11 "__ XING"
19 Be worthy of
21 On the same wavelength
23 Director/producer Serling
24 Not do so well
25 Timeline segment
26 Decay
27 "All for __ and . . ."
29 Fury
30 "Nothing but __" (without using the rim or backboard)
31 "Mares __ oats, and . . ."
32 __ date
34 Huge
36 Fire-breather of stories
38 One way to stand
39 VCR __
40 It counts more than a quiz
41 Short skirt
42 "Hey, buddy!"
44 Makes a hit
45 Piece of linoleum
46 Coat rack
47 Time's "Man of the __"
50 Elect

Clump of earth

solution on page 328

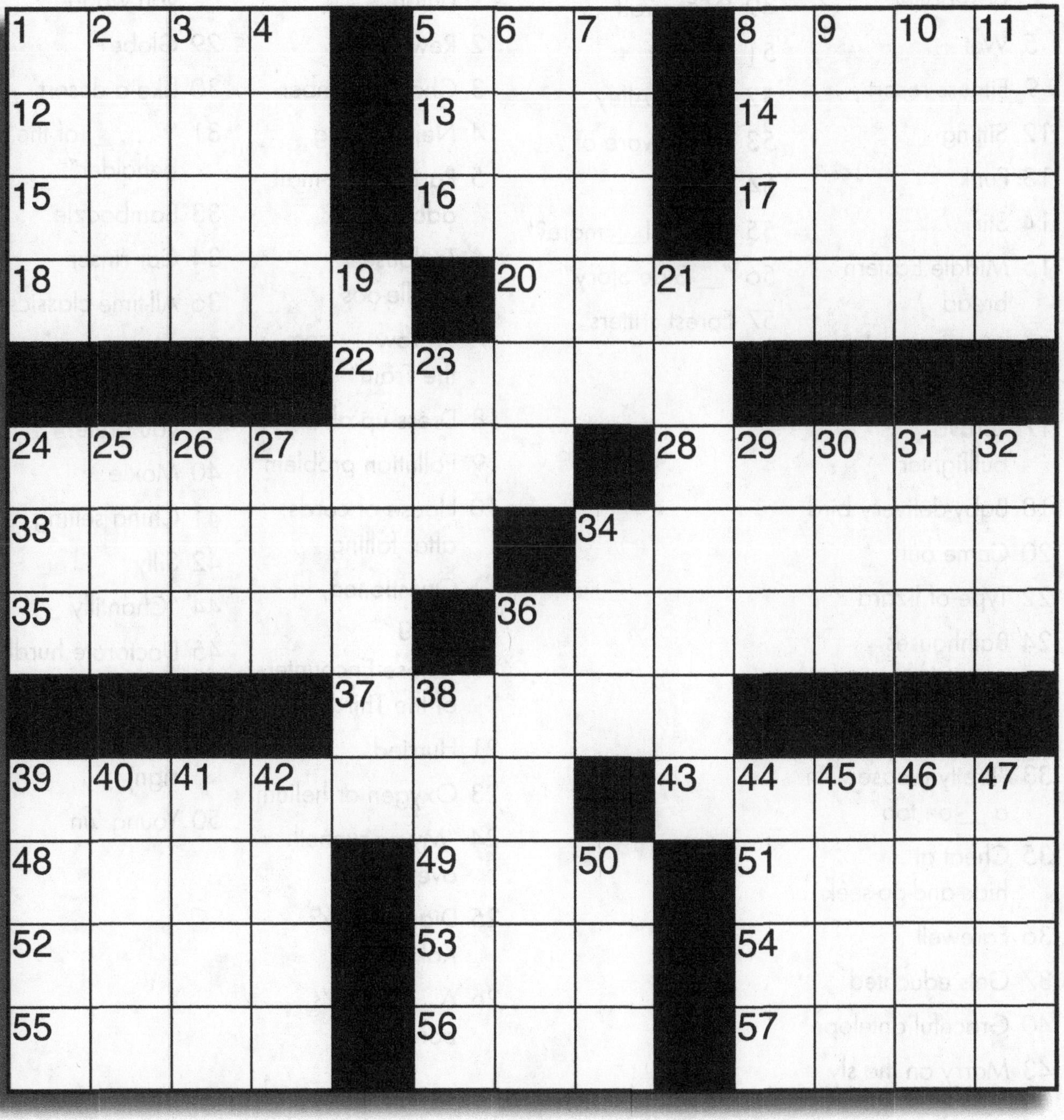

ACROSS

1 "Dizzy" baseballer
5 Wet
9 Fitness resort
12 Sitting __
13 Funk
14 Stir
15 Middle Eastern bread
16 "Get Me to the Church on __"
17 "Bravo, bullfighter!"
18 Baby-delivery bird
20 Came out
22 Type of lizard
24 Bathhouses
28 Cryptogram
32 Turns over
33 "Pretty please with a __ on top"
35 Cheat at hide-and-go-seek
36 Farewell
37 Gets educated
40 Graceful antelope
43 Marry on the sly
48 Patriotic chant
49 Watercraft
51 Precinct
52 __ Pan Alley
53 Well aware of
54 Go-__
55 "Need I __ more?"
56 "__ Side Story"
57 Forest critters

DOWN

1 Salsa and French onion
2 Reword
3 Chorus member
4 Neighboring
5 Part of an e-mail address
6 Toulouse's toodle-oos
7 "Throw __ from the Train"
8 Dress up all fancy
9 Pollution problem
10 House of cards, after falling
11 Questioned, in slang
19 "Close Encounters of the Third __"
21 Hurried
23 Oxygen or helium
24 "My __ runneth over"
25 Dian Fossey's Koko
26 A __ in one's bonnet
27 It gets wet when you wade
29 Globe
30 Like a desert
31 ". . . __ of the beholder"
33 Bamboozle
34 Car rinser
36 All-time classics
38 __ macaroni
39 "Leave him __, you brute!"
40 Moxie
41 China setting
42 Silly
44 "Chantilly __"
45 Doctorate hurdle
46 __ up (get happy)
47 Good __ (diner sign)
50 Young 'un

"Dizzy" baseballer

solution on page 328

ACROSS

1 Electric swimmer
4 "__ over matter"
8 Bluenose
12 Place, as a bet
13 Thought
14 __ conquers all
15 Like Peppermint Patty
17 Hot chamber
18 Cattail kin
19 Begin
20 Hard-bed bear
23 __ shot (hockey move)
25 Maze finales
27 Blew, like a volcano
32 One of the Seven Dwarves
34 Theatrical road company
35 Yorkshire __ (dog breed)
37 Gin and __
38 __ one, purl two
40 Shortage
41 Soup server
45 Store sign
47 Ambience
48 Water channel of ancient Rome
52 "__ on a dime"
53 Respiratory organ
54 __ shu pork
55 Little leaps
56 Gives one's blessing to
57 "Wham!"

DOWN

1 Wee one
2 Pulled item for Carol Burnett
3 Pipe cleaner
4 Concealed __
5 Does nothing
6 Tailor's tool
7 Poppa
8 Letter drop
9 Big bang
10 "Don't cry __ spilt milk"
11 Like a mishammered nail
16 Moon hole
19 Sudden burst
20 Nudnik
21 Wheel shaft
22 Docking spot
24 Comic actor Carney
26 Railroad nail
28 Combined, as money
29 __ melt (type of sandwich)
30 Adventure tale
31 __ of cards
33 Desire
36 Racy
39 Ridicule
41 Whip end
42 Ferry fare
43 "__ and give me twenty!"
44 Drinks like a dog
46 Frog's __
48 "My heart's __ aflutter!"
49 Diamond expert
50 Speak lovingly
51 Bring to the mechanic

Electric swimmer

solution on page 328

solution on page 328

ACROSS

1 Atlas page
4 "A __ a minute"
8 "Born and __"
12 Sounds of relief
13 Showy bloom
14 "__ and learn"
15 "Let's call it a __"
16 Land parcels
17 __ a can of worms
18 Extended family
20 Restaurant
22 Hurted
24 Inch or centimeter
25 Church goers
26 The Dead Sea __
30 Lob's path
31 Boston Cream __
32 Granola bit
33 "Court is now in __"
36 "Klepto-" follower
38 Wooden shoe
39 Mad
40 Supported
43 Improve __ age
44 City light
45 __ an egg (did awful)
47 One who is all thumbs
50 Arena roof
51 Otherwise
52 Baker's loaf
53 "The Defiant __"
54 " . . . be __ and not heard"
55 "__ and improved"

DOWN

1 Alfred E. Neuman's magazine
2 "Caught you in the act!"
3 Mentalists
4 Her, in England
5 Anvil
6 Ignited
7 "Ebony" rival
8 Totally drunk
9 At its peak
10 Never __ (at no time)
11 Claim to be untrue
19 "Live and __ Die" (Bond film)
21 Hot-__ balloon
22 "Too bad!"
23 "Not a __ in the world"
24 Putting to work
27 Breed of cattle
28 Burrow
29 Overnight visit
31 Small, curly-haired dogs
34 Tantrums
35 "An __ wind blows"
36 "I'll save you, fair __!"
37 __ farm (critter cage)
40 Nullify
41 Unskilled worker
42 "There's no place like __"
43 Like village elders
46 Suds at a saloon
48 Vote in favor
49 Not many

Atlas page

solution on page 328

ACROSS

1 Periphery
5 "__ and polish"
9 Dole who ran for President in '96
12 Bodybuilder's exercise
13 __ duck presidency
14 Blow away
15 __ over heels in love
16 Yodeler's home
17 Lobster color in cartoons, but when alive
18 Most ancient
20 Tiny particle
22 Hitchcock's "The 39 __"
24 Yellow jacket
27 Item for Hans Brinker
30 Stupid
32 Hostel
33 Gave comfort to
35 "Can you __ it?"
36 Brings back
38 Makes it to the end
40 Mas that baa
41 "Well, I __!"
43 Fix up
45 Builds
49 Area 51 item
51 Sailor's assents
53 Manicured item
54 Slime
55 Hiker's dwelling
56 Fluffy hairstyle
57 __ in (confine)
58 Continues, in talk
59 Ooze

DOWN

1 Parrot
2 Old West fight
3 Alumnus, for short
4 Most mature
5 "Let's wipe the __ clean"
6 Friend
7 Standoff
8 __ pilot
9 Tavern waitresses
10 Be in the red
11 Cot or hammock
19 Take the wheel
21 __ up to (confess)
23 Antiquated
25 Huff
26 Cribbage needs
27 Beget
28 "If You __ Susie"
29 Lobby
31 One who loafs
34 Bothered
37 "What's the __ of worrying . . . "
39 Sports centers
42 Suit parts
44 It's collected for a census
46 Bistro
47 Radial __
48 __ the hogs
49 "Yuck!"
50 Rival
52 Bring to a close

Periphery

solution on page 328

ACROSS

1 Social dud
5 Little shaver
8 "Been there, done __"
12 " . . . and the dish ran __ with the spoon"
13 Crude metal
14 Skelton or Chaplin persona
15 Make
17 Function
18 Had supper
19 Canticles
20 "The Eagle __ landed"
23 Human being
25 Fraternal order member
26 Take a stab at
27 Takes five
31 Courtroom excuses
33 Item drawn in the Old West
34 Entered data
35 "__ you for real?"
36 Long __ (yore)
37 Sluggish
39 Q key neighbor
40 Past the pier
43 Gambling game
45 Talk online
46 Supposed
50 Raced
51 Farm female
52 Talk excitedly
53 Auction ender
54 State further
55 Beef dish

DOWN

1 Kvetch
2 Ma that baas
3 Skedaddled
4 Recolored
5 Courtesy cars
6 Blood vessel
7 "Mr. __ Goes to Town"
8 King's seats
9 Little Red Riding __
10 Skilled
11 On one's __ (alert)
16 Boating hazard
20 __-seeking missile
21 Buddy
22 Go without
24 Turns in the right direction
28 "Pronto!"
29 Frat-party cry
30 Untidy one
32 Like some birthday greetings
33 Play make-believe
35 Idolized
38 __ Centauri
40 Deeds
41 "Buzz off!"
42 Chief Justice Warren
44 Belonging to us
47 It prevents slipping in the tub
48 Holiday night
49 Frost above freezing

Social dud

solution on page 329

Appendix A

Glossary

#:
Crosswords are called by the number of rows and columns they have, which tend to be the same in the crossword world (a newspaper's daily puzzle is usually a 15, and a newspaper's Sunday crossword is usually a 21; almost always a square puzzle and an odd number).

American-style:
See construction.

anagram:
Rearranging letters to spell something else; occasionally used in a theme.

British-style:
See construction.

byline:
A constructor credit.

cheater:
A black square that maintains word count, making the grid easier to fill in.

construction/constructor:
In an American-style crossword, a constructor constructs using the art of construction. For British-style crosswords, setters set crossword puzzles. British-style puzzles DO NOT have cross-checking, and the clues have a straight half and a cryptic half (there are about a half-dozen different styles of acceptable cryptic form).

cross-checking:
Having all white boxes used in both across and down entries, so that you can check a square against valid entries going in both directions.

crossword:
The first crossword, created by Arthur Wynn, appeared in the December 21, 1913, edition of New York World. Word squares go back at least to early Rome.

crosswordese:
Words that you rarely encounter outside the crossword world.

cruciverbalism:
The art/science of crosswords.

cruciverbalist:
Crossword constructor.

entry:
An across or down answer.

fill:
The entries stuffed into a grid.

grid:
A crossword's black/white square pattern.

interconnectedness:
Grid quality where black squares don't chop the puzzle into separate pieces.

isle of white:
Cut-off part of a grid that is not interconnected.

knothole:
A square that's hard to break open, because you have no clue about the across and down entries crossing there.

Margaret Farrar:
The world's first crossword editor (for the New York Times); she laid down the first ground rules, giving legitimacy to the field.

mirror-symmetry:
The feature of a grid where if you chop it in half, then spin it around on its center, it'll match up.

Monday:
Traditionally, an easy

crossword in a daily newspaper.

new wave:
A construction style where entries go beyond your typical dictionary and atlas (more pop culture, arts, business names, IT terms, very recent news, and clues apropos for Jeopardy and Trivial Pursuit).

open:
A dense concentration of white squares in a grid.

palindrome:
Something that is the same spelled forward and backward; occasionally used in a theme or clue.

partial:
A fill-in-the-blank where multiple words go in the blank.

patch:
A minor grid rework.

Ray Hamel:
Keeper of a great crossword reference list at *www.primate.wisc.edu/people/hamel/cp.html*

Saturday:
Traditionally, a tough-as-nails crossword in a daily newspaper; a Monday would be the easy puzzle.

Scrabble:
A word game where one can stack across and down words, forming a crude crossword puzzle. When I was a kid, I would jot down good open areas.

square:
A box in a grid.

stacking:
Putting long answers side by side.

Stephen Sondheim:
Lyricist credited for popularizing cryptic crosswords in the U.S.

sticky:
Adjective describing a square or section that's hard to break open.

tag:
A clue about an entry's form, such as ": 2 wds." or ": Fr." or ": var."

teardown:
A major grid rework.

theme:
Common concept that runs throughout a puzzle's long entries or even the whole puzzle; such a puzzle is said to be themed.

Tom Swifty:
Swapping the initial consonant sounds/blends on the starts of words; occasionally used in a theme.

Unch:
Short for "unchecked letter" (see cross-checking).

Will Shortz:
Current New York Times crossword editor (who added bylines and made the puzzles more new wave), host of NPR's "The Puzzler Presents," and someone who actually got a college degree in enigmatology (the study of puzzles).

Will Weng:
Former New York Times crossword editor.

word count:
The number of entries in a grid; some publishers specify word count limits.

word square:
A crossword variant (dating back at least to ancient Rome) where the downs and acrosses are the same. It may be well advised to attempt making these before tackling the construction of a whole puzzle. An example of a word square is as follows:

```
START
TABOO
ABOUT
ROUGE
TOTEM
```

Appendix B

Answers

1. Off to a Good Start

Skirt edges

H	E	M	S	■	P	L	A	N	■	Z	I	P
I	R	O	N	■	R	I	D	E	■	I	C	E
P	A	P	A	■	I	M	I	T	A	T	O	R
■	■	■	G	L	O	B	E	■	P	I	N	K
L	I	P	■	A	R	O	U	S	E	■	■	■
A	D	A	P	T	S	■	S	U	M	M	I	T
S	E	L	A	H	■	■	■	P	A	U	S	E
T	A	S	T	E	S	■	G	E	N	T	L	E
■	■	■	T	R	E	M	O	R	■	T	E	N
E	D	G	E	■	C	U	B	B	Y	■	■	■
D	O	O	R	B	E	L	L	■	O	P	E	N
I	N	N	■	I	D	L	E	■	L	U	G	E
T	E	E	■	N	E	S	T	■	K	N	O	W

Body covering

S	K	I	N	■	C	O	S	Y	■	T	A	P
U	N	D	O	■	O	N	T	O	■	A	G	E
P	E	O	N	■	N	E	I	G	H	B	O	R
S	E	L	E	C	T	■	L	A	Y	■	■	■
■	■	■	■	O	R	A	L	■	P	L	O	T
T	R	A	C	T	O	R	■	■	H	I	D	E
H	E	R	O	■	L	E	G	■	E	V	E	N
U	S	E	R	■	■	N	E	W	N	E	S	S
S	T	A	R	■	S	A	N	E	■	■	■	■
■	■	■	A	S	H	■	E	D	I	T	E	D
C	E	L	L	U	L	A	R	■	T	R	A	Y
R	Y	E	■	D	E	L	I	■	C	U	R	E
Y	E	T	■	S	P	E	C	■	H	E	L	D

Close loudly

S	L	A	M	■	R	O	W	■	R	E	E	F
N	O	T	E	■	A	P	E	■	U	R	G	E
A	G	O	N	I	Z	E	D	■	S	A	G	E
P	O	P	■	T	O	N	G	U	E	S	■	■
■	■	■	V	E	R	S	E	S	■	U	F	O
T	O	T	E	M	S	■	S	A	C	R	E	D
O	G	R	E	■	■	■	■	■	H	E	E	D
A	L	A	R	M	S	■	T	W	I	S	T	S
D	E	W	■	O	U	T	E	A	T	■	■	■
■	■	L	O	B	B	I	E	D	■	T	H	E
O	V	E	N	■	M	A	T	E	R	I	A	L
W	I	R	E	■	I	R	E	■	I	R	I	S
L	E	S	S	■	T	A	R	■	M	E	R	E

Combine, in math

A	D	D	■	S	P	A	R	■	S	W	A	B
W	E	E	■	T	A	L	E	■	L	A	C	E
E	N	D	■	O	W	L	S	■	A	I	R	S
■	■	U	P	O	N	■	T	A	B	L	E	T
F	O	C	A	L	■	H	O	T	■	■	■	■
A	X	I	S	■	B	A	R	E	B	A	C	K
R	E	N	T	■	E	V	E	■	A	C	H	E
E	N	G	E	N	D	E	R	■	C	H	I	P
■	■	■	■	U	R	N	■	P	O	I	N	T
T	O	M	A	T	O	■	G	E	N	E	■	■
A	K	I	N	■	O	M	E	N	■	V	O	W
P	A	N	T	■	M	O	R	N	■	E	W	E
E	Y	E	S	■	S	O	M	E	■	S	E	T

Prison cell walls

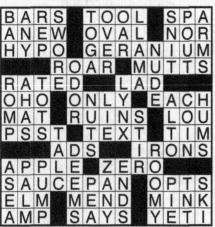

B	A	R	S	■	T	O	O	L	■	S	P	A
A	N	E	W	■	O	V	A	L	■	N	O	R
H	Y	P	O	■	G	E	R	A	N	I	U	M
■	■	■	R	O	A	R	■	M	U	T	T	S
R	A	T	E	D	■	■	L	A	D	■	■	■
O	H	O	■	O	N	L	Y	■	E	A	C	H
M	A	T	■	R	U	I	N	S	■	L	O	U
P	S	S	T	■	T	E	X	T	■	T	I	M
■	■	■	A	D	S	■	■	I	R	O	N	S
A	P	P	L	E	■	Z	E	R	O	■	■	■
S	A	U	C	E	P	A	N	■	O	P	T	S
E	L	M	■	M	E	N	D	■	M	I	N	K
A	M	P	■	S	A	Y	S	■	Y	E	T	I

Groundhog __

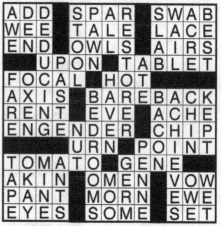

D	A	Y	■	S	O	B	S	■	S	A	S	H
O	R	E	■	H	A	L	O	■	E	C	H	O
E	M	A	N	A	T	E	D	■	V	E	E	P
S	Y	R	U	P	■	W	A	G	E	■	■	■
■	■	■	M	E	T	■	■	I	N	L	E	T
G	L	O	B	■	H	O	O	F	■	A	R	E
L	A	B	■	C	R	A	F	T	■	V	A	N
U	S	E	■	H	U	F	F	■	F	A	S	T
T	H	Y	M	E	■	■	S	I	R	■	■	■
■	■	■	O	W	E	D	■	M	E	R	G	E
W	A	I	T	■	A	E	R	A	T	I	N	G
A	X	L	E	■	S	M	O	G	■	G	A	G
D	E	L	L	■	T	O	T	E	■	S	T	Y

Ball

O	R	B		R	O	D	S		A	F	R	O
P	A	Y		A	W	A	Y		L	U	A	U
T	W	E	E	T	E	R	S		O	M	I	T
			A	S	S	E	T		H	E	N	S
A	L	P	S				E	R	A			
R	O	L	E	S		A	M	U	S	I	N	G
T	O	E		P	R	I	S	M		D	U	O
S	T	A	D	I	U	M		P	O	L	K	A
			I	T	S				P	E	E	L
S	L	U	G		T	R	A	D	E			
L	I	N	E		L	A	M	I	N	A	T	E
O	A	T	S		E	V	E	R		S	E	A
T	R	O	T		D	E	N	T		P	A	T

Family group

C	L	A	N		A	D	D	S		M	O	P
O	I	L	Y		H	E	R	E		A	L	E
R	O	S	E		S	P	A	N		N	E	W
K	N	O	T	S		A	I	D	E	D		
			S	W	O	R	N		D	A	W	N
R	I	P		A	N	T		A	G	R	E	E
A	S	H	O	R	E		T	H	E	I	R	S
G	L	E	A	M		D	I	E		N	E	T
S	E	A	T		S	O	N	A	R			
		S	H	O	T	S		D	I	T	T	O
A	H	A		O	R	A	L		G	R	I	D
W	O	N		P	A	G	E		H	I	D	E
L	E	T		S	P	E	D		T	O	Y	S

Not young

O	L	D		E	V	I	L		B	I	D	S
A	Y	E		L	O	N	E		A	R	E	A
K	E	G		S	I	N	G		L	O	A	F
		R	E	E	L			G	E	N	R	E
S	L	A	M		A	C	H	Y				
T	I	D	E			R	U	M	M	A	G	E
E	V	E	N		F	E	E		A	Q	U	A
M	E	D	D	L	E	D			P	U	T	T
				I	D	O	L		L	E	S	S
C	L	U	M	P			U	S	E	D		
L	A	N	E		T	A	C	T		U	G	H
A	I	D	S		O	G	R	E		C	O	O
P	R	O	S		P	E	E	P		T	O	W

Thanks a __!

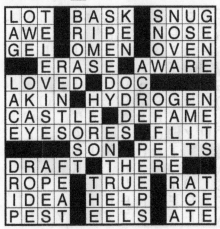

L	O	T		B	A	S	K		S	N	U	G
A	W	E		R	I	P	E		N	O	S	E
G	E	L		O	M	E	N		O	V	E	N
		E	R	A	S	E		A	W	A	R	E
L	O	V	E	D		D	O	C				
A	K	I	N		H	Y	D	R	O	G	E	N
C	A	S	T	L	E		D	E	F	A	M	E
E	Y	E	S	O	R	E	S		F	L	I	T
				S	O	N		P	E	L	T	S
D	R	A	F	T		T	H	E	R	E		
R	O	P	E		T	R	U	E		R	A	T
I	D	E	A		H	E	L	P		I	C	E
P	E	S	T		E	E	L	S		A	T	E

Baby cow

C	A	L	F		A	N	E	W		A	R	T
O	V	A	L		D	A	M	E		L	O	W
D	A	T	A		I	M	B	E	C	I	L	E
	R	E	P		E	E	L		A	B	L	E
A	I	R		N	U	D	E		L	I	S	T
S	C	A	L	E	S		M	U	M			
H	E	L	L	O				P	E	A	C	H
			A	N	D		M	O	D	U	L	E
P	R	I	M		I	C	O	N		R	I	M
A	U	R	A		S	A	T		D	O	E	
C	R	O	S	S	C	U	T		U	R	N	S
T	A	N		P	O	L	O		M	A	T	E
S	L	Y		A	S	K	S		P	S	S	T

Change to another house

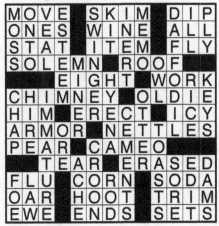

M	O	V	E		S	K	I	M		D	I	P
O	N	E	S		W	I	N	E		A	L	L
S	T	A	T		I	T	E	M		F	L	Y
S	O	L	E	M	N		R	O	O	F		
			E	I	G	H	T		W	O	R	K
C	H	I	M	N	E	Y		O	L	D	I	E
H	I	M		E	R	E	C	T		I	C	Y
A	R	M	O	R		N	E	T	T	L	E	S
P	E	A	R		C	A	M	E	O			
		T	E	A	R		E	R	A	S	E	D
F	L	U		C	O	R	N		S	O	D	A
O	A	R		H	O	O	T		T	R	I	M
E	W	E		E	N	D	S		S	E	T	S

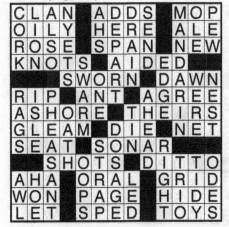

Poison __

I	V	Y	■	S	N	I	P	■	S	C	A	R
S	E	E	■	T	O	N	E	■	T	A	X	I
N	E	T	W	O	R	K	S	■	O	W	E	D
T	R	I	A	L	■	Y	O	Y	O	■	■	■
■	■	■	S	E	W	■	■	A	D	D	E	D
B	L	A	H	■	O	V	E	R	■	A	C	E
O	U	R	■	B	R	E	A	D	■	S	H	E
S	A	M	■	L	E	T	S	■	S	H	O	P
S	U	S	H	I	■	■	Y	A	K	■	■	■
■	■	■	O	P	T	S	■	P	I	N	C	H
B	E	A	R	■	H	A	B	A	N	E	R	O
I	R	I	S	■	E	V	E	R	■	W	E	B
G	A	M	E	■	M	E	E	T	■	T	W	O

Eye impolitely

O	G	L	E	■	E	T	C	H	■	F	A	R
F	A	I	L	■	C	O	L	A	■	L	I	E
F	L	E	D	■	L	O	O	T	■	A	D	D
S	A	N	E	■	I	N	T	E	N	T	■	■
■	■	■	S	A	P	■	■	■	O	I	L	S
E	G	O	T	I	S	T	■	S	T	R	I	P
Y	O	U	■	R	E	A	C	H	■	O	N	E
E	N	T	R	Y	■	P	R	E	E	N	E	D
S	E	M	I	■	■	■	O	D	D	■	■	■
■	■	O	P	E	R	A	S	■	I	T	C	H
L	I	D	■	G	U	M	S	■	T	I	L	E
A	R	E	■	G	L	E	E	■	O	R	A	L
B	E	D	■	Y	E	N	S	■	R	E	N	D

James __ Jones

E	A	R	L	■	S	A	W	■	G	R	I	N
G	L	U	E	■	O	L	E	■	R	I	S	E
G	E	N	T	■	F	A	T	■	I	D	L	E
■	■	■	T	S	A	R	S	■	F	E	E	D
G	R	O	U	P	■	M	U	T	T	■	■	■
O	U	N	C	E	■	S	I	R	■	S	O	D
A	S	L	E	E	P	■	T	A	T	T	O	O
T	H	Y	■	C	U	B	■	G	A	U	Z	E
■	■	■	T	H	R	U	■	I	N	N	E	R
A	F	R	O	■	S	L	I	C	K	■	■	■
S	L	O	T	■	E	L	F	■	A	L	T	O
E	A	S	E	■	R	E	F	■	R	A	I	L
A	G	E	D	■	S	T	Y	■	D	Y	E	D

2. Start-up

Gain in return for labor

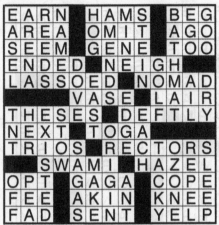

E	A	R	N	■	H	A	M	S	■	B	E	G
A	R	E	A	■	O	M	I	T	■	A	G	O
S	E	E	M	■	G	E	N	E	■	T	O	O
E	N	D	E	D	■	N	E	I	G	H	■	■
L	A	S	S	O	E	D	■	N	O	M	A	D
■	■	■	■	V	A	S	E	■	L	A	I	R
T	H	E	S	E	S	■	D	E	F	T	L	Y
N	E	X	T	■	T	O	G	A	■	■	■	■
T	R	I	O	S	■	R	E	C	T	O	R	S
■	■	S	W	A	M	I	■	H	A	Z	E	L
O	P	T	■	G	A	G	A	■	C	O	P	E
F	E	E	■	A	K	I	N	■	K	N	E	E
F	A	D	■	S	E	N	T	■	Y	E	L	P

Watermelon shape

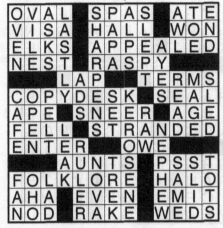

O	V	A	L	■	S	P	A	S	■	A	T	E
V	I	S	A	■	H	A	L	L	■	W	O	N
E	L	K	S	■	A	P	P	E	A	L	E	D
N	E	S	T	■	R	A	S	P	Y	■	■	■
■	■	■	L	A	P	■	■	T	E	R	M	S
C	O	P	Y	D	E	S	K	■	S	E	A	L
A	P	E	■	S	N	E	E	R	■	A	G	E
F	E	L	L	■	S	T	R	A	N	D	E	D
E	N	T	E	R	■	■	O	W	E	■	■	■
■	■	■	A	U	N	T	S	■	P	S	S	T
F	O	L	K	L	O	R	E	■	H	A	L	O
A	H	A	■	E	V	E	N	■	E	M	I	T
N	O	D	■	R	A	K	E	■	W	E	D	S

Lasso

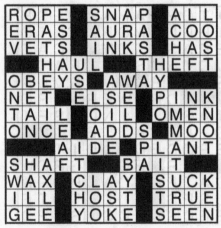

R	O	P	E	■	S	N	A	P	■	A	L	L
E	R	A	S	■	A	U	R	A	■	C	O	O
V	E	T	S	■	I	N	K	S	■	H	A	S
■	■	H	A	U	L	■	■	T	H	E	F	T
O	B	E	Y	S	■	A	W	A	Y	■	■	■
N	E	T	■	E	L	S	E	■	P	I	N	K
T	A	I	L	■	O	I	L	■	O	M	E	N
O	N	C	E	■	A	D	D	S	■	M	O	O
■	■	■	A	I	D	E	■	P	L	A	N	T
S	H	A	F	T	■	■	B	A	I	T	■	■
W	A	X	■	C	L	A	Y	■	S	U	C	K
I	L	L	■	H	O	S	T	■	T	R	U	E
G	E	E	■	Y	O	K	E	■	S	E	E	N

Hammered item

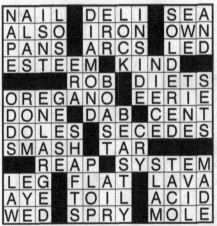

N	A	I	L	■	D	E	L	I	■	S	E	A
A	L	S	O	■	I	R	O	N	■	O	W	N
P	A	N	S	■	A	R	C	S	■	L	E	D
E	S	T	E	E	M	■	K	I	N	D	■	■
■	■	■	■	R	O	B	■	D	I	E	T	S
O	R	E	G	A	N	O	■	E	E	R	I	E
D	O	N	E	■	D	A	B	■	C	E	N	T
D	O	L	E	S	■	S	E	C	E	D	E	S
S	M	A	S	H	■	T	A	R	■	■	■	■
■	■	R	E	A	P	■	S	Y	S	T	E	M
L	E	G	■	F	L	A	T	■	L	A	V	A
A	Y	E	■	T	O	I	L	■	A	C	I	D
W	E	D	■	S	P	R	Y	■	M	O	L	E

__ Wednesday

A	S	H	■	S	C	A	R	■	A	C	R	E
W	O	O	■	T	R	I	O	■	C	H	U	G
E	L	M	■	R	O	D	S	■	H	A	N	G
■	■	E	P	I	C	■	E	N	E	R	G	Y
S	H	L	E	P	■	A	M	I	D	■	■	■
P	E	A	R	■	P	L	A	N	■	S	H	E
U	R	N	■	C	H	O	R	E	■	P	A	N
R	E	D	■	Z	A	N	Y	■	Y	A	R	D
■	■	■	M	A	R	E	■	L	O	R	D	S
A	F	F	I	R	M	■	T	O	U	R	■	■
C	O	R	N	■	A	H	O	Y	■	O	D	D
T	R	E	E	■	C	O	L	A	■	W	O	E
S	E	E	R	■	Y	E	L	L	■	S	E	W

Yawn-inducer

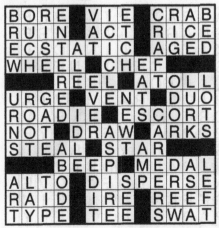

B	O	R	E	■	V	I	E	■	C	R	A	B
R	U	I	N	■	A	C	T	■	R	I	C	E
E	C	S	T	A	T	I	C	■	A	G	E	D
W	H	E	E	L	■	C	H	E	F	■	■	■
■	■	■	R	E	E	L	■	A	T	O	L	L
U	R	G	E	■	V	E	N	T	■	D	U	O
R	O	A	D	I	E	■	E	S	C	O	R	T
N	O	T	■	D	R	A	W	■	A	R	K	S
S	T	E	A	L	■	S	T	A	R	■	■	■
■	■	■	B	E	E	P	■	M	E	D	A	L
A	L	T	O	■	D	I	S	P	E	R	S	E
R	A	I	D	■	I	R	E	■	R	E	E	F
T	Y	P	E	■	T	E	E	■	S	W	A	T

Line-__ veto

I	T	E	M		R	A	M	P		E	L	K
N	O	P	E		A	R	E	A		G	U	N
K	N	I	T		S	E	N	T		O	L	E
		S	A	S	H			I	S	S	U	E
T	R	O	L	L		S	O	O	N			
H	A	D		Y	A	W	N		O	A	T	S
I	R	I	S		F	O	E		W	I	R	E
N	E	C	K		R	O	S	E		R	O	W
			I	C	O	N		V	E	S	T	S
G	R	A	P	E			H	E	L	P		
R	A	N		A	R	T	Y		V	A	T	S
I	C	E		S	O	U	P		E	C	H	O
P	E	W		E	D	G	E		S	E	E	D

Bite __ more than you can chew

O	F	F		H	A	R	E		C	R	A	W
L	I	E		O	X	E	N		H	O	B	O
D	R	E	S	S	I	N	G		I	S	L	E
			P	E	S	T	O		E	Y	E	S
G	A	G	A				R	E	F			
L	I	A	R	S		A	G	E		W	O	W
A	R	M		L	A	P	E	L		H	U	H
D	Y	E		O	U	T		S	P	O	R	E
			I	T	S				E	A	S	Y
S	W	A	N		T	A	B	L	E			
T	A	C	T		E	Q	U	A	L	L	E	D
O	V	E	R		R	U	N	S		O	A	R
P	E	S	O		E	A	S	T		T	R	Y

Give the __-over

O	N	C	E		U	N	T	O		C	A	P
P	E	A	L		P	E	O	N		O	U	R
T	A	G	S		D	I	K	E		A	T	E
S	T	E	E	R	A	G	E		S	L	O	P
				E	T	H	N	I	C			
W	O	B	B	L	E		S	T	O	M	P	S
A	W	A	R	E				C	R	O	A	K
S	E	D	A	N	S		T	H	E	O	R	Y
			S	T	O	G	I	E				
P	O	S	H		C	E	N	S	O	R	E	D
A	P	E		P	I	N	G		M	O	V	E
P	E	A		E	A	R	L		E	V	E	N
A	N	T		G	L	E	E		N	E	S	T

Mosquito bite symptom

I	T	C	H		A	H	A		M	E	S	H
T	H	R	U		N	O	R		I	N	T	O
E	R	A	S		T	O	M		S	C	A	T
M	O	T	H		S	P	A		E	A	T	
S	W	E	E	P			M	U	R	M	U	R
			D	R	A	W	E	R		P	R	O
T	A	G		I	C	I	N	G		S	E	T
O	I	L		M	A	T	T	E	R			
E	R	O	D	E	D			D	I	T	T	O
	B	A	R		E	G	O		G	R	O	W
D	A	T	E		M	O	W		H	O	R	N
U	S	E	S		I	L	L		T	O	T	E
B	E	D	S		A	D	S		S	P	E	D

You have a certain __ about you

A	U	R	A		O	P	T		T	R	E	E
S	N	A	G		R	A	W		H	E	R	E
K	I	T	E		C	L	I	N	I	C	A	L
S	T	E	N	C	H		T	O	N	E		
			T	O	A	D		S	K	I	L	L
H	I	D		T	R	A	S	H		V	I	A
O	R	E			D	I	P			E	L	M
P	O	P		A	S	S	E	T		R	Y	E
S	N	A	F	U		Y	E	A	R			
		R	A	N	T		D	R	A	P	E	D
A	T	T	I	T	U	D	E		D	O	V	E
S	E	E	R		B	U	R		A	K	I	N
P	A	D	S		A	H	S		R	E	L	Y

Diner's food catalog

M	E	N	U		S	U	P	S		F	O	R
O	V	E	N		E	P	I	C		B	A	A
R	E	A	D		E	T	E	R	N	I	T	Y
E	R	R	E	D		A	S	E	A			
			R	A	C	K		W	I	L	T	S
A	R	F		D	U	E	T		V	E	I	L
C	E	L	L	A	R		A	G	E	N	D	A
I	D	E	A		T	O	M	E		D	E	W
D	O	E	R	S		P	E	E	P			
			G	A	Z	E		K	E	B	A	B
D	A	T	E	L	I	N	E		A	L	S	O
O	W	N		S	T	E	W		R	U	I	N
G	E	T		A	I	D	E		L	E	A	K

Laser __

B	E	A	M		P	R	O	F		B	A	G
U	R	G	E		H	E	R	O		A	L	L
G	O	A	L		O	V	A	L		L	O	O
	S	I	T		N	E	C	K		S	O	B
T	I	N		W	E	L	L		C	A	F	E
H	O	S	T	E	D		E	Y	E			
E	N	T	E	R				E	L	B	O	W
			S	E	W		S	A	L	A	M	I
B	L	O	T		E	A	T	S		B	E	G
Y	O	U		P	A	L	E		S	O	L	
L	O	G		U	S	E	R		H	O	E	D
A	S	H		M	E	R	E		O	N	T	O
W	E	T		A	L	T	O		P	S	S	T

Money

C	A	S	H		R	A	S	H		U	S	A
A	C	H	E		A	R	E	A		N	A	G
R	E	E	L		T	E	N	D		D	I	E
			P	O	I	N	T		F	O	L	D
H	E	R		C	O	A	R	S	E			
A	D	O	P	T	S		Y	E	L	L	O	W
T	I	A	R	A				R	O	U	G	E
S	T	R	I	V	E		S	I	N	G	L	E
			D	E	M	O	T	E		E	E	K
W	I	N	E		P	U	R	S	E			
I	C	E		M	I	N	E		A	N	E	W
D	O	E		A	R	C	S		S	A	L	E
E	N	D		T	E	E	S		T	Y	K	E

Enjoyed the buffet

A	T	E		S	H	U	T		S	N	O	B
G	E	L		T	U	N	E		H	O	P	E
E	N	F	E	E	B	L	E		E	V	E	N
			R	I	S	E		P	L	A	N	T
S	P	U	R	N		S	O	I	L			
T	A	P			T	S	U	N	A	M	I	S
E	N	O	U	G	H		R	E	C	E	D	E
M	E	N	T	I	O	N	S			O	L	E
			T	R	U	E		M	O	W	E	D
L	I	B	E	L		C	R	O	W			
O	D	O	R		S	T	I	P	E	N	D	S
T	O	R	E		E	A	S	E		O	U	T
S	L	E	D		A	R	K	S		T	O	Y

3. Head Start

Joke

G	A	G		S	T	A	T		P	E	S	T
O	H	O		P	O	L	O		A	C	H	Y
B	A	T	H	R	O	O	M		S	H	I	P
			O	A	T	H		A	T	O	N	E
S	T	O	R	Y		A	I	R	Y			
W	I	G	S		I	S	N	T		A	Y	E
A	R	R	E	S	T		C	Y	M	B	A	L
B	E	E		M	E	S	H		E	L	K	S
			F	U	M	E		G	E	E	S	E
S	H	R	U	G		S	P	O	T			
T	O	E	S		P	A	R	A	S	O	L	S
U	S	E	S		E	M	I	T		A	I	L
D	E	F	Y		P	E	G	S		K	E	Y

Fill to the __

B	R	I	M		G	A	P		C	H	I	T
R	A	R	E		O	R	E		A	U	T	O
A	T	O	M		A	M	P		N	E	S	T
G	E	N	E		T	E	P	E	E			
			N	E	E	D	E	D		A	R	C
T	A	T	T	L	E		R	I	T	U	A	L
A	C	H	O	O				B	O	N	G	O
C	R	I	S	P	Y		F	L	U	T	E	D
K	E	N		E	A	S	I	E	R			
			A	D	M	I	T		I	T	C	H
G	R	E	W		M	E	T		S	H	O	E
A	U	R	A		E	V	E		T	E	A	M
S	T	A	Y		R	E	D		S	E	T	S

Groaner

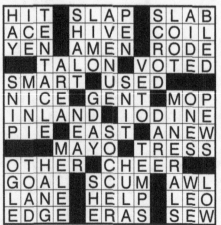

P	U	N		C	A	P	S		O	P	T	S
I	R	E		O	M	E	N		D	R	O	P
T	N	T		L	O	G	O		D	A	M	E
		W	E	A	N		O	B	E	Y	E	D
S	C	O	W		G	A	Z	E	S			
C	O	R	E	D		H	E	A	T	E	R	S
A	S	K		R	O	O	S	T		L	A	P
M	Y	S	T	E	R	Y		S	A	L	S	A
			W	A	I	S	T		R	I	P	S
S	T	R	I	D	E		R	A	M	P		
I	R	I	S		N	E	A	T		S	A	T
T	I	N	T		T	A	C	O		E	G	O
E	G	G	Y		S	T	E	P		S	O	N

James __ Carter

E	A	R	L		S	I	F	T		S	K	Y
A	S	I	A		K	N	E	E		T	I	E
R	E	N	T		I	S	L	E		A	N	T
N	A	K	E	D		U	T	T	E	R		
			R	O	L	L		H	A	S	T	Y
S	P	A		D	A	T	E		S	H	O	O
C	U	S	T	O	M		T	R	Y	I	N	G
A	R	C	H		P	A	C	E		P	E	A
T	R	E	E	S		S	H	E	D			
		N	Y	E	T	S		D	E	M	O	N
A	D	D		C	R	U	D		C	O	V	E
L	Y	E		T	I	M	E		O	V	E	R
L	E	D		S	P	E	W		R	E	N	D

__ the deck!

H	I	T		S	L	A	P		S	L	A	B
A	C	E		H	I	V	E		C	O	I	L
Y	E	N		A	M	E	N		R	O	D	E
		T	A	L	O	N		V	O	T	E	D
S	M	A	R	T		U	S	E	D			
N	I	C	E		G	E	N	T		M	O	P
I	N	L	A	N	D		I	O	D	I	N	E
P	I	E		E	A	S	T		A	N	E	W
			M	A	Y	O		T	R	E	S	S
O	T	H	E	R		C	H	E	E	R		
G	O	A	L		S	C	U	M		A	W	L
L	A	N	E		H	E	L	P		L	E	O
E	D	G	E		E	R	A	S		S	E	W

Tarot suit

C	U	P	S		Y	A	P		A	D	D	S
A	F	R	O		E	R	R		S	E	E	P
T	O	O	L		S	E	A		S	E	M	I
			E	S	S	A	Y		U	P	O	N
A	H	S		P	E	S	E	T	A			
C	E	A	S	E	S		D	I	G	E	S	T
E	A	G	L	E				R	E	V	U	E
S	T	E	E	D	S		L	A	S	E	R	S
			E	Y	E	L	I	D		N	E	T
S	L	O	P		C	A	V	E	D			
H	O	P	E		R	Y	E		U	N	T	O
U	S	E	R		E	E	L		C	O	O	L
T	E	N	S		T	R	Y		T	R	O	D

Spat

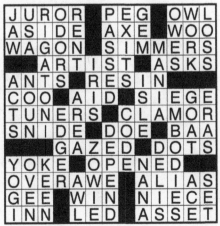

T	I	F	F		E	Y	E		I	D	O	L
O	D	O	R		S	O	L		N	I	N	E
W	E	R	E		C	U	B		F	E	E	T
N	A	M	E		A	R	O	M	A			
			Z	I	P		W	I	N	C	E	S
B	A	S	E	M	E	N		S	T	O	V	E
A	H	A		P	E	A	C	E		P	E	W
T	E	M	P	O		B	O	R	D	E	R	S
S	M	E	A	R	S		A	Y	E			
			S	T	E	P	S		F	R	O	G
M	I	T	T		L	I	T		A	I	R	Y
A	C	H	E		A	L	E		C	L	A	M
D	Y	E	D		H	E	R		E	E	L	S

__ and far between

F	E	W		A	R	C		F	A	S	T	S
E	A	R		T	E	A		A	C	H	O	O
U	S	E	L	E	S	S		C	R	O	W	D
D	E	N	Y		C	E	N	T	E	R		
			R	E	U	S	E			T	E	E
O	F	F	I	C	E		W	I	D	E	L	Y
G	U	L	C	H				R	I	N	S	E
R	E	A	S	O	N		H	O	R	S	E	S
E	L	M			A	T	O	N	E			
		I	M	A	G	E	S		C	O	T	S
M	O	N	E	Y		S	T	A	T	U	R	E
A	L	G	A	E		T	E	N		C	U	E
P	E	O	N	S		S	L	Y		H	E	N

Couples

D	U	O	S		A	D	S		S	W	A	P
I	S	N	T		H	U	H		T	A	L	E
P	E	S	O		O	H	O		R	I	S	E
		C	I	T	Y		E	D	I	T	O	R
L	U	R	C	H		S	L	I	P			
O	R	E		E	A	T	E	N		C	A	W
A	G	E		A	R	O	S	E		A	W	E
D	E	N		T	R	U	S	T		L	A	B
			B	E	A	T		T	R	A	Y	S
R	E	T	U	R	N		S	E	E	M		
O	V	A	L		G	I	N		S	A	S	H
P	I	L	L		E	R	A		T	R	I	O
E	L	K	S		R	E	P		S	I	T	E

"Planet of the __"

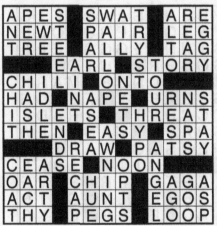

A	P	E	S		S	W	A	T		A	R	E
N	E	W	T		P	A	I	R		L	E	G
T	R	E	E		A	L	L	Y		T	A	G
			E	A	R	L		S	T	O	R	Y
C	H	I	L	I		O	N	T	O			
H	A	D		N	A	P	E		U	R	N	S
I	S	L	E	T	S		T	H	R	E	A	T
T	H	E	N		E	A	S	Y		S	P	A
			D	R	A	W		P	A	T	S	Y
C	E	A	S	E		N	O	O	N			
O	A	R		C	H	I	P		G	A	G	A
A	C	T		A	U	N	T		E	G	O	S
T	H	Y		P	E	G	S		L	O	O	P

1 of 12 in court

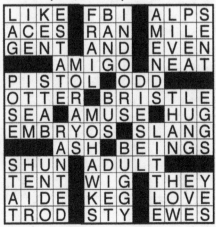

J	U	R	O	R		P	E	G		O	W	L
A	S	I	D	E		A	X	E		W	O	O
W	A	G	O	N		S	I	M	M	E	R	S
		A	R	T	I	S	T		A	S	K	S
A	N	T	S		R	E	S	I	N			
C	O	O		A	I	D		S	I	E	G	E
T	U	N	E	R	S		C	L	A	M	O	R
S	N	I	D	E		D	O	E		B	A	A
			G	A	Z	E	D		D	O	T	S
Y	O	K	E		O	P	E	N	E	D		
O	V	E	R	A	W	E		A	L	I	A	S
G	E	E		W	I	N		N	I	E	C	E
I	N	N		L	E	D		A	S	S	E	T

__ two peas in a pod

L	I	K	E		F	B	I		A	L	P	S
A	C	E	S		R	A	N		M	I	L	E
G	E	N	T		A	N	D		E	V	E	N
			A	M	I	G	O		N	E	A	T
P	I	S	T	O	L		O	D	D			
O	T	T	E	R		B	R	I	S	T	L	E
S	E	A		A	M	U	S	E		H	U	G
E	M	B	R	Y	O	S		S	L	A	N	G
			A	S	H		B	E	I	N	G	S
S	H	U	N		A	D	U	L	T			
T	E	N	T		W	I	G		T	H	E	Y
A	I	D	E		K	E	G		L	O	V	E
T	R	O	D		S	T	Y		E	W	E	S

Cereal type

O	A	T		S	A	P	S		S	H	O	P
W	H	O		T	H	O	U		N	A	G	S
L	E	T		O	O	P	S		A	I	L	S
S	M	E	L	L	Y		P	I	G	L	E	T
			L	E	S	S	E	N				
A	R	E	A	S		I	C	K	I	E	S	T
H	E	L	M		A	R	T		D	E	E	R
A	F	F	A	B	L	E		A	L	L	E	Y
				I	G	N	I	T	E			
S	T	R	O	B	E		M	O	R	A	L	E
L	I	O	N		B	R	A	N		N	O	D
I	D	O	L		R	A	G	E		E	G	G
D	E	F	Y		A	G	E	D		W	O	E

I hate to __ and run . . .

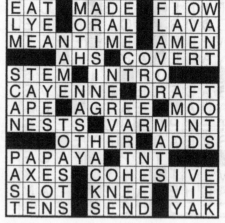

E	A	T		M	A	D	E		F	L	O	W
L	Y	E		O	R	A	L		L	A	V	A
M	E	A	N	T	I	M	E		A	M	E	N
			A	H	S		C	O	V	E	R	T
S	T	E	M		I	N	T	R	O			
C	A	Y	E	N	N	E		D	R	A	F	T
A	P	E		A	G	R	E	E		M	O	O
N	E	S	T	S		V	A	R	M	I	N	T
			O	T	H	E	R		A	D	D	S
P	A	P	A	Y	A		T	N	T			
A	X	E	S		C	O	H	E	S	I	V	E
S	L	O	T		K	N	E	E		V	I	E
T	E	N	S		S	E	N	D		Y	A	K

Quiet, please!

H	U	S	H		S	L	A	P		F	I	G
I	N	T	O		H	E	R	O		O	L	E
S	T	U	N		E	G	G	S	H	E	L	L
S	O	B	E	R		A	U	T	O			
			D	U	N	C	E		M	A	R	K
G	A	S		B	O	Y		F	E	L	O	N
O	C	C	U	L	T		T	I	R	A	D	E
S	H	A	P	E		M	A	N		S	E	W
H	E	R	S		C	O	R	A	L			
			E	M	I	T		L	A	B	E	L
L	E	F	T	O	V	E	R		R	A	V	E
O	R	E		L	I	L	Y		G	R	I	N
W	A	D		E	L	S	E		E	E	L	S

4. Jump Start

Whitewater __

RAFT SOB BEAT
ASIA TWO OGRE
SERGEANT DOME
HAM PRETTY
GIRDLE DAB
IDIOCY ENTICE
FARE WARN
FROSTY TOILED
YEN OUTEAT
TYPIST SKI
ALSO PATHETIC
BEAM IRE YANK
COME EAR EGGY

Prod

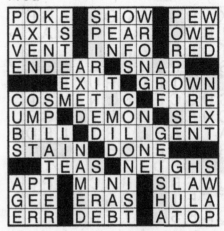

POKE SHOW PEW
AXIS PEAR OWE
VENT INFO RED
ENDEAR SNAP
EXIT GROWN
COSMETIC FIRE
UMP DEMON SEX
BILL DILIGENT
STAIN DONE
TEAS NEIGHS
APT MINI SLAW
GEE ERAS HULA
ERR DEBT ATOP

"Well, __ me down!"

BLOW AMP AHAS
LIVE BAA RULE
OMEN RICOCHET
TEND INERT
END BITES
BANDAGES COVE
ARE PELTS NEW
SEAT SKIPPERS
HARES PAL
EAGLE AURA
PLANTAIN SPUR
RATS LED MOST
OBEY ADS ANTS

Place to play darts

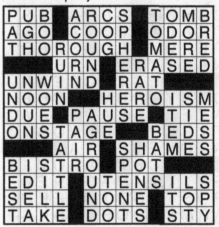

PUB ARCS TOMB
AGO COOP ODOR
THOROUGH MERE
URN ERASED
UNWIND RAT
NOON HEROISM
DUE PAUSE TIE
ONSTAGE BEDS
AIR SHAMES
BISTRO POT
EDIT UTENSILS
SELL NONE TOP
TAKE DOTS STY

Wise bird

OWL AFRO BOGS
VIE CROP ROOK
ART TILE AHOY
LESS DERBY
QUASAR HUM
OCCUPY SUTURE
PLAID TINGE
TURBAN MARKET
SEE TAMALE
BEGUN DISK
LAKE GDAY THE
OPEN EDGE COP
GENT DYES HOT

"Can we? Can we? Huh?" person

PEST SPRY ASH
INTO THEE COO
EVEN EAST HIS
RYE CASE PELT
ROULETTE
AWARDS SORTED
RIGID SURGE
KNEELS ASSIGN
NEWSREEL
PAST OATS LID
ACE YOGI WIDE
PIN APES HOOF
ADD PSST ONLY

Billy the __

K	I	D		H	E	R	O		P	A	G	E
I	R	E		E	M	I	T		A	W	A	Y
T	O	L	E	R	A	N	T		E	L	S	E
S	N	I	P		I	D	E	A	L			
			I	L	L		R	U	L	E	R	S
S	U	C	C	E	E	D		N	A	V	A	L
O	N	E		A	D	O	P	T		I	C	E
A	T	L	A	S		T	R	I	F	L	E	D
R	O	L	L	E	R		E	E	L			
			E	D	I	T	S		A	R	T	Y
U	S	E	R		F	R	A	C	T	U	R	E
F	E	E	T		T	O	G	A		N	E	T
O	A	K	S		S	T	E	W		S	K	I

Busy insect

B	E	E		A	R	M	S		D	E	B	T
Y	A	M		L	E	A	N		O	G	R	E
E	R	A		T	A	L	E		M	O	A	N
		N	O	O	D	L	E		I	S	N	T
L	I	A	R				R	U	N			
A	C	T	E	D		R	E	S	O	R	T	S
T	O	E		E	R	O	D	E		E	A	T
E	N	D	O	W	E	D		D	O	G	M	A
			D	Y	E				L	I	S	T
S	L	I	D		L	A	S	H	E	S		
T	U	N	E		E	C	H	O		T	A	P
A	R	K	S		C	H	I	P		E	W	E
R	E	S	T		T	Y	P	E		R	E	P

Soak up the sun

B	A	S	K		A	S	P		B	E	T	S
O	R	A	L		D	U	O		A	S	E	A
R	E	P	U	L	S	E	D		S	P	E	D
N	A	S	T	Y			S	T	I	R		
			Z	E	S	T		O	C	E	A	N
D	E	N	Y		P	U	M	A		S	H	E
A	X	E		S	A	L	A	D		S	A	W
T	I	P		P	R	I	G		M	O	S	T
A	T	O	N	E		P	I	T	A			
		T	U	C	K			A	R	O	M	A
S	N	I	T		I	M	A	G	I	N	E	D
P	O	S	T		N	O	T		N	E	E	D
A	R	M	Y		D	O	E		A	S	K	S

Boxing punch

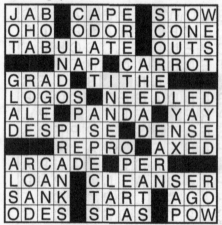

J	A	B		C	A	P	E		S	T	O	W
O	H	O		O	D	O	R		C	O	N	E
T	A	B	U	L	A	T	E		O	U	T	S
			N	A	P		C	A	R	R	O	T
G	R	A	D		T	I	T	H	E			
L	O	G	O	S		N	E	E	D	L	E	D
A	L	E		P	A	N	D	A		Y	A	Y
D	E	S	P	I	S	E		D	E	N	S	E
			R	E	P	R	O		A	X	E	D
A	R	C	A	D	E		P	E	R			
L	O	A	N		C	L	E	A	N	S	E	R
S	A	N	K		T	A	R	T		A	G	O
O	D	E	S		S	P	A	S		P	O	W

Slippery

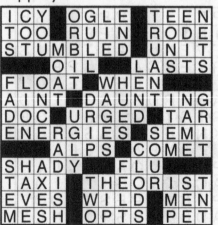

I	C	Y		O	G	L	E		T	E	E	N
T	O	O		R	U	I	N		R	O	D	E
S	T	U	M	B	L	E	D		U	N	I	T
			O	I	L			L	A	S	T	S
F	L	O	A	T		W	H	E	N			
A	I	N	T		D	A	U	N	T	I	N	G
D	O	C		U	R	G	E	D		T	A	R
E	N	E	R	G	I	E	S		S	E	M	I
			A	L	P	S		C	O	M	E	T
S	H	A	D	Y			F	L	U			
T	A	X	I		T	H	E	O	R	I	S	T
E	V	E	S		W	I	L	D		M	E	N
M	E	S	H		O	P	T	S		P	E	T

"I don't think so!"

N	O	P	E		T	W	A	S		O	F	F
O	V	A	L		R	I	P	E		W	E	E
S	E	N	D		U	N	R	E	I	N	E	D
E	N	T	E	R	S		O	D	D			
			S	A	T	I	N		E	A	S	T
P	A	R	T	I	E	D		S	A	U	C	Y
U	S	E		N	E	I	G	H		R	A	P
P	I	E	T	Y		O	R	E	G	A	N	O
S	A	F	E		S	T	O	L	E			
			A	I	M		S	L	I	G	H	T
E	L	A	S	T	I	C	S		S	L	U	R
R	A	G		C	L	U	E		H	O	L	E
R	Y	E		H	E	E	D		A	B	L	E

Swan __ (ballet)

L	A	K	E		S	L	O	B		G	E	T
O	P	E	N		C	I	A	O		E	V	E
T	E	N	D		E	N	T	W	I	N	E	S
			S	O	N	G			G	E	N	T
A	P	T		D	E	E	P	E	N			
C	L	O	U	D		R	E	S	I	S	T	S
T	O	N	S	I	L		A	T	T	I	R	E
S	W	E	A	T	E	R		E	E	R	I	E
			B	Y	G	O	N	E		S	O	N
E	V	I	L			D	O	M	E			
R	E	C	E	I	V	E	S		A	W	A	Y
A	S	K		L	I	N	E		C	O	R	E
S	T	Y		L	E	T	S		H	O	E	S

Deli sandwich

H	E	R	O		S	L	A	P		T	U	B
I	C	O	N		L	A	I	R		E	R	A
S	H	O	W		A	R	R	O	G	A	N	T
S	O	F	A		N	I	P	P	Y			
			R	E	G	A	L		M	A	L	L
S	T	U	D	Y		T	A	P		C	O	O
K	I	S	S	E	R		Y	A	C	H	T	S
I	R	E		S	O	W		T	R	Y	S	T
T	E	R	M		M	A	C	H	O			
			E	L	A	T	E		P	U	L	P
F	A	S	T	E	N	E	D		P	R	O	S
I	C	E		A	C	R	E		E	G	O	S
B	E	T		K	E	Y	S		D	E	N	T

__ Isaac Newton

S	I	R		A	M	I	D		D	A	S	H
U	S	A		M	A	N	E		A	R	T	Y
E	L	K		P	L	E	A		R	E	A	P
D	E	E	R		I	R	R	I	T	A	T	E
			A	R	C	T	I	C				
S	U	B	D	U	E		E	I	G	H	T	S
A	G	A	I	N				C	R	O	O	K
T	H	R	O	N	G		S	L	O	P	P	Y
				E	L	A	T	E	S			
P	A	S	T	R	A	M	I		S	O	D	A
O	K	A	Y		R	I	N	D		A	I	R
R	I	N	K		E	G	G	Y		R	A	M
K	N	E	E		D	O	S	E		S	L	Y

5. Flying Start

Rowing blade

O	A	R		B	L	O	B		O	G	R	E
A	H	A		L	A	N	E		C	L	A	W
T	O	M		A	G	E	D		C	O	N	E
H	Y	P	E	D			S	N	U	B		
			V	E	I	N		E	R	U	P	T
D	I	C	E		N	E	S	T		L	O	O
O	D	O	R		C	A	T		H	A	L	O
E	L	M		T	H	R	U		I	R	O	N
R	E	P	R	O		S	N	A	G			
		A	U	N	T			P	H	A	S	E
A	D	D	S		A	T	O	P		L	E	D
C	U	R	E		C	A	L	L		S	A	G
T	O	E	S		O	B	E	Y		O	R	E

Lunch or dinner

M	E	A	L		C	H	E	W		T	H	E
A	X	L	E		H	E	A	R		N	U	N
P	I	T	A		A	R	R	E	S	T	E	D
S	T	O	P		P	E	N	N	E			
			T	I	E				E	G	G	S
A	D	S		S	A	P		T	R	O	L	L
R	U	T		N	U	R	S	E		S	E	A
K	N	E	L	T		Y	A	M		H	E	M
S	E	M	I				S	P	A			
			M	A	R	C	H		R	O	T	S
S	A	Y	O	N	A	R	A		O	M	I	T
O	W	E		T	R	A	Y		M	E	M	O
D	E	N		S	E	W	S		A	N	E	W

"__, humbug!"

B	A	H		B	E	E	P		A	T	O	M
E	G	O		R	O	A	R		F	I	N	E
E	E	L		O	N	T	O		F	E	E	L
		I	R	I	S		T	H	I	R	S	T
P	A	N	E	L		D	O	O	R			
U	S	E	D		D	O	C	U	M	E	N	T
T	I	S		T	E	N	O	R		N	O	R
T	A	S	T	E	F	U	L		C	L	U	E
			H	A	L	T		B	R	I	N	K
C	A	M	E	R	A		W	A	Y	S		
A	C	E	S		T	A	I	L		T	A	N
T	H	E	E		E	L	S	E		E	Y	E
S	E	T	S		D	E	E	D		D	E	W

At the drop of a __

H	A	T		I	D	O	L		S	P	A	R
A	S	H		D	E	L	I		T	A	X	I
S	K	I		E	N	D	S		E	P	I	C
		E	R	A	S		T	H	R	A	S	H
W	A	V	E		I	S	S	U	E			
E	L	E	V	A	T	E		N	O	S	E	S
E	A	R		C	Y	N	I	C		P	E	A
P	S	Y	C	H		S	C	H	O	O	L	S
			L	E	V	E	E		W	I	S	H
P	A	G	O	D	A		P	O	L	L		
O	U	R	S		L	O	A	D		E	L	F
T	R	E	E		V	I	C	E		R	Y	E
S	A	Y	S		E	L	K	S		S	E	W

Do __ give it another thought

N	O	T		A	S	K	S		G	A	G	A
A	P	E		C	H	I	T		L	I	A	R
V	E	X		T	I	D	E		U	R	G	E
A	R	T		S	E	D	A	T	E	D		
L	A	S	T		L	I	L	Y		R	E	P
			A	I	D	E		P	R	O	V	E
A	D	O	P	T	S		W	E	E	P	E	R
P	U	R	E	E		C	A	S	E			
T	E	E		M	A	L	L		D	A	T	E
		G	O	S	L	I	N	G		D	A	M
F	L	A	P		A	Q	U	A		U	M	P
L	I	N	E		R	U	T	S		L	E	T
U	P	O	N		M	E	S	H		T	R	Y

Underhanded

S	L	Y		A	R	M	S		R	A	Y	S
P	I	E		H	O	O	T		I	C	O	N
A	N	T		S	C	A	R		M	A	G	I
S	K	I	M		K	N	I	T		D	I	P
			A	T	E		C	A	R	E		
B	O	A	T	E	R		T	H	E	M	E	D
A	U	N	T	S				I	C	I	E	R
G	R	E	E	T	S		S	N	E	A	K	Y
		C	R	E	W		H	I	D			
P	A	D		D	E	E	R		E	A	R	L
L	I	O	N		A	C	I	D		F	E	E
U	N	T	O		T	H	E	Y		R	A	W
S	T	E	W		Y	O	K	E		O	D	D

Not given away

KEPT■ACT■WAIL
IDLE■SHE■ACRE
DIES■SUN■NEED
STAT■ENDED■■■
■■■YANK■NEWER
ITS■STY■CRAVE
NEIGHS■FOSSIL
KAZOO■COD■PLY
SMEAR■OXEN■■■
■■■TEACH■AHAS
CAFE■MOO■VISA
OGLE■SOL■EVEN
TOYS■ONE■LEAK

Sector

AREA■HATH■AHA
NORM■OKAY■GUM
GURU■LIMP■IMP
EGOS■INSECT■■
REREAD■■■OAFS
■■■DUAL■UNTIE
GAP■NYETS■ERA
EXIST■GEEK■■■
MENU■■■ARENAS
■■HECTIC■EASE
TOO■HUSH■PIKE
AWL■ABLE■EVER
GEE■PEER■REDS

Verve

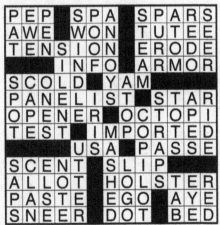

PEP■SPA■SPARS
AWE■WON■TUTEE
TENSION■ERODE
■■■INFO■ARMOR
SCOLD■YAM■■■■
PANELIST■STAR
OPENER■OCTOPI
TEST■IMPORTED
■■■■USA■PASSE
SCENT■SLIP■■■
ALLOT■HOLSTER
PASTE■EGO■AYE
SNEER■DOT■BED

Lamb's dad

RAM■GYPS■SCOW
OLE■RAIL■TORE
TENTACLE■OVAL
■■■ACHED■DELL
ANKLET■DIG■■■
NONE■■RECYCLE
TOE■PRIDE■HAM
SNEERED■■ZITI
■■■DOG■PLANET
SNUG■APRON■■■
NOSE■TRICYCLE
OVER■TACK■AIL
WADS■AYES■REF

Patch of grassy ground

SOD■ERAS■SLAW
WOO■RASP■TAXI
APE■RISE■EVES
PSST■DECREASE
■■■HASTIER■■■
BATON■SAD■FAB
ENOUGH■LIABLE
GYP■LUG■AGILE
■■■DEBACLE■■■
ENCIRCLE■DRAG
GALE■ALAS■USE
GNAT■POSE■SIN
YAPS■SPEW■EAT

Tie the __ (marry)

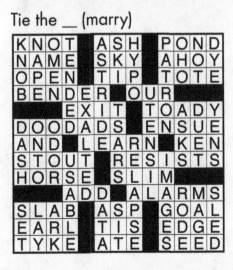

KNOT■ASH■POND
NAME■SKY■AHOY
OPEN■TIP■TOTE
BENDER■OUR■■■
■■■EXIT■TOADY
DOODADS■ENSUE
AND■LEARN■KEN
STOUT■RESISTS
HORSE■SLIM■■■
■■■ADD■ALARMS
SLAB■ASP■GOAL
EARL■TIS■EDGE
TYKE■ATE■SEED

Lost traction

S	L	I	D		S	A	W	S		P	A	Y
N	U	D	E		O	G	R	E		U	F	O
O	G	L	E		L	E	A	D		T	R	Y
B	E	E	P	E	D		T	A	T	T	O	O
				E	I	G	H	T	H			
W	H	I	S	K	E	R		E	A	G	E	R
H	U	L	A		R	U	M		W	O	V	E
Y	E	L	L	S		M	I	S	S	T	E	P
			S	T	A	P	L	E				
R	E	T	A	I	L		E	X	H	A	L	E
A	C	E		T	O	G	A		O	X	E	N
T	H	E		C	H	U	G		B	E	N	D
S	O	N		H	A	T	E		O	D	D	S

Tried to put out the birthday candles

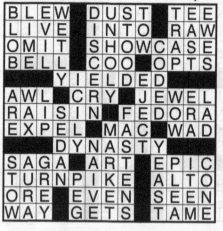

B	L	E	W		D	U	S	T		T	E	E
L	I	V	E		I	N	T	O		R	A	W
O	M	I	T		S	H	O	W	C	A	S	E
B	E	L	L		C	O	O		O	P	T	S
			Y	I	E	L	D	E	D			
A	W	L		C	R	Y		J	E	W	E	L
R	A	I	S	I	N		F	E	D	O	R	A
E	X	P	E	L		M	A	C		W	A	D
			D	Y	N	A	S	T	Y			
S	A	G	A		A	R	T		E	P	I	C
T	U	R	N	P	I	K	E		A	L	T	O
O	R	E		E	V	E	N		S	E	E	N
W	A	Y		G	E	T	S		T	A	M	E

Scuttlebutt

I	N	F	O		W	A	S		M	I	L	D
R	U	I	N		H	U	H		A	R	E	A
E	N	T	I	R	E	T	Y		T	I	N	T
			O	A	T	H		P	A	S	S	E
G	R	A	N	T		O	W	E	D			
A	I	M			P	R	I	S	O	N	E	R
S	P	I	R	A	L		F	O	R	A	G	E
P	E	D	I	C	U	R	E			P	O	D
			V	I	S	A		L	A	S	S	O
H	I	R	E	D		R	E	E	D			
E	D	I	T		V	I	A	D	U	C	T	S
R	O	L	E		I	T	S		L	U	A	U
B	L	E	D		E	Y	E		T	E	R	M

6. Start with a Bang

Pleads

B	E	G	S		R	A	R	E		A	R	F
A	X	L	E		I	D	E	A		S	E	A
N	E	O	N		F	O	G	S		I	N	N
	C	A	T		T	R	A	Y		D	E	N
P	U	T		I	S	N	T		D	E	W	Y
I	T	E	M	S		S	T	I	R			
P	E	D	A	L	S		A	R	I	S	E	N
			N	E	E	D		O	P	E	R	A
S	P	R	Y		D	A	W	N		M	O	P
P	E	A		M	U	S	H		B	I	T	
U	R	N		A	C	H	E		U	N	I	T
R	I	D		M	E	E	T		L	A	C	E
S	L	Y		A	D	D	S		B	R	A	N

Owl's call

H	O	O	T		I	C	O	N		A	N	Y
U	N	D	O		M	O	V	E		W	O	E
S	T	E	W		P	L	A	T	T	E	R	S
H	O	S	E	S		A	L	S	O			
			R	E	F				O	F	F	S
M	A	S	S	E	U	R		G	L	A	R	E
E	L	K		D	R	O	V	E		W	E	T
S	L	I	M	Y		T	E	N	A	N	T	S
H	Y	P	E				T	U	G			
			L	O	A	F		S	E	N	D	S
O	B	S	T	A	C	L	E		N	O	U	N
R	A	P		F	R	E	E		D	O	D	O
B	A	Y		S	E	A	L		A	N	E	W

__ Scotia

N	O	V	A		S	T	Y		S	T	A	B
E	V	I	L		T	O	E		P	A	P	A
W	E	S	T		E	R	A		A	X	E	S
T	R	I	O		E	R	R		R	I	S	K
		T	S	A	R	I	N	A	S			
D	U	O		R	E	D		R	E	I	G	N
A	F	R	A	I	D		C	O	R	N	E	A
D	O	S	E	S		H	A	M		F	L	Y
			R	E	S	O	N	A	T	E		
M	E	M	O		M	A	N		A	R	M	S
A	C	E	S		A	G	E		K	N	E	E
S	H	O	O		S	I	R		E	A	R	N
H	O	W	L		H	E	Y		S	L	E	D

Cost an __ and a leg

A	R	M		P	O	S	H		B	L	A	B
B	O	O		H	A	L	O		A	I	D	E
L	A	P		O	R	A	L		N	E	S	T
E	R	E	C	T		N	E	R	D			
			L	O	S	T		O	S	C	A	R
G	A	L	A		T	Y	P	O		A	G	O
O	R	A	N	G	E		A	T	O	N	E	D
A	C	T		U	P	O	N		W	E	D	S
T	H	E	I	R		B	E	E	N			
			M	U	S	T		A	S	S	E	T
A	T	O	P		O	A	T	S		O	L	E
M	I	N	E		D	I	N	E		U	S	A
P	E	E	L		A	N	T	S		P	E	R

Dwarf with glasses

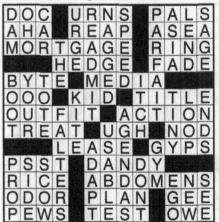

D	O	C		U	R	N	S		P	A	L	S
A	H	A		R	E	A	P		A	S	E	A
M	O	R	T	G	A	G	E		R	I	N	G
			H	E	D	G	E		F	A	D	E
B	Y	T	E		M	E	D	I	A			
O	O	O		K	I	D		T	I	T	L	E
O	U	T	F	I	T		A	C	T	I	O	N
T	R	E	A	T		U	G	H		N	O	D
			L	E	A	S	E		G	Y	P	S
P	S	S	T		D	A	N	D	Y			
R	I	C	E		A	B	D	O	M	E	N	S
O	D	O	R		P	L	A	N		G	E	E
P	E	W	S		T	E	S	T		O	W	E

Pill portion

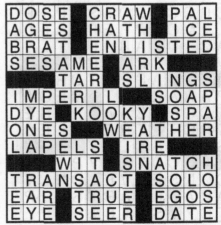

D	O	S	E		C	R	A	W		P	A	L
A	G	E	S		H	A	T	H		I	C	E
B	R	A	T		E	N	L	I	S	T	E	D
S	E	S	A	M	E		A	R	K			
			T	A	R		S	L	I	N	G	S
I	M	P	E	R	I	L			S	O	A	P
D	Y	E		K	O	O	K	Y		S	P	A
O	N	E	S			W	E	A	T	H	E	R
L	A	P	E	L	S		I	R	E			
			W	I	T		S	N	A	T	C	H
T	R	A	N	S	A	C	T		S	O	L	O
E	A	R		T	R	U	E		E	G	O	S
E	Y	E		S	E	E	R		D	A	T	E

Frosty

I	C	Y	■	H	O	O	P	■	S	T	A	G
T	O	O	■	A	F	R	O	■	C	O	I	L
E	N	G	U	L	F	E	D	■	R	O	L	E
M	E	A	N	T	■	■	■	S	E	N	S	E
■	■	■	I	S	O	L	A	T	E	■	■	■
S	T	A	T	■	L	A	M	I	N	A	T	E
H	E	R	■	C	I	G	A	R	■	S	E	A
E	N	C	L	A	V	E	S	■	W	H	A	T
■	■	■	O	V	E	R	S	E	E	■	■	■
A	L	G	A	E	■	■	■	R	E	A	P	S
R	E	A	D	■	S	T	R	A	D	D	L	E
T	A	M	E	■	O	W	E	S	■	D	E	N
S	P	E	D	■	N	O	P	E	■	S	A	T

Illuminated

L	I	T	■	S	T	A	R	■	T	A	C	T
O	N	E	■	A	I	D	E	■	H	U	L	A
A	T	E	■	M	A	M	A	■	O	R	A	L
D	O	N	E	■	R	I	D	■	R	A	N	K
■	■	A	V	I	A	T	I	O	N	■	■	■
C	A	G	E	D	■	S	E	W	■	A	H	S
O	P	E	N	E	D	■	D	I	S	M	A	L
P	E	R	■	A	I	R	■	N	E	E	D	Y
■	■	■	A	L	L	E	R	G	E	N	■	■
P	E	G	S	■	A	L	E	■	D	A	M	S
A	L	A	S	■	T	I	N	T	■	B	A	T
I	S	L	E	■	E	V	E	R	■	L	I	E
R	E	S	T	■	D	E	W	Y	■	E	L	M

Not right

L	E	F	T	■	C	A	M	E	■	L	A	W
I	D	L	E	■	A	M	E	N	■	E	W	E
A	G	E	D	■	U	P	S	T	A	G	E	D
R	E	D	I	A	L	■	H	E	X	■	■	■
■	■	■	U	N	D	O	■	R	I	F	L	E
S	U	B	M	E	R	G	E	■	S	A	I	L
A	G	O	■	W	O	R	S	T	■	I	N	K
G	L	A	D	■	N	E	T	W	O	R	K	S
S	Y	R	U	P	■	S	E	A	R	■	■	■
■	■	■	T	O	M	■	E	S	C	R	O	W
P	L	A	Y	R	O	O	M	■	H	I	D	E
R	I	P	■	C	L	U	E	■	I	D	E	A
O	P	T	■	H	E	R	D	■	D	E	S	K

Sear

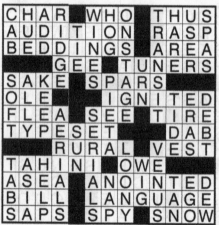

C	H	A	R	■	W	H	O	■	T	H	U	S
A	U	D	I	T	I	O	N	■	R	A	S	P
B	E	D	D	I	N	G	S	■	A	R	E	A
■	■	■	G	E	E	■	T	U	N	E	R	S
S	A	K	E	■	S	P	A	R	S	■	■	■
O	L	E	■	■	■	I	G	N	I	T	E	D
F	L	E	A	■	S	E	E	■	T	I	R	E
T	Y	P	E	S	E	T	■	■	■	D	A	B
■	■	■	R	U	R	A	L	■	V	E	S	T
T	A	H	I	N	I	■	O	W	E	■	■	■
A	S	E	A	■	A	N	O	I	N	T	E	D
B	I	L	L	■	L	A	N	G	U	A	G	E
S	A	P	S	■	S	P	Y	■	S	N	O	W

Gator kin

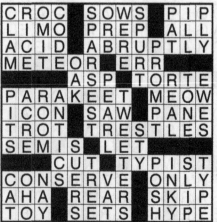

C	R	O	C	■	S	O	W	S	■	P	I	P
L	I	M	O	■	P	R	E	P	■	A	L	L
A	C	I	D	■	A	B	R	U	P	T	L	Y
M	E	T	E	O	R	■	E	R	R	■	■	■
■	■	■	■	A	S	P	■	T	O	R	T	E
P	A	R	A	K	E	E	T	■	M	E	O	W
I	C	O	N	■	S	A	W	■	P	A	N	E
T	R	O	T	■	T	R	E	S	T	L	E	S
S	E	M	I	S	■	L	E	T	■	■	■	■
■	■	■	C	U	T	■	T	Y	P	I	S	T
C	O	N	S	E	R	V	E	■	O	N	L	Y
A	H	A	■	R	E	A	R	■	S	K	I	P
T	O	Y	■	S	E	T	S	■	H	Y	P	E

Lodge member

E	L	K	■	B	I	A	S	■	C	A	S	T
R	A	N	■	E	T	C	H	■	A	L	T	O
A	G	E	■	E	C	H	O	■	N	O	O	N
■	■	E	I	T	H	E	R	■	D	O	V	E
F	A	C	T	■	■	■	T	W	O	F	E	R
B	R	A	S	H	■	W	E	A	R	■	■	■
I	M	P	■	I	C	I	N	G	■	S	P	A
■	■	■	A	K	I	N	■	E	A	T	E	N
M	A	L	L	E	T	■	■	■	C	O	P	Y
E	D	I	T	■	A	C	H	I	E	R	■	■
N	I	N	E	■	D	I	E	S	■	A	D	S
D	E	E	R	■	E	A	R	N	■	G	O	O
S	U	N	S	■	L	O	O	T	■	E	E	L

Unexciting

B	L	A	H		U	M	P		F	A	I	L
A	U	T	O		F	O	R		O	N	C	E
S	L	O	P		O	R	I	E	N	T	E	D
S	U	P	E	R		T	E	X	T			
				E	R	A	S	E		U	S	A
S	N	A	P	P	E	R		C	U	R	E	D
P	E	R	I	O	D		H	U	G	G	E	D
E	A	T	E	R		M	O	T	H	E	R	S
D	R	Y		T	R	I	P	E				
			T	E	E	N		D	E	P	T	H
T	O	L	E	R	A	N	T		G	L	E	E
I	R	O	N		C	O	O		G	E	A	R
P	E	T	S		T	W	O		Y	A	M	S

Cry at the villain

B	O	O		O	A	R		P	R	I	S	M
A	N	D		S	H	E		R	A	D	I	I
D	E	D	U	C	E	D		O	D	O	R	S
			S	A	M	E		T	A	L	E	S
F	L	O	U	R		E	V	E	R			
L	A	V	A		S	M	O	G		T	H	E
O	M	E	L	E	T		L	E	G	I	O	N
P	E	R		L	A	S	T		R	E	E	D
			B	A	B	Y		B	I	R	D	S
S	W	E	E	P		S	L	O	T			
W	A	L	L	S		T	O	N	S	I	L	S
A	I	S	L	E		E	G	G		V	I	A
B	L	E	E	D		M	O	O		Y	E	T

Fill-in worker

T	E	M	P		P	A	N		S	T	A	Y
O	D	O	R		I	R	E		C	A	P	E
O	G	L	E		E	R	A	S	U	R	E	S
T	E	E	S		T	O	T	E	M			
			U	N	A	W	E	D		A	S	H
S	H	A	M	U	S		R	U	M	B	L	E
A	I	M	E	D				C	O	L	O	N
C	R	E	D	I	T		R	E	N	E	W	S
K	E	N		S	H	R	E	D	S			
			S	T	E	E	P		T	O	M	B
A	B	R	A	S	I	V	E		E	V	I	L
S	E	A	L		R	U	N		R	A	K	E
K	E	P	T		S	E	T		S	L	E	D

7. Make a Fresh Start

Write a bit

J	O	T		O	O	H		A	S	S	E	T
A	W	E		A	T	E		R	O	U	G	E
W	E	A	L	T	H	Y		M	O	R	O	N
			U	S	E		L	A	T	E	S	T
D	O	W	N		R	A	I	D				
A	R	E	A			M	E	A	N	I	N	G
T	A	L	C		S	I	N		A	S	E	A
A	L	L	Y	I	N	G			G	L	O	P
				R	O	O	K		G	E	N	E
H	O	L	L	O	W		A	L	E			
U	N	I	O	N		B	R	I	D	L	E	D
S	T	O	N	E		A	M	P		A	Y	E
H	O	N	E	D		H	A	S		P	E	W

Bulls-eye flyer

D	A	R	T		T	E	E		S	L	A	W
U	S	E	R		H	A	Y		P	I	N	E
O	P	P	O	S	I	T	E		O	V	E	N
		R	U	T	S		S	H	R	E	W	D
G	R	I	P	E		M	O	A	T			
R	I	S	E	N		U	R	N		P	A	R
O	L	E		C	A	R	E	D		A	G	O
W	E	D		I	N	K		R	A	T	E	D
			P	L	A	Y		A	R	I	S	E
A	T	T	E	S	T		F	I	R	E		
L	O	O	N		O	P	U	L	E	N	C	E
S	O	O	N		M	E	N		S	C	A	N
O	N	L	Y		Y	A	K		T	E	N	D

Plaster dressing

C	A	S	T		D	E	N	S		T	A	N
A	X	L	E		E	X	I	T		O	H	O
R	E	E	L		T	I	N	Y		G	A	P
		E	L	D	E	S	T		E	A	S	E
P	E	P		A	N	T	H	E	M			
E	V	E		I	T	S		L	I	S	T	S
S	E	R	E	N	E		S	A	T	I	R	E
O	N	S	E	T		P	U	P		G	I	N
			L	Y	R	I	C	S		H	O	T
W	O	W	S		A	C	C	E	N	T		
E	G	O		P	I	K	E		A	S	I	A
E	R	R		U	S	E	S		Y	E	L	L
P	E	N		B	E	T	S		S	E	L	L

Capitol top

D	O	M	E		P	L	O	T		S	P	A
A	K	I	N		L	A	W	N		T	A	P
S	A	N	E		U	N	I	T		R	Y	E
H	Y	D	R	O	G	E	N		L	E	S	S
			G	I	G		G	R	I	N		
A	R	G	Y	L	E	S		E	D	G	E	S
N	O	R		I	D	I	O	M		T	W	O
T	W	I	N	E		T	R	A	S	H	E	D
		D	I	R	T		B	I	N			
C	L	I	P		E	M	I	N	E	N	C	E
O	U	R		G	N	A	T		A	I	R	Y
P	R	O		O	O	Z	E		K	N	E	E
Y	E	N		B	R	E	D		S	E	W	S

Start of FBI

F	E	D		A	R	T	S		D	I	S	C
A	R	E		L	O	O	T		E	C	H	O
T	A	N	D	O	O	R	I		B	O	O	T
			I	N	F	E	R		A	N	T	S
S	T	O	V	E			R	O	T			
A	I	D	E		B	R	U	N	E	T	T	E
G	E	E		C	O	U	P	E		A	H	A
A	S	S	A	U	L	T	S		S	C	A	R
			L	E	D			C	L	O	W	N
P	R	I	M		N	A	C	H	O			
R	E	D	O		E	L	L	I	P	S	I	S
O	N	E	S		S	T	U	N		A	C	E
S	T	A	T		S	O	B	S		D	Y	E

What a sharpshooter does

A	I	M		A	T	O	P		O	P	T	S
C	R	Y		P	I	T	A		F	L	E	A
T	O	N		E	A	T	S		F	A	N	G
S	N	A	G		R	E	T	E	S	T		
			N	E	A	R	E	D		O	R	E
A	P	R	O	N	S		S	I	G	N	A	L
D	E	E	M	S				B	R	I	C	K
D	E	V	E	I	N		S	L	I	C	E	S
S	K	I		G	O	S	P	E	L			
		S	I	N	G	L	E		L	O	R	D
S	H	I	N		G	I	L	L		W	E	E
K	O	O	K		I	D	L	E		L	A	W
Y	E	N	S		N	E	S	T		S	L	Y

Small branch

```
TWIG■AQUA■TEA
HIDE■MUMS■RAG
UPON■NAPS■IRE
DELIVER■ELM■■
■■■EAST■TIMES
ADD■SIZE■FELT
FIESTA■AVERSE
REST■CASE■SEW
OSCAR■WINE■■■
■■EYE■ANDIRON
BAN■SAKE■GENE
OLD■EWES■HATE
YES■TENS■TROD
```

Consider

```
DEIGN■USE■MAP
IGLOO■PHASERS
DOLLS■SATIRES
■■■FEVER■NEAT
OFF■■ITEM■■■■
ALIASES■ENDED
FOLLOW■SLEEVE
SWELL■BETWEEN
■■■■OGRE■■PRY
MASH■RUDDY■■■
ASPIRIN■OATHS
TEATIME■SWEET
HAS■MET■ENEMY
```

Classic "Star Trek" episode

```
NOMAD■AHA■ARM
AWARE■RUN■SEA
PERKS■ENTRIES
■■ASKING■HALT
FLU■■TARRY■■■
RADIUS■YAMMER
OVENS■■■GEODE
GARNET■ASSIGN
■■■IDOLS■■SET
DOWN■MOPPET■■
ENIGMAS■AMUSE
ELF■ATE■SIREN
RYE■NOR■STEED
```

Sits for a portrait

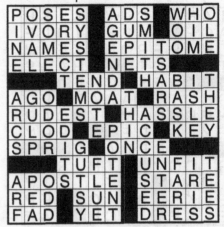

```
POSES■ADS■WHO
IVORY■GUM■OIL
NAMES■EPITOME
ELECT■NETS■■■
■■■TEND■HABIT
AGO■MOAT■RASH
RUDEST■HASSLE
CLOD■EPIC■KEY
SPRIG■ONCE■■■
■■■TUFT■UNFIT
APOSTLE■STARE
RED■SUN■EERIE
FAD■YET■DRESS
```

Item ridden by Huckleberry Finn

```
RAFT■ACT■SCOW
ACRE■THE■YOGI
THEN■TAN■CALL
SETTLERS■AXED
■■■■ESTEEM■■■
RECENT■SMORES
IRONS■■■BRAVO
PROVES■BEEPED
■■■EDITED■■■■
DUAL■ERASABLE
INTO■SAM■BRAY
STOP■TIE■LANE
HOME■AND■ENDS
```

Tiny cooking amount

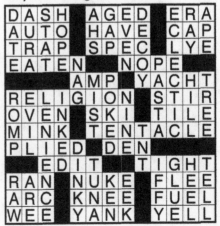

```
DASH■AGED■ERA
AUTO■HAVE■CAP
TRAP■SPEC■LYE
EATEN■■NOPE■■
■■■■AMP■YACHT
RELIGION■STIR
OVEN■SKI■TILE
MINK■TENTACLE
PLIED■DEN■■■■
■■EDIT■■TIGHT
RAN■NUKE■FLEE
ARC■KNEE■FUEL
WEE■YANK■YELL
```

Insert __ A in slot B

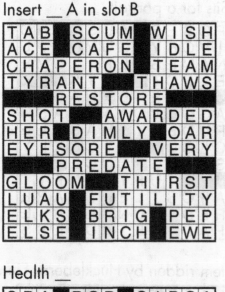

T	A	B	■	S	C	U	M	■	W	I	S	H
A	C	E	■	C	A	F	E	■	I	D	L	E
C	H	A	P	E	R	O	N	■	T	E	A	M
T	Y	R	A	N	T	■	■	T	H	A	W	S
■	■	■	R	E	S	T	O	R	E	■	■	■
S	H	O	T	■	■	A	W	A	R	D	E	D
H	E	R	■	D	I	M	L	Y	■	O	A	R
E	Y	E	S	O	R	E	■	■	V	E	R	Y
■	■	■	P	R	E	D	A	T	E	■	■	■
G	L	O	O	M	■	■	T	H	I	R	S	T
L	U	A	U	■	F	U	T	I	L	I	T	Y
E	L	K	S	■	B	R	I	G	■	P	E	P
E	L	S	E	■	I	N	C	H	■	E	W	E

Star that goes boom

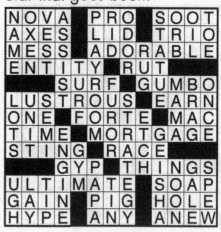

N	O	V	A	■	P	R	O	■	S	O	O	T
A	X	E	S	■	L	I	D	■	T	R	I	O
M	E	S	S	■	A	D	O	R	A	B	L	E
E	N	T	I	T	Y	■	R	U	T	■	■	■
■	■	■	S	U	R	F	■	G	U	M	B	O
L	U	S	T	R	O	U	S	■	E	A	R	N
O	N	E	■	F	O	R	T	E	■	M	A	C
T	I	M	E	■	M	O	R	T	G	A	G	E
S	T	I	N	G	■	R	A	C	E	■	■	■
■	■	■	G	Y	P	■	T	H	I	N	G	S
U	L	T	I	M	A	T	E	■	S	O	A	P
G	A	I	N	■	P	I	G	■	H	O	L	E
H	Y	P	E	■	A	N	Y	■	A	N	E	W

Health __

S	P	A	■	R	O	B	■	C	I	R	C	A
K	I	T	■	A	W	E	■	O	C	E	A	N
Y	E	T	■	P	E	G	■	M	I	D	S	T
■	■	A	S	I	D	E	■	P	E	S	T	S
A	R	C	E	D	■	T	I	E	R	■	■	■
T	A	K	E	■	P	S	S	T	■	U	M	P
O	V	E	R	D	O	■	N	E	C	T	A	R
P	E	R	■	O	M	I	T	■	H	E	R	O
■	■	■	H	O	P	S	■	W	A	N	T	S
P	A	C	E	D	■	L	A	I	R	S	■	■
U	S	U	A	L	■	A	R	T	■	I	M	P
S	E	R	V	E	■	N	E	T	■	L	O	U
H	A	T	E	D	■	D	A	Y	■	S	O	N

8. Start the Ball Rolling

"__ She Sweet?"

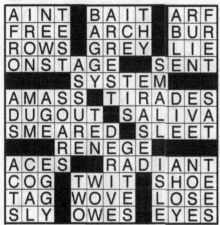

A	I	N	T		B	A	I	T		A	R	F
F	R	E	E		A	R	C	H		B	U	R
R	O	W	S		G	R	E	Y		L	I	E
O	N	S	T	A	G	E			S	E	N	T
				S	Y	S	T	E	M			
A	M	A	S	S		T	I	R	A	D	E	S
D	U	G	O	U	T		S	A	L	I	V	A
S	M	E	A	R	E	D		S	L	E	E	T
			R	E	N	E	G	E				
A	C	E	S			R	A	D	I	A	N	T
C	O	G		T	W	I	T		S	H	O	E
T	A	G		W	O	V	E		L	O	S	E
S	L	Y		O	W	E	S		E	Y	E	S

Use a beeper

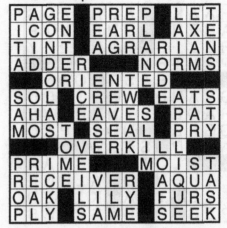

P	A	G	E		P	R	E	P		L	E	T
I	C	O	N		E	A	R	L		A	X	E
T	I	N	T		A	G	R	A	R	I	A	N
A	D	D	E	R				N	O	R	M	S
		O	R	I	E	N	T	E	D			
S	O	L		C	R	E	W		E	A	T	S
A	H	A		E	A	V	E	S		P	A	T
M	O	S	T		S	E	A	L		P	R	Y
			O	V	E	R	K	I	L	L		
P	R	I	M	E				M	O	I	S	T
R	E	C	E	I	V	E	R		A	Q	U	A
O	A	K		L	I	L	Y		F	U	R	S
P	L	Y		S	A	M	E		S	E	E	K

A retainer fixes the upper one

J	A	W		T	Y	P	O		B	A	T	S
O	L	E		R	O	A	D		E	M	I	T
B	E	T	R	A	Y	E	D		G	O	N	E
			I	D	O	L		L	U	N	G	E
G	A	F	F	E		L	O	U	N	G	E	D
O	R	A	L		S	A	I	L				
B	E	R	E	F	T		N	U	D	G	E	D
				R	A	C	K		R	A	R	E
M	A	M	M	O	T	H		B	Y	L	A	W
I	D	I	O	M		R	O	L	E			
S	I	L	O		C	O	V	E	R	A	G	E
E	E	L	S		A	M	E	N		T	E	E
R	U	S	E		T	E	N	D		E	L	K

Sounded a bell

R	A	N	G		A	R	C		S	A	G	A
U	S	E	R		M	A	Y		O	P	E	N
N	I	C	E		P	I	N		R	E	E	D
T	A	K	E	N		S	I	T	E			
			T	U	N	I	C	S		T	O	O
P	E	L	I	C	A	N		A	P	R	O	N
E	V	E	N	L	Y		F	R	E	E	Z	E
S	I	N	G	E		S	O	I	R	E	E	S
O	L	D		A	S	C	E	N	T			
			T	R	A	Y		A	U	D	I	O
E	C	H	O		I	T	S		R	E	D	O
N	O	U	N		T	H	E		B	E	E	P
D	O	M	E		H	E	X		S	P	A	S

__ Largo

K	E	Y		F	B	I		S	L	E	P	T
I	V	O	R	I	E	S		W	A	G	O	N
N	E	G	A	T	E	S		A	D	O	P	T
D	R	I	P		R	U	G	B	Y			
				U	S	E	D			U	F	O
W	I	P	E	R		S	A	V	O	R	E	D
E	N	R	A	G	E		Y	A	W	N	E	D
S	T	E	R	E	O	S		T	E	S	T	S
T	O	Y			N	A	B	S				
			B	A	S	I	L		B	A	S	E
W	A	V	E	R		L	A	B	E	L	E	D
A	G	E	N	T		O	R	I	G	A	M	I
D	O	T	T	Y		R	E	D		S	I	T

Ridicule

M	O	C	K		P	O	O	H		L	A	W
A	C	H	E		E	D	G	E		A	W	E
Y	E	A	R		R	E	L	I	A	B	L	E
B	A	R	N		U	S	E	R	S			
E	N	T	E	R	S				E	A	S	Y
			L	E	A	F		P	A	R	K	A
A	I	D		E	L	U	D	E		T	I	P
D	R	I	L	L		N	E	A	T			
D	E	M	O				S	K	E	T	C	H
			S	P	A	T	S		A	I	R	Y
P	R	E	S	S	U	R	E		S	T	E	P
R	A	Y		S	T	I	R		E	L	S	E
O	N	E		T	O	O	T		S	E	T	S

Warmongers

H	A	W	K	S	■	A	S	H	■	A	D	S
A	R	E	N	A	■	S	H	E	■	L	I	P
R	E	L	I	C	■	P	A	R	S	L	E	Y
P	A	L	T	R	Y	■	L	E	O	■	■	■
■	■	■	■	E	A	S	T	■	O	W	N	S
G	R	A	N	D	P	A	■	■	T	H	O	U
R	A	C	E	■	S	I	N	■	H	I	V	E
O	G	R	E	■	■	N	O	T	E	P	A	D
W	E	E	D	■	S	T	O	W	■	■	■	■
■	■	■	L	O	T	■	N	E	C	T	A	R
L	I	K	E	N	E	D	■	A	L	O	N	E
A	C	E	■	T	E	A	■	K	I	T	E	D
P	E	G	■	O	R	B	■	S	P	E	W	S

Signs of things to come

O	M	E	N	S	■	S	E	A	■	S	P	A
H	A	V	O	C	■	E	R	R	■	T	A	P
O	P	E	R	A	■	R	U	M	M	A	G	E
■	■	■	■	R	U	M	P	■	E	Y	E	S
S	T	A	G	■	N	O	T	E	D	■	■	■
H	A	I	R	P	I	N	■	V	I	T	A	L
U	P	R	O	O	T	■	S	E	C	U	R	E
N	E	S	T	S	■	T	E	N	A	N	T	S
■	■	■	T	E	P	E	E	■	L	A	S	S
A	L	T	O	■	R	A	K	E	■	■	■	■
F	I	A	S	C	O	S	■	A	M	A	S	S
R	A	M	■	U	S	E	■	R	O	G	U	E
O	R	E	■	B	E	D	■	S	W	E	P	T

Prepare to drag race

R	E	V	■	C	O	I	N	■	A	B	L	E
A	X	E	■	R	I	L	E	■	C	R	O	W
P	I	T	F	A	L	L	S	■	T	U	N	E
S	T	O	U	T	■	■	T	H	O	N	G	S
■	■	■	N	E	E	D	■	A	R	E	■	■
P	O	R	K	■	A	I	N	T	■	T	W	O
A	L	E	■	I	S	S	U	E	■	T	O	W
N	E	W	■	D	E	C	K	■	S	E	E	N
■	■	O	W	L	■	S	E	W	N	■	■	■
A	G	R	E	E	D	■	■	R	I	G	O	R
N	U	D	E	■	A	L	T	I	T	U	D	E
T	R	E	K	■	D	Y	E	S	■	S	O	L
S	U	D	S	■	S	E	N	T	■	T	R	Y

Story with a punch line

J	O	K	E	■	S	A	F	E	■	C	O	N
A	X	I	S	■	C	L	A	W	■	A	P	E
B	E	T	S	■	H	A	L	E	■	P	E	W
S	N	E	A	K	E	R	S	■	I	S	N	T
■	■	■	Y	A	M	M	E	R	S	■	■	■
O	F	F	■	Y	E	S	■	A	L	I	B	I
P	U	L	S	A	R	■	A	P	E	M	E	N
T	R	U	C	K	■	N	I	P	■	P	E	N
■	■	■	A	S	S	U	M	E	D	■	■	■
C	L	A	M	■	H	A	L	L	O	W	E	D
O	O	H	■	C	A	N	E	■	W	O	V	E
T	O	O	■	A	R	C	S	■	S	K	I	N
S	T	Y	■	T	E	E	S	■	E	E	L	S

The __ (information superhighway)

N	E	T	■	P	A	L	S	■	A	L	A	S
A	G	O	■	R	U	I	N	■	L	I	M	O
P	O	D	■	I	D	E	A	■	B	O	I	L
■	■	D	O	Z	I	N	G	■	U	N	D	O
B	A	L	L	E	T	■	G	Y	M	■	■	■
U	S	E	D	■	■	W	E	A	S	E	L	S
S	I	R	■	B	E	A	D	Y	■	M	O	P
T	A	S	T	E	R	S	■	■	V	I	S	A
■	■	■	A	T	E	■	T	W	I	S	T	S
S	T	A	B	■	C	H	O	R	E	S	■	■
W	A	I	L	■	T	Y	P	E	■	A	C	T
A	X	L	E	■	E	P	I	C	■	R	U	N
M	I	S	T	■	D	O	C	K	■	Y	E	T

The __ is up!

J	I	G	■	C	O	E	D	■	E	N	D	S
E	R	A	■	A	W	A	Y	■	N	E	A	T
T	E	L	E	V	I	S	E	■	S	O	D	A
■	■	■	V	E	N	T	■	L	U	N	A	R
E	D	G	E	■	G	E	N	I	E	■	■	■
T	A	R	R	Y	■	R	U	M	■	A	R	F
C	R	A	Y	O	N	■	T	I	S	S	U	E
H	E	M	■	D	O	T	■	T	H	E	S	E
■	■	■	M	E	D	I	C	■	E	A	T	S
F	E	T	A	L	■	T	R	O	D	■	■	■
I	C	O	N	■	P	L	E	A	S	U	R	E
S	H	O	E	■	R	E	E	F	■	S	O	Y
T	O	T	S	■	O	D	D	S	■	A	W	E

Scrabble tile holder

R	A	C	K		H	I	G	H		S	A	P
O	R	A	L		A	C	R	E		T	I	E
M	E	N	U		N	E	A	R		U	M	P
P	A	S	T	E	D		V	O	I	D		
			Z	E	S	T	Y		T	I	P	S
S	H	E		L	A	W			C	O	O	L
C	O	S	T		W	I	T		H	U	L	A
A	U	T	O			R	I	B		S	O	B
T	R	I	G		P	L	A	I	N			
		M	A	G	I		R	O	U	S	E	D
B	A	A		A	Q	U	A		M	O	L	E
A	N	T		P	U	R	E		B	A	S	E
R	Y	E		S	E	N	D		S	P	E	D

Less modern

O	L	D	E	R		I	T	S		P	O	P
M	A	U	V	E		O	W	E		E	A	R
I	N	K	E	D		D	I	E	T	A	R	Y
T	E	E		W	H	I	S	K	S			
			P	O	I	N	T		A	T	O	M
I	M	P	L	O	R	E		D	R	O	V	E
D	E	L	U	D	E		S	U	I	T	E	S
O	M	E	N	S		R	U	N	N	E	R	S
L	O	A	D		C	O	N	G	A			
			E	N	R	A	G	E		L	O	T
B	A	R	R	O	O	M		O	L	I	V	E
O	H	O		T	O	E		N	A	V	A	L
W	A	D		E	N	D		S	P	E	L	L

Run easily

J	O	G		V	I	N	E		R	O	W	S
A	L	E		I	R	O	N		E	D	I	T
Y	E	N		S	I	N	G		C	O	L	A
		E	R	A	S	E	R		A	R	T	Y
A	C	R	E	S			A	L	L			
L	O	A	F		C	A	V	A	L	I	E	R
T	O	T		T	A	X	E	D		M	O	O
O	P	E	R	A	T	E	D		B	I	N	S
			A	R	C			G	U	T	S	Y
S	U	M	P		A	R	M	A	D	A		
T	R	A	P		L	E	A	P		T	A	B
O	G	R	E		L	A	Z	E		O	R	E
P	E	E	R		S	L	E	D		R	E	D

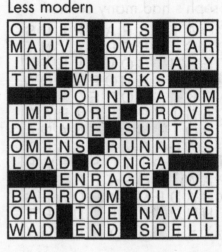

9. Start from Scratch

Joseph's had many colors

C	O	A	T		S	P	A		P	L	U	S
O	N	C	E		E	R	R		A	I	N	T
T	E	E	N		C	O	M	P	L	E	T	E
			T	R	E	M	O	R		S	O	W
A	R	K		A	D	O	R	E	D			
C	A	N	I	N	E		S	P	I	R	A	L
T	R	O	T						N	A	N	A
S	E	W	E	R	S		N	U	G	G	E	T
			M	O	T	T	O	S		E	W	E
P	A	W		P	O	R	T	E	R			
A	C	A	D	E	M	I	A		O	W	L	S
T	H	R	U		P	A	R		D	I	E	T
H	Y	P	E		S	L	Y		E	G	G	Y

Symbol of peace

D	O	V	E		A	R	T	S		F	R	Y
A	X	E	S		D	E	N	T		L	E	O
T	E	E	S		H	A	T	E		O	A	K
E	N	R	A	G	E	D		A	D	O	R	E
			Y	A	R	D		K	I	D		
A	G	E		L	I	S	T		S	L	A	P
S	E	A	M	A	N		R	E	C	I	P	E
P	E	S	O		G	D	A	Y		T	E	N
		I	L	L		E	V	E	S			
P	A	N	D	A		N	E	S	T	L	E	D
L	I	E		S	T	I	R		R	O	V	E
A	D	S		E	W	E	S		A	S	I	A
Y	E	S		R	O	S	E		W	E	L	L

Toss and turn

F	R	E	T		A	H	E	M		C	A	B
L	A	M	E		S	O	R	E		H	U	E
A	K	I	N		H	E	A	D	W	I	N	D
P	E	T	A	L			S	A	I	N	T	S
			N	I	C	K	E	L	S			
F	O	O	T	M	A	N			P	U	F	F
O	W	L		E	N	E	M	Y		S	U	E
E	N	D	S			L	E	O	P	A	R	D
			W	H	I	T	T	L	E			
A	T	T	A	I	N			K	A	R	M	A
S	H	I	N	G	L	E	S		L	I	A	R
K	E	N		H	E	R	E		E	P	I	C
S	E	E		S	T	A	T		D	E	N	S

Log slicer

S	A	W		P	S	S	T		P	A	D	S
P	I	E		L	U	A	U		A	R	E	A
I	R	E		A	R	M	S		T	R	E	K
T	Y	P	I	N	G		S	P	H	E	R	E
			N	E	E	D	L	E	S	S		
E	J	E	C	T		R	E	P		T	E	A
G	O	S	H		T	I	S		M	E	E	T
G	Y	P		A	R	F		S	I	D	L	E
		R	E	G	A	T	T	A	S			
P	H	E	N	O	M		R	U	S	S	E	T
E	A	S	T		P	O	U	T		L	A	Y
E	L	S	E		L	I	N	E		A	S	K
P	O	O	R		E	L	K	S		B	Y	E

__ the riot act

R	E	A	D		D	A	B		B	A	W	L
A	X	L	E		U	F	O		A	H	O	Y
P	A	S	S	W	O	R	D		S	A	N	E
S	M	O	K	E		A	Y	E	S			
			S	E	M	I		V	I	S	O	R
T	A	G			A	D	H	E	S	I	V	E
A	C	R	O	S	S		E	N	T	R	E	E
C	H	A	R	I	S	M	A			E	N	D
T	E	M	P	T		A	T	O	P			
			H	E	A	L		H	A	R	S	H
T	U	B	A		M	I	N	O	R	I	T	Y
O	M	E	N		I	C	E		C	L	A	P
O	P	T	S		D	E	W		H	E	R	O

"God's Little __"

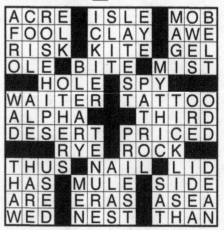

A	C	R	E		I	S	L	E		M	O	B
F	O	O	L		C	L	A	Y		A	W	E
R	I	S	K		K	I	T	E		G	E	L
O	L	E		B	I	T	E		M	I	S	T
		H	O	L	E		S	P	Y			
W	A	I	T	E	R		T	A	T	T	O	O
A	L	P	H	A				T	H	I	R	D
D	E	S	E	R	T		P	R	I	C	E	D
			R	Y	E		R	O	C	K		
T	H	U	S		N	A	I	L		L	I	D
H	A	S		M	U	L	E		S	I	D	E
A	R	E		E	R	A	S		A	S	E	A
W	E	D		N	E	S	T		T	H	A	N

Guinea __

P	I	G		R	A	C	E		G	O	L	F
E	V	E		I	C	O	N		O	R	A	L
T	O	N		D	I	R	T		O	G	R	E
	R	E	F		D	R	A	I	N	A	G	E
F	I	R	E			A	I	R		N	E	T
B	E	A	T		A	L	L	O	T			
I	S	L	A	N	D		E	N	R	A	P	T
			L	O	V	E	D		E	C	H	O
S	P	A		T	A	N			S	T	A	Y
C	U	R	R	E	N	C	Y		S	I	R	
U	R	G	E		C	O	O	P		O	A	T
F	E	U	D		E	D	G	E		N	O	R
F	E	E	S		D	E	A	R		S	H	Y

__and haw

H	E	M		A	D	D	S		T	R	A	P
I	V	Y		D	R	O	P		R	A	I	L
P	I	N	T	S	I	Z	E		U	G	L	Y
S	L	A	W		V	E	N	U	E			
			E	M	E	N	D	S		J	A	W
A	P	P	L	E	S		S	E	W	A	G	E
L	A	R	V	A				F	R	I	E	D
P	R	E	E	N	S		B	U	I	L	D	S
S	K	Y		I	N	S	U	L	T			
			R	E	A	C	T		H	U	S	H
D	A	T	A		P	A	T	I	E	N	C	E
U	P	O	N		P	L	O	T		T	A	R
G	E	E	K		Y	E	N	S		O	R	B

Face cover for Halloween

M	A	S	K		C	R	Y		S	L	O	B
O	X	E	N		L	I	E		H	A	V	E
P	I	N	E		I	M	A	G	I	N	E	D
E	S	T	E	E	M		R	E	F	E	R	S
			C	A	B	I	N	E	T			
S	E	D	A	T	E	D				O	A	K
T	R	I	P		R	I	B		R	U	L	E
Y	A	P				O	R	D	E	R	L	Y
			P	R	E	M	I	U	M			
A	F	F	A	I	R		S	H	O	C	K	S
B	R	A	G	G	A	R	T		D	O	N	E
L	O	N	E		S	O	L		E	M	I	T
E	G	G	S		E	W	E		L	E	T	S

It reeks

O	D	O	R		S	I	T		W	H	A	M
N	U	D	E		O	N	E		R	I	C	E
C	A	D	S		A	G	E		A	R	E	A
E	L	S	E		P	O	T		P	E	S	T
			R	H	Y	T	H	M	S			
W	E	A	V	E		S	E	E		P	U	B
A	G	R	E	E	D		S	T	A	R	R	Y
G	O	T		L	I	P		A	T	O	N	E
			A	S	S	A	U	L	T			
S	P	E	W		A	P	T		I	T	C	H
N	O	V	A		B	A	T		R	A	R	E
U	S	E	R		L	Y	E		E	X	A	M
B	E	N	D		E	A	R		D	I	M	S

Ocean Jail

B	R	I	G		P	A	P	A		A	C	E
L	A	C	E		E	R	A	S		R	A	Y
A	T	O	M		L	I	S	P		O	R	E
M	E	N		K	I	S	S		G	U	M	
E	S	S	E	N	C	E			A	S	I	A
			R	O	A	S	T		R	E	N	D
D	I	S	O	W	N		R	I	N	S	E	D
U	S	E	D		S	P	A	D	E			
B	O	N	E			O	V	E	R	A	W	E
	L	A	D		P	L	E	A		S	I	X
P	A	T		H	E	I	R		M	I	N	I
A	T	E		O	A	T	S		O	D	E	S
Y	E	S		T	R	E	E		W	E	S	T

Leaf collection for jumping into

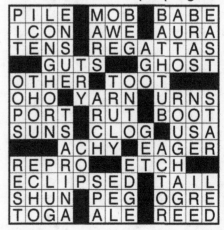

P	I	L	E		M	O	B		B	A	B	E
I	C	O	N		A	W	E		A	U	R	A
T	E	N	S		R	E	G	A	T	T	A	S
		G	U	T	S			G	H	O	S	T
O	T	H	E	R		T	O	O	T			
O	H	O		Y	A	R	N		U	R	N	S
P	O	R	T		R	U	T		B	O	O	T
S	U	N	S		C	L	O	G		U	S	A
			A	C	H	Y		E	A	G	E	R
R	E	P	R	O			E	T	C	H		
E	C	L	I	P	S	E	D		T	A	I	L
S	H	U	N		P	E	G		O	G	R	E
T	O	G	A		A	L	E		R	E	E	D

"All You Need Is __" (Beatle song)

L	O	V	E	■	A	J	A	R	■	I	M	P
I	R	O	N	■	N	A	N	A	■	N	O	R
M	A	I	D	■	T	R	E	K	■	S	P	Y
O	L	D	E	R	■	S	W	E	A	T	■	■
■	■	■	A	I	M	■	■	D	R	A	G	S
O	V	E	R	C	O	A	T	■	K	N	E	E
V	A	N	■	H	A	I	R	Y	■	C	A	W
A	R	T	S	■	T	R	O	O	P	E	R	S
L	Y	R	I	C	■	■	D	U	E	■	■	■
■	■	A	P	R	O	N	■	R	E	L	A	Y
R	A	N	■	E	G	O	S	■	L	I	F	E
A	R	C	■	A	L	T	O	■	E	A	R	L
W	E	E	■	K	E	E	N	■	D	R	O	P

Cay

I	S	L	E	■	A	D	S	■	A	I	D	E
N	A	I	L	■	N	U	T	■	T	R	A	Y
T	I	E	D	■	Y	O	U	■	T	I	M	E
O	L	D	E	S	T	■	C	R	I	S	E	S
■	■	■	S	T	I	N	K	E	R	■	■	■
C	O	S	T	U	M	E	■	P	E	S	T	S
O	A	K	■	F	E	V	E	R	■	A	H	A
G	R	I	E	F	■	E	X	I	S	T	E	D
■	■	■	R	E	F	R	E	S	H	■	■	■
A	R	C	A	D	E	■	R	E	A	R	E	D
M	O	O	S	■	A	C	T	■	M	A	M	A
I	D	L	E	■	T	O	E	■	A	C	I	D
D	E	A	R	■	S	O	D	■	N	E	T	S

Had feelings

F	E	L	T	■	O	F	F	■	P	A	D	S
L	A	I	R	■	P	I	E	■	E	X	I	T
A	S	E	A	■	E	N	S	H	R	I	N	E
P	E	N	S	■	R	A	T	E	■	S	E	W
■	■	■	H	E	A	L	E	R	■	■	■	■
A	L	L	E	Y	■	E	R	R	■	T	O	P
H	O	O	D	E	D	■	S	I	G	N	A	L
S	U	B	■	S	E	T	■	N	U	T	T	Y
■	■	■	■	O	R	A	N	G	E	■	■	■
Y	A	P	■	R	I	L	E	■	S	P	A	R
A	C	H	I	E	V	E	R	■	S	A	K	E
W	H	E	T	■	E	N	D	■	E	V	I	L
N	E	W	S	■	S	T	Y	■	D	E	N	Y

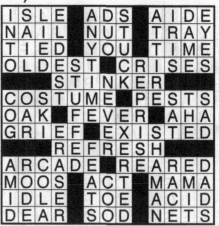

10. Start Over

Tofu is made from it

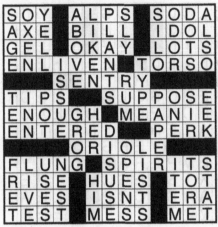

S	O	Y	■	A	L	P	S	■	S	O	D	A
A	X	E	■	B	I	L	L	■	I	D	O	L
G	E	L	■	O	K	A	Y	■	L	O	T	S
E	N	L	I	V	E	N	■	T	O	R	S	O
■	■	■	S	E	N	T	R	Y	■	■	■	■
T	I	P	S	■	■	S	U	P	P	O	S	E
E	N	O	U	G	H	■	M	E	A	N	I	E
E	N	T	E	R	E	D	■	■	P	E	R	K
■	■	■	■	O	R	I	O	L	E	■	■	■
F	L	U	N	G	■	S	P	I	R	I	T	S
R	I	S	E	■	H	U	E	S	■	T	O	T
E	V	E	S	■	I	S	N	T	■	E	R	A
T	E	S	T	■	M	E	S	S	■	M	E	T

Lie low

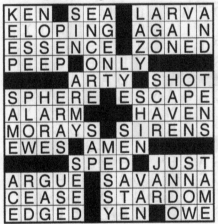

H	I	D	■	P	A	C	T	■	A	R	M	S
O	L	E	■	S	P	R	Y	■	B	E	E	T
E	L	F	■	S	E	E	P	■	L	A	M	E
■	■	E	A	T	■	D	E	V	E	L	O	P
C	H	A	R	■	V	I	S	A	■	■	■	■
A	U	T	O	M	A	T	■	P	R	O	W	L
P	R	E	S	E	T	■	S	O	I	R	E	E
E	L	D	E	R	■	E	A	R	N	I	N	G
■	■	■	■	R	O	S	Y	■	S	E	T	S
A	N	A	L	Y	S	T	■	D	E	N	■	■
W	I	R	E	■	C	A	N	E	■	T	E	A
A	C	E	S	■	A	T	O	M	■	E	G	G
Y	E	A	S	■	R	E	D	O	■	D	O	E

__ thumbs (clumsy)

A	L	L	■	A	G	E	D	■	S	T	A	Y
H	U	E	■	D	E	L	I	■	H	E	R	E
A	R	F	■	I	N	K	S	■	O	A	T	S
S	E	T	T	E	E	■	P	R	O	S	■	■
■	■	■	R	U	S	T	L	E	■	P	A	R
C	L	A	U	S	■	R	A	V	I	O	L	I
H	A	I	L	■	M	A	Y	■	T	O	A	D
A	C	R	Y	L	I	C	■	T	E	N	S	E
P	E	W	■	E	S	T	E	E	M	■	■	■
■	■	A	D	D	S	■	L	E	S	S	E	E
N	O	V	A	■	I	C	O	N	■	O	D	D
A	H	E	M	■	N	A	P	S	■	F	I	G
B	O	S	S	■	G	R	E	Y	■	A	T	E

Understanding

K	E	N	■	S	E	A	■	L	A	R	V	A
E	L	O	P	I	N	G	■	A	G	A	I	N
E	S	S	E	N	C	E	■	Z	O	N	E	D
P	E	E	P	■	O	N	L	Y	■	■	■	■
■	■	■	■	A	R	T	Y	■	S	H	O	T
S	P	H	E	R	E	■	E	S	C	A	P	E
A	L	A	R	M	■	■	■	H	A	V	E	N
M	O	R	A	Y	S	■	S	I	R	E	N	S
E	W	E	S	■	A	M	E	N	■	■	■	■
■	■	■	■	S	P	E	D	■	J	U	S	T
A	R	G	U	E	■	S	A	V	A	N	N	A
C	E	A	S	E	■	S	T	A	R	D	O	M
E	D	G	E	D	■	Y	E	N	■	O	W	E

Blind as a __

B	A	T	■	S	P	U	R	■	S	A	P	S
A	L	E	■	L	A	N	E	■	H	E	R	O
S	I	P	■	I	R	I	S	■	I	R	O	N
E	V	E	■	T	R	O	T	■	P	I	P	■
D	E	E	D	■	O	N	E	S	■	A	H	A
■	■	■	A	P	T	■	D	U	L	L	E	D
S	H	A	W	L	■	■	■	R	U	S	T	S
E	A	R	N	E	R	■	B	E	G	■	■	■
E	L	M	■	A	I	R	Y	■	E	A	S	T
■	F	O	E	■	B	O	G	S	■	L	I	E
T	W	I	N	■	A	T	O	P	■	O	R	E
H	A	R	D	■	L	O	N	E	■	H	E	N
E	Y	E	S	■	D	R	E	W	■	A	N	Y

Item by Scott Joplin

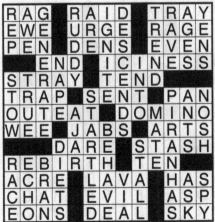

R	A	G	■	R	A	I	D	■	T	R	A	Y
E	W	E	■	U	R	G	E	■	R	A	G	E
P	E	N	■	D	E	N	S	■	E	V	E	N
■	■	E	N	D	■	I	C	I	N	E	S	S
S	T	R	A	Y	■	T	E	N	D	■	■	■
T	R	A	P	■	S	E	N	T	■	P	A	N
O	U	T	E	A	T	■	D	O	M	I	N	O
W	E	E	■	J	A	B	S	■	A	R	T	S
■	■	■	D	A	R	E	■	S	T	A	S	H
R	E	B	I	R	T	H	■	T	E	N	■	■
A	C	R	E	■	L	A	V	A	■	H	A	S
C	H	A	T	■	E	V	I	L	■	A	S	P
E	O	N	S	■	D	E	A	L	■	S	K	Y

Lymph __

N	O	D	E	S		S	H	E		P	E	G
O	U	I	J	A		W	O	R	D	A	G	E
T	R	E	E	S		A	P	R	I	C	O	T
			C	H	I	M	P		M	E	S	S
S	T	A	T		V	I	E	D				
P	A	C	I	F	Y		R	E	H	A	S	H
A	C	H	O	O				N	A	S	T	Y
S	T	E	N	O	S		S	T	R	E	A	M
				D	I	S	K		D	A	R	N
H	A	T	S		C	L	I	M	B			
U	N	A	L	I	K	E		O	A	S	I	S
R	E	C	Y	C	L	E		P	L	U	M	E
T	W	O		E	E	K		S	L	E	P	T

"Dizzy" baseballer

D	E	A	N		D	A	M	P		S	P	A
I	D	L	E		O	D	O	R		M	I	X
P	I	T	A		T	I	M	E		O	L	E
S	T	O	R	K		E	M	E	R	G	E	D
				I	G	U	A	N	A			
C	A	B	A	N	A	S			C	O	D	E
U	P	E	N	D	S		C	H	E	R	R	Y
P	E	E	K			G	O	O	D	B	Y	E
			L	E	A	R	N	S				
G	A	Z	E	L	L	E		E	L	O	P	E
U	S	A		B	O	A	T		A	R	E	A
T	I	N		O	N	T	O		C	A	R	T
S	A	Y		W	E	S	T		E	L	K	S

Atlas page

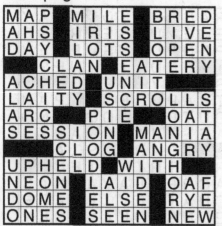

M	A	P		M	I	L	E		B	R	E	D
A	H	S		I	R	I	S		L	I	V	E
D	A	Y		L	O	T	S		O	P	E	N
		C	L	A	N		E	A	T	E	R	Y
A	C	H	E	D		U	N	I	T			
L	A	I	T	Y		S	C	R	O	L	L	S
A	R	C			P	I	E			O	A	T
S	E	S	S	I	O	N		M	A	N	I	A
			C	L	O	G		A	N	G	R	Y
U	P	H	E	L	D		W	I	T	H		
N	E	O	N		L	A	I	D		O	A	F
D	O	M	E		E	L	S	E		R	Y	E
O	N	E	S		S	E	E	N		N	E	W

Clump of earth

C	L	O	D		B	U	S		T	R	O	D
L	I	M	O		A	S	H		W	A	G	E
A	K	I	N		G	E	E		I	S	L	E
M	E	T	E	D		F	E	A	T	H	E	R
				E	R	U	P	T				
A	E	R	O	S	O	L		T	I	N	E	D
I	R	O	N	E	D		B	U	R	E	A	U
L	A	T	E	R		D	I	N	E	T	T	E
				V	E	R	G	E				
T	E	M	P	E	R	A		D	O	T	T	Y
A	X	I	S		E	G	O		F	I	R	E
P	A	N	S		C	O	P		F	L	E	A
E	M	I	T		T	N	T		S	E	E	R

Electric swimmer

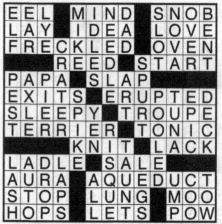

E	E	L		M	I	N	D		S	N	O	B
L	A	Y		I	D	E	A		L	O	V	E
F	R	E	C	K	L	E	D		O	V	E	N
			R	E	E	D		S	T	A	R	T
P	A	P	A		S	L	A	P				
E	X	I	T	S		E	R	U	P	T	E	D
S	L	E	E	P	Y		T	R	O	U	P	E
T	E	R	R	I	E	R		T	O	N	I	C
				K	N	I	T		L	A	C	K
L	A	D	L	E		S	A	L	E			
A	U	R	A		A	Q	U	E	D	U	C	T
S	T	O	P		L	U	N	G		M	O	O
H	O	P	S		L	E	T	S		P	O	W

Periphery

E	D	G	E		S	P	I	T		B	O	B
C	U	R	L		L	A	M	E		A	W	E
H	E	A	D		A	L	P	S		R	E	D
O	L	D	E	S	T		A	T	O	M		
			S	T	E	P	S		W	A	S	P
S	K	A	T	E		A	S	I	N	I	N	E
I	N	N		E	A	S	E	D		D	I	G
R	E	T	U	R	N	S		L	A	S	T	S
E	W	E	S		N	E	V	E	R			
		R	E	D	O		E	R	E	C	T	S
U	F	O		A	Y	E	S		N	A	I	L
G	O	O		T	E	N	T		A	F	R	O
H	E	M		A	D	D	S		S	E	E	P

Social dud

N	E	R	D		L	A	D		T	H	A	T
A	W	A	Y		O	R	E		H	O	B	O
G	E	N	E	R	A	T	E		R	O	L	E
			D	I	N	E	D		O	D	E	S
H	A	S		P	E	R	S	O	N			
E	L	K		T	R	Y		R	E	S	T	S
A	L	I	B	I	S		P	I	S	T	O	L
T	Y	P	E	D		A	R	E		A	G	O
			L	E	A	D	E	N		T	A	B
A	S	E	A		L	O	T	T	O			
C	H	A	T		P	R	E	S	U	M	E	D
T	O	R	E		H	E	N		R	A	V	E
S	O	L	D		A	D	D		S	T	E	W